Little VISITS

VOLUME THREE

365 FAMILY DEVOTIONS

CONCORDIA PUBLISHING HOUSE • SAINT LOUIS

Copyright © 2004 Concordia Publishing House

Published by Concordia Publishing House
3558 S. Jefferson Avenue
St. Louis, MO 63118-3968

Manufactured in the United States of America

Library of Congress Cataloging-in-Publication Data

365 family devotions.
       p. cm. -- (Little visits ; v. 3)
    ISBN 0-7586-0685-0
    1. Family--Prayer-books and devotions--English. 2. Devotional
calendars. I. Series.
    BV255 .A14 2002
    249--dc21   2002006608

1 2   3   4   5   6   7   8   9   10   13 12 11 10 09 08 07 06 05 04

Versions of these devotions originally appeared in various volumes of the magazine *My Devotions*. This book is dedicated to the authors of these devotions, who have contributed their God-given time and talents to nurturing the faith of God's children. ❧

Preface

For a number of years, the title *Little Visits* has been associated with devotions that share the saving Gospel of Jesus Christ with children. From the very first edition of *Little Visits with God* to this current volume, these devotions reinforce scriptural truths and faith concepts centered on God's love for us through Christ.

Setting aside time for devotions is an excellent way to lead children to the Savior and to bring them face-to-face with God's Word. In Romans 10:7, we read that "faith comes from hearing the message, and the message is heard through the word of Christ." Find a time that best suits your family and be consistent. Set a format that is most harmonious with the ages and stages of your children. Using the order of worship provided on the facing page will build a sense of tradition and ritual into your family devotions. Developing such rituals or traditions helps to lay important building blocks for faith formation and creates a link between worship in the family of faith and worship within your own family.

These devotions have been written by pastors and educators who have drawn upon their experiences to provide illustrations from daily life and link them to God's Word. May you and your children be blessed as the Holy Spirit works through these words to teach your minds and to touch your hearts.

The Editors

Daily Devotion for Family Use

Parents may feel free to adapt according to the children's ages and ability to participate.

____ The Invocation

The parent may open the devotion with a call to worship.
Leader: In the name of the Father and of the Son and of the Holy Spirit.
Family: Amen.

____ The Hymn

The family may sing together a related hymn or song of praise.

____ The Scripture Reading

The designated Scripture may be read by parent or child.

____ The Devotional Reading

The designated devotion may be read by parent or child.
The parent may lead the family in discussion using the questions provided.

____ The Closing Prayer

The parent may lead the family in the closing prayer.

january

Contributors for this month:

Jennifer AlLee

Carol Delph

Carla Fast

Judy C. Thompson

The Silver Trumpets

Today we remember last year and celebrate a new start.

God prepared His Old Testament people for a new start as they left for the Promised Land. God would direct people by the sound of silver trumpets.

His people were to listen carefully to the trumpet calls. The first call signaled the Israelites to gather at the Tent of Meeting. At the trumpet's *blast*, the people were to set out. God attached a promise to the blast. "You will be remembered by the LORD your God and rescued from your enemies." God assured the people of His saving aid.

Jesus fulfilled God's promises in His ministry on earth. Through Jesus' death and resurrection we have saving aid from our enemies—sin, death, and the devil. On the Last Day the trumpet will sound to lead us to heaven.

Like the people of the Old Testament, we gather to worship. We use the invocation; we call on the Lord—the same words used in Baptism. We leave worship, not with the blast of trumpets, but with a benediction: "The LORD bless you and keep you" (Numbers 6:24).

The New Year is when the church celebrates the naming of Jesus, who would live out the meaning of His name by saving His people from their sins. Celebrate God's power and victory!

Read from God's Word

The Lord said to Moses: "Make two trumpets of hammered silver, and use them for calling the community together and for having the camps set out. When both are sounded, the whole community is to assemble before you at the entrance to the Tent of Meeting. If only one is sounded, the leaders—the heads of the clans of Israel—are to assemble before you. When a trumpet blast is sounded, the tribes camping on the east are to set out. At the sounding of a second blast, the camps on the south are to set out. The blast will be the signal for setting out. To gather the assembly, blow the trumpets, but not with the same signal. The sons of Aaron, the priests, are to blow the trumpets. This is to be a lasting ordinance for you and the generations to come. When you go into battle in your own land against an enemy who is oppressing you, sound a blast on the trumpets. Then you will be remembered by the LORD your God and rescued from your enemies." Numbers 10:1–9 ✑

_____Let's do: Make a special design using the name *Jesus*.

_____Let's pray: How sweet Your name sounds in my ear, Jesus. Amen.

C. D.

Read from God's Word

Simeon took Him in his arms and praised God, saying: "Sovereign Lord, as You have promised, You now dismiss Your servant in peace. For my eyes have seen Your salvation, which You have prepared in the sight of all people, a light for revelation to the Gentiles and for glory to Your people Israel." The child's father and mother marveled at what was said about Him. Luke 2:28–33

Treasures of the Heart

Some people collect rocks, dolls, or baseball cards as treasures. Mary collected words about Jesus as her treasures.

An angel told Mary she would be the mother of the Savior. The shepherds told her about many angels who announced her Son's birth, calling Him the Savior, Christ the Lord. "Mary treasured up all these things and pondered them in her heart" (Luke 2:19).

Years later, Mary heard more words to collect and treasure. She heard Jesus say He had to be in His Father's house. The house He was talking about was the temple, where God was present for His people.

God helped Mary understand that Jesus was her Savior as well as her child. Her child was God's child, the Savior of the world. The words she heard and collected from the angel, the shepherds, Simeon, and from Jesus helped her learn about Jesus as the Savior.

Like Mary, God gives us time to hear the Gospel of Jesus in church, family devotions, and Sunday school. God's Word is used by the Spirit to work faith in our hearts.

"Do not store up for yourselves treasures on earth, where moth and rust destroy. ... But store up for yourselves treasures in heaven. ... For where your treasure is, there your heart will be also" (Matthew 6:19–21).

_____Let's do: What words of Jesus do you treasure? Write out your favorite verse.

_____Let's pray: Lord, help me keep Your Word as my true treasure. Amen.

C. D.

His Star

In the beginning God created the stars. Although these heavenly bodies shine constantly, they are visible only at night.

The prophet Balaam foretold a special star: "A star will come out of Jacob; a scepter will rise out of Israel" (Numbers 24:17). He was talking about the promised Messiah.

More than 2,000 years ago a star, "His star" (Matthew 2:2), appeared over Judea. Some Wise Men spotted it and connected it with something special. God led them to follow His star until they saw the prophet's promise fulfilled in Bethlehem.

God used His star to announce the arrival of Jesus. The light of the star broadcast the news of the Christmas story beyond Bethlehem. God used a star to reveal the birth of the Savior to the entire world.

From the baby King's manger, God's saving love for us twinkles. This baby would overcome sin, death, and the power of the devil. His death and resurrection provide eternal life for all.

The message of Jesus still shines brightly today. God uses simple means—water, bread, wine—connected with His Word to show our Savior to us. God uses His Word to shine in our hearts.

Like the Wise Men of old, let us worship the King, who turns the darkness of our sin into light.

Read from God's Word

And God said, "Let there be lights in the expanse of the sky to separate the day from the night, and let them serve as signs to mark seasons and days and years, and let them be lights in the expanse of the sky to give light on the earth." And it was so. God made two great lights—the greater light to govern the day and the lesser light to govern the night. He also made the stars. God set them in the expanse of the sky to give light on the earth, to govern the day and the night, and to separate light from darkness. And God saw that it was good. And there was evening, and there was morning—the fourth day. Genesis 1:14–19 〰

_____Let's do: Draw five stars. Think of five people who have
               shared the Gospel with you. Thank God for them.

_____Let's pray: By Your holy Word, shine in my life, Lord. Amen.

C. D.

Read from God's Word

After Jesus was born in Bethlehem in Judea, during the time of King Herod, Magi from the east came to Jerusalem and asked, "Where is the one who has been born King of the Jews? We saw His star in the east and have come to worship Him." When King Herod heard this he was disturbed, and all Jerusalem with him. Matthew 2:1–3 ⮜

Hidden

The tower and spire of the Church of Our Saviour in Copenhagen, Denmark, is 295 feet high. During World War II, the Danish Resistance used that tower and spire as a hiding place. The weapons were right there, yet they were hidden.

Jesus was born during the time when wicked King Herod ruled. Herod killed many people. He built altars where people would worship false gods. He didn't realize that the true God was visible but hiding in his land.

The Wise Men's question shocked him: "Where is the one who has been born king of the Jews?"

Herod thought, *I am the king of the Jews!* The Wise Men wanted to worship this King. "When King Herod heard this he was disturbed, and all Jerusalem with him."

Why would a king and a whole city be so upset about a baby?

The world was ruined by sin. Then Jesus, God's Word in human form, came into the world. God came to rescue His people in the life of a real baby. People heard about the new King and were stirred to faith or to fear.

Church spires point to heaven as reminders that Jesus has come. He is our weapon against sin, death, and the devil. He is our Savior—a truth we don't want to hide!

———Let's do: Look for church steeples to draw. When you draw them, remember Jesus is your strength.

———Let's pray: "O LORD … I hide myself in You" (Psalm 143:9). Amen.

C. D.

Missed It!

The children of Israel had been watching for the Messiah since the early times. They knew their need to be saved, and they looked forward to their Savior's coming.

God's Word had been written down and preserved by the scribes. They studied the words and taught the people about the Messiah and the peace and restoration He would bring.

But some people in Jerusalem were upset that a new king of the Jews had been born. Herod asked the chief priests and teachers of the law to pinpoint the place where Christ was born. Herod gave the information to the Wise Men. Herod knew what they said, but he missed Jesus. The scribes knew, but they missed Him too. The Bible doesn't tell us that the Jewish leaders went with the Wise Men to worship Jesus. They missed out on worshiping the One they had been teaching about and looking for.

Our Lord doesn't let us miss out on His salvation. He has called us by the Gospel and made us His own in Baptism. Through His Word we learn about Jesus.

Read from God's Word

When he had called together all the people's chief priests and teachers of the law, he asked them where the Christ was to be born. "In Bethlehem in Judea," they replied, "for this is what the prophet has written: 'But you, Bethlehem, in the land of Judah, are by no means least among the rulers of Judah; for out of you will come a ruler who will be the shepherd of My people Israel.'" Then Herod called the Magi secretly and found out from them the exact time the star had appeared. He sent them to Bethlehem and said, "Go and make a careful search for the child. As soon as you find Him, report to me, so that I too may go and worship Him." After they had heard the king, they went on their way, and the star they had seen in the east went ahead of them until it stopped over the place where the child was. When they saw the star, they were overjoyed. Matthew 2:4–10 ✍

We look forward to when our Lord will come again. By His grace, we are confident we will not miss out on eternal life.

_____Let's do: Thank God for the people who share the message of Jesus the Savior with you—so you do not miss out.

_____Let's pray: "O my Strength, I watch for You" (Psalm 59:9). Amen.

C. D.

Read from God's Word

On coming to the house, they saw the child with His mother Mary, and they bowed down and worshiped Him. Then they opened their treasures and presented Him with gifts of gold and of incense and of myrrh. And having been warned in a dream not to go back to Herod, they returned to their country by another route. Matthew 2:11–12 ✍

The Epiphany Gifts

Imagine Mary's surpise when strangers brought gold as a gift for her Son! Gold was scarce in her land. It was used by kings not by babies. But Jesus, the Christ, was worthy of this royal gift.

Frankincense is a sweet, pine-like scent used in worship. God told the Israelites to mix frankincense with fragrant spices as incense to mark His presence (Exodus 30:34–37). The high priest burned some every morning. King David talks of this ritual, "May my prayer be set before You like incense" (Psalm 141:2). Jesus is our High Priest; He offered Himself as our sacrifice. Jesus was worthy of this special gift.

The sweet-smelling sap of the myrrh bush was used to make anointing oil. This oil was used in consecrating (or setting things apart for God's special use) things in the tabernacle, the high priest and his sons. Jesus was worthy of this unusual gift.

Today the church celebrates Epiphany and highlights the truth that Jesus is the Savior of the whole world. The Wise Men's gifts tell us who Jesus is. Gold shows He is our King. Frankincense reminds us He is our High Priest. Myrrh tells us He was our Savior who died for our sins. Thank God for the gifts Jesus has given to you.

_____Let's do: Draw three symbols for the Wise Men's gifts.

_____Let's pray: Dear heavenly Father, thank You for Your gift
of Jesus to every nation. Amen.

C. D.

A Hope and a Plan

Can you draw a picture of danger? Jean-François Millet did. In his drawing called *The Flight into Egypt*, he captured the danger of that story. The picture is dark with the shadows of Joseph and Mary holding Jesus and hurrying to Egypt. The sketch gives feelings of danger—and *love!*

Their escape to Egypt was filled with real danger. It was also filled with love because Mary and Joseph trusted God's plan. God sent an angel to warn Joseph to leave in the night. The family fled to safety so the soldiers of King Herod would not kill Jesus, who was a very young child.

About 30 years later, Jesus was in the Garden of Gethsemane at night. There was danger again. This time the soldiers found Jesus. He was arrested and crucified. Why? Because of love. God loves us and had a plan to rescue us from the punishment of our sin.

Read from God's Word

When they had gone, an angel of the Lord appeared to Joseph in a dream. "Get up," he said, "take the child and His mother and escape to Egypt. Stay there until I tell you, for Herod is going to search for the child to kill Him." So he got up, took the child and His mother during the night and left for Egypt, where he stayed until the death of Herod. And so was fulfilled what the Lord had said through the prophet: "Out of Egypt I called My Son." Matthew 2:13–15

As you think about the dangers in your life, you do not need to panic. God gives you a plan to escape the danger and He gives you hope in His Son. Jesus defeated sin and won salvation for us when He rose from the grave on Easter. He offers the victory to us by grace through faith in Him.

_____Let's do: Thank God for His loving plan. Then pray for someone who needs to hear the message of God's saving love. (Check out the painting by Millet on the Internet.)

_____Let's pray: "Christ who lived for us and died, By the Spirit was revived; By that Spirit we shall too Rise from death to life anew" (*HS98* 835:12). Amen.

C. D.

Read from God's Word

Now there was a man in Jerusalem called Simeon, who was righteous and devout. ... It had been revealed to him by the Holy Spirit that he would not die before he had seen the Lord's Christ. Moved by the Spirit, he went into the temple courts. When the parents brought in the child Jesus ... Simeon took Him in his arms and praised God, saying: "Sovereign Lord, as You have promised, You now dismiss Your servant in peace. For my eyes have seen Your salvation, which You have prepared in the sight of all people, a light for revelation to the Gentiles and for glory to Your people Israel." The child's father and mother marveled at what was said about Him. Then Simeon blessed them and said to Mary, His mother: "This child is destined to cause the falling and rising of many in Israel, and to be a sign that will be spoken against, so that the thoughts of many hearts will be revealed. And a sword will pierce your own soul too." Luke 2:25–35 ✑

The Nunc Dimittis

Can anyone be happy and sad at the same time?

Think about how happy you might be to move, but how sad you would be to leave your friends. Think about how eager you might be to welcome a new baby, but how unsure you might be of how your family would change.

In the temple courts Simeon held a baby, Jesus, and praised God. Simeon waited a long time to see his Savior. After that, Simeon was ready to be dismissed in peace and die. The words he spoke have been called the Nunc Dimittis. Once his eyes saw the salvation of the world, he was happy.

Simeon told Mary that Jesus would be great, like a light for the world and the glory for the people of Israel. Simeon also revealed that Jesus and Mary would suffer deep anguish.

The joy and the sadness were mixed together. Jesus came for the sin, death, and struggles we have. He would sadly die on Good Friday. But He would rise to life again on Easter. How glad we are! He brings us joy!

During the Divine Service we sing the Nunc Dimittis. As you sing its words of celebration, may you see Christ as your joy always.

———Let's do: Write a poem about Jesus, who takes away the sin of the whole world. Mention the joy He gives.

———Let's pray: Dear Jesus, thank You for suffering so I might have eternal joy and a home with You in heaven. Amen.

C. D.

Our Private Tree

Under their "private tree," Heidi and Danielle confessed things like failed tests and talking back. After listening and sharing hugs, they felt better—but they didn't feel perfect.

People in Jesus' time went to John the Baptist to confess. "Confessing their sins, they were baptized by him in the Jordan River" (Matthew 3:6). To "confess" means to admit a fault, guilt, or sin. To "repent" is to feel sorry for that sin and stop doing it. It's hard to confess. Sometimes we make excuses or blame others. But if we avoid confession, we miss out on the peace and forgiveness God has for sinners.

John the Baptist came to show repentant sinners their Savior. John told the Pharisees, "Produce fruit in keeping with repentance" (Matthew 3:8). He wanted the Pharisees to believe in Jesus and not rely on their own rules. Many who ignored John's call missed out on Jesus' offer of forgiveness.

Read from God's Word

"What do you think? There was a man who had two sons. He went to the first and said, 'Son, go and work today in the vineyard.' 'I will not,' he answered, but later he changed his mind and went. Then the father went to the other son and said the same thing. He answered, 'I will, sir,' but he did not go. Which of the two did what his father wanted?" "The first," they answered. Jesus said to them, "I tell you the truth, the tax collectors and the prostitutes are entering the kingdom of God ahead of you. For John came to you to show you the way of righteousness, and you did not believe him, but the tax collectors and the prostitutes did. And even after you saw this, you did not repent and believe him." Matthew 21:28–32 ✍

With God's help, we are able to admit our sins and confess our need for a Savior. Jesus is the Savior who died to save us from sins.

We have a place where we can go to tell God our sins and hear His words of forgiveness. God invites us to worship Him with our whole heart. We receive forgiveness from God through the words our pastor speaks.

_____Let's talk: What are some words to use when you confess a sin?

_____Let's pray: Show me, Lord, what it means to be forgiven. In Jesus' name. Amen.

C. D.

Know Me

Read from God's Word

The next day Jesus decided to leave for Galilee. Finding Philip, He said to him, "Follow Me." Philip, like Andrew and Peter, was from the town of Bethsaida. Philip found Nathanael and told him, "We have found the one Moses wrote about in the Law, and about whom the prophets also wrote—Jesus of Nazareth, the son of Joseph." "Nazareth! Can anything good come from there?" Nathanael asked. "Come and see," said Philip. When Jesus saw Nathanael approaching. He said of him, "Here is a true Israelite, in whom there is nothing false." "How do You know me?" Nathanael asked. Jesus answered, "I saw you while you were still under the fig tree before Philip called you." Then Nathanael declared, "Rabbi, You are the Son of God; You are the King of Israel." Jesus said, "You believe because I told you I saw you under the fig tree. You shall see greater things than that." He then added, "I tell you the truth, you shall see heaven open, and the angels of God ascending and descending on the Son of Man." John 1:43–51 ✍

Introducing newcomers helps them feel welcome and become familiar with others. Introductions aren't always easy, especially if we don't know the people very well. But they are helpful and make us feel like we belong.

In our Bible reading, Philip was a new follower of Jesus. Philip found Nathanael and asked him to come and see Jesus, the promised Christ. After seeing Nathanael, Jesus took care of all the introductions. Jesus said He had seen Nathanael under the fig tree. He knew Nathanael was a man of truth, not of lies.

Jesus knows us too. He knows our deepest fears, our inmost needs, and our darkest sins. He knows our desperate need for a Savior.

Through His Word, Jesus finds us and tells us that He is our Savior. He never wants us to feel left out or unloved. Through Holy Baptism, He welcomes us into the family of His heavenly Father, who loves us with a boundless love. He gives us His Holy Spirit, helping us grow in faith. His Holy Spirit helps us know our Savior and His ways. He invites us to introduce others to Jesus.

To see Jesus is to see the Father. Jesus coming in the flesh introduces us to God—Father, Son, and Holy Spirit. That's some introduction!

_____Let's do: Practice introducing someone to a friend today.

_____Let's pray: "Father, who the crown shall give, Savior by whose death we live, Spirit guide through all our days: Three in One, Your name we praise" (*LW* 126:8). Amen.

C. D.

A Family Business

Read from God's Word

"Why were you searching for Me?" He asked. "Didn't you know I had to be in My Father's house?" But they did not understand what He was saying to them. Then He went down to Nazareth with them and was obedient to them. But His mother treasured all these things in her heart. And Jesus grew in wisdom and stature, and in favor with God and men. Luke 2:49–52

When some children grow up, they take over the family business. Some children may take over the family farm or the family bakery or factory. Some join the family's law practice or become doctors or teachers like their parents.

When Jesus was a boy, He was taught the family business. His earthly father, Joseph, was a carpenter. No doubt Jesus learned the trade, but His main task was to do His heavenly Father's work.

Jesus had already begun to learn the family business by the time He was 12. He told Mary and Joseph that He had to be in the temple because it was His Father's house—where the family business continued.

What is Jesus' family business? It's our salvation! The business God the Father has with this world is redemption. Everything is centered on saving us from our sins. God promised Adam and Eve that He would send a Savior. His Son, Jesus, completed the Father's plan.

Jesus did everything His Father asked Him to do. Because of His redeeming work, we're part of His family and inherit the rewards. By faith, we inherit eternal life with Him in heaven. On earth, we are given the opportunity to love, serve, and share God's message as part of the family of God.

_____Let's do: Whom can you tell about Jesus' death and resurrection?

_____Let's pray: Dear God, thank You for being in the business of saving us. Amen.

C. F.

Read from God's Word

Then the man and his wife heard the sound of the LORD God as He was walking in the garden in the cool of the day, and they hid from the LORD God among the trees of the garden. But the LORD God called to the man, "Where are you?" He answered, "I heard you in the garden, and I was afraid because I was naked; so I hid." And He said, "Who told you that you were naked? Have you eaten from the tree that I commanded you not to eat from?" The man said, "The woman You put here with me—she gave me some fruit from the tree, and I ate it." Then the LORD God said to the woman, "What is this you have done?" The woman said, "The serpent deceived me, and I ate."
Genesis 3:1–13

The Blaming Game

Kids! Come here!" Mrs. Saleeby's voice was stern. The trio arrived and stood in a line facing their mother. "Well?" she asked.

Brianne spoke first. "It wasn't me, Mom. I was in my room playing. Katie's the one who broke—"

"Uh-uh!" Katie blurted. "I did not! It was Chris's fault."

Chris made a face at his sister. "Well, if she would have let go of it when I asked her, it wouldn't have fallen."

Mrs. Saleeby thought a bit and then picked up the family Bible. "This situation sounds familiar to me." (Read Genesis 3:1–13 to find out why.)

Mrs. Saleeby continued: "The sin of passing the blame began with Adam and Eve. Rather than admitting our wrong, we blame others to make ourselves feel better. But that doesn't work. God knows the truth. God is just, and because Adam and Eve sinned, they were punished. But God loved them (and us) so much that He passed their sin and ours onto—"

"Jesus?" Katie asked.

"That's right. Jesus took the punishment on the cross. Now we are forgiven and blameless in God's eyes."

"We're sorry for breaking the vase," chimed in all three.

"You're forgiven," she said, "because Jesus is willing to take the blame. Now how about helping me clean up this mess?"

_____Let's talk: Read Genesis 3:1–13. When we do something wrong, why do we want to blame it on someone else?

_____Let's pray: Dear Lord, thank You for sending Jesus to take the blame for our sins. Amen.

C. F.

Healthful Eating

Read from God's Word

Like newborn babies, crave pure spiritual milk, so that by it you may grow up in your salvation, now that you have tasted that the Lord is good. 1 Peter 2:2–3

Some people made a study of babies' eating habits. They placed a variety of foods in front of each baby to choose from. Amazingly, the babies ate healthful foods.

Many doctors tell mothers not to worry about what their babies eat. Babies seem to crave (and eat) what their bodies need for proper nutrition. As we grow, we remain much like babies. We still crave food. But in addition to physical food, Christians want another type of nourishment. All believers crave spiritual milk. God's nourishing Word helps us grow into the fullness of our salvation.

Sometimes we slip into eating spiritual "junk food." We may look for spiritual nourishment by trusting in ourselves, our good grades, our possessions, and even our good looks. None of this is healthful food. It leads to starvation and death.

How blessed are the children of God! God nourishes our faith by creating in us a craving for spiritual food. We receive this spiritual milk as we learn more about our Savior's love for us.

We are fed by words from Christ. Through His Word and His body and blood in Holy Communion, we receive the forgiveness of sins and the gift of eternal life. Christ is the only one who can satisfy our hunger. And He does it gladly!

_____Let's talk: What kind of nourishment does Jesus give in the eating and drinking of the Lord's Supper?

_____Let's pray: Dear Lord, thank You for providing us with the nourishment we need, both spiritually and physically. We praise You for Your goodness to us. In Jesus' name. Amen.

C. F.

Grin and Bear It

After the suffering of His soul, He will see the light of life and be satisfied; by His knowledge My righteous servant will justify many, and He will bear their iniquities. Isaiah 53:11

Why are you like a man taken by surprise, like a warrior powerless to save? You are among us, O LORD, and we bear your name; do not forsake us! Jeremiah 14:9

"Cheer up! It'll get better." These words encourage us to be positive when we have problems.

Everyone has problems. Sometimes they seem too big to solve. Sometimes they seem like too much for us to handle. We worry, lose sleep, or even get sick because of them.

The advice we often receive is, "Grin and bear it; things will work out." Although these words remind us how we want to live, they can't make us feel that way. Only Jesus can.

The solution for our troubles is Jesus. Read Isaiah 53:11. Jesus came into the world to bear our iniquities. He took our problems upon Himself. What we could not handle, He did. Our sins cost Jesus His life. He suffered, died, and rose again so our sins would be removed forever.

Jesus also gives us something to carry. Read Jeremiah 14:9. As children of God we bear Jesus' name, the name of the One who bore our sins. Whatever comes our way, we are safe in God's hands. Our salvation is a promise from Him.

God helps us look at our troubles in a new way. Things may get tough, but we know Jesus has taken our problems upon Himself. Now we can "grin and bear it" because we bear His name.

_____Let's do: Whenever a problem gets you down, talk to your parents, teachers, or pastor. They are God's gift to you.

_____Let's pray: Dear Lord, thank You for caring for us. Thank You for taking our troubles upon Yourself, especially our largest problem—sin. In Jesus' name. Amen.

C. F.

The Heart Is the Problem

Read from God's Word

"But the things that come out of the mouth come from the heart, and these make a man 'unclean.' For out of the heart come evil thoughts, murder, adultery, sexual immorality, theft, false testimony, slander." Matthew 15:18–19

Cruel words seem to jump out of our mouth before we realize what we're saying. It's as if our tongue has a mind of its own. That's because when our tongue speaks, the words are coming from deep within our heart. Read Matthew 15:18–19.

Evil things are already in our hearts. Our tongues say what we think, feel, and how we really are. It's no wonder that we say rude things and argue with people.

Often you will hear someone exclaim, "I can't believe I said that!" or "If only I could take back those words!" We try to make ourselves feel better, but there is only One who takes our guilt away.

Jesus took all our evil words, thoughts, and actions with Him to the cross. Our hateful hearts and tongues were buried with Him in the tomb. His resurrection means that we, too, will have a life in heaven, where our mouths will speak only words of love and praise. Our hearts will overflow with what is inside—love for our Savior.

For now, we're in a sinful world—but our guilt is taken away. When we say something wrong, what a comfort and joy it is to hear Jesus say, "I love you. You are forgiven!"

_____Let's talk: If you get angry with someone, how could it help to count to 10 before you speak? What are other ways to deal with the situation?

_____Let's pray: Dear Father in heaven, help me use my tongue for good. Help me tell others of Your forgiving love. In Jesus' name. Amen.

C. F.

You're Forgiven

Read from God's Word

Blessed is he whose transgressions are forgiven, whose sins are covered. Blessed is the man whose sin the LORD does not count against him and in whose spirit is no deceit. When I kept silent, my bones wasted away through my groaning all day long. For day and night Your hand was heavy upon me; my strength was sapped as in the heat of summer. Then I acknowledged my sin to You and did not cover up my iniquity. I said, "I will confess my transgressions to the LORD"— and You forgave the guilt of my sin. Psalm 32:1–5 ✍

Mom had said that playing in the living room was off limits. But Carla had broken the rule and played there anyway. She thought Mom would never know.

Unfortunately, Carla cracked the coffee table.

She tried to cover it up by carefully arranging magazines over the crack. Then she waited. She knew Mom had found out because the magazines had been moved. But Mom never said a word about it.

Finally Carla admitted her guilt. The most amazing thing happened. Mom simply forgave her.

Read Psalm 32:1–5. Carla tried to hide her sin from her mom and from God. But the guilt weighed more heavily than the actual deed and she really wanted Mom to find out.

God knows we try to hide from our sins; it is our way of dealing with sin. But it doesn't work. There is a better way—God's way. He tells us that He will not hold our sins against us. Instead, He held them against His Son, Jesus, on the cross. We don't need to cover up our sins. They have been wrapped in the burial cloth of Jesus' death. They have been taken away.

What a surprise it was when Carla's mother forgave her! What a greater joy it is to hear God say, "You are forgiven!"

_____Let's talk: When we forgive others for wrongs they have done, how are we showing the love of Christ in us?

_____Let's pray: Dear Father, thank You for forgiving my sins. I don't have to try to hide them from You. You have forgiven them once and for all through Your Son. And in Jesus' name I come to You. Amen.

C. F.

Call upon Me

Read from God's Word

"And call upon Me in the day of trouble: I will deliver you, and you will honor Me." Psalm 50:15

S tay with me until I fall asleep," whispered Jaime to her father.

"I'll stay. Now get some rest," he said. Jaime closed her eyes. Her father said a silent prayer asking for healing for his daughter.

Hours later he awoke to the sound of "Daddy! Daddy!" He rushed to Jaime's side. "Daddy, I feel much better; but my pajamas are damp."

He laughed. "Jaime, you're wet from sweating. That's how your body got rid of the fever. I'm so thankful that you're feeling better."

"Me too, Dad. And I'm thankful that you were here when I called you. I don't like to be alone."

"None of us likes that. You called on me, but I also did some calling of my own. I called on Jesus. I need Him just like you need me. I prayed for Him to help you."

"And He always does, right?"

"Even in ways we don't always understand. If you had not recovered, we would still know that Jesus is helping us. He died on the cross for us. We have His promise that He will take us to heaven to live with Him eternally. No matter what happens, we can call upon Him, and He will take care of us. Why don't we thank Him for answering our prayer?"

_____Let's talk: Jesus called upon His Father in prayer. We are God's children through faith in Christ. Isn't it great to know that we can speak directly with our Father anytime?

_____Let's pray: Dear Father, what a comfort it is to have You as our Dad! We know You are always near. Thank You for making us Your children through Jesus' sacrifice. Amen.

C. F.

Read from God's Word

How great is the love the Father has lavished on us, that we should be called children of God! And that is what we are! The reason the world does not know us is that it did not know Him. Dear friends, now we are children of God, and what we will be has not yet been made known. But we know that when He appears, we shall be like Him, for we shall see Him as He is. Everyone who has this hope in Him purifies himself, just as He is pure. 1 John 3:1–3

Who Are You?

Who are you? You are a son or daughter, a student, perhaps a sister or a brother. Are you a ballplayer? a pianist? a gymnast? a scout? The list could go on and on.

Sometimes we have an endless list of identities. We may feel torn because we are many different things at one time. Children are sometimes torn between being good students or good athletes. We may be anxious about what we hope to be when we grow up.

We wonder who we really are and which part of us is the most important. Some people handle identity problems in a different way. They add more descriptions to their list. A dad might have a full-time job and coach your soccer team. A child might add swimming lessons to an already full schedule. But when people are too busy or not focused on what is really important, they are not happy with any part of their lives.

We don't have to wonder who we are. We are children of God. We became His children through Baptism into the death and resurrection of Jesus.

God claims us as His own. Our true identity is that of God's family member. And all our other names are gifts He has given us to enjoy.

_____Let's talk: When you feel worried or under pressure, how can knowing that you're a child of God make your life more peaceful?

_____Let's pray: Dear Lord, thank You for making me Your own. Knowing that I am Your child gives me the assurance of Your love for me and the certainty that I will live with You in heaven forever. In Jesus' name I praise You. Amen.

C. F.

Why We Can Be Unafraid

Read from God's Word

The LORD is my light and my salvation—whom shall I fear? The LORD is the stronghold of my life—of whom shall I be afraid? When evil men advance against me to devour my flesh, when my enemies and my foes attack me, they will stumble and fall. Though an army besiege me, my heart will not fear; though war break out against me, even then will I be confident. One thing I ask of the LORD, this is what I seek: that I may dwell in the house of the LORD all the days of my life, to gaze upon the beauty of the LORD and to seek Him in His temple. For in the day of trouble He will keep me safe in His dwelling; He will hide me in the shelter of His tabernacle and set me high upon a rock. Psalm 27:1–5 〰

Mrs. Gibson asked her students to describe one thing they were afraid of. Kyle was afraid of tornadoes. Kaitlin was afraid of sickness. John was afraid of criminals. Krista was afraid of war. No one had difficulty thinking of something.

Mrs. Gibson then picked up a newspaper clipping. "This article lists 10 of the most common fears that people have. Many of your fears are on this list. Can anyone guess what many people fear the most?"

After a moment of silence, Bill raised his hand. "Death?"

"Yes," replied Mrs. Gibson. "Many people list death as their greatest fear. Fear is a part of living in a sinful world. But as Christians we know that God is with us to calm our fears, even the fear of death. Listen to this psalm verse: 'The LORD is my light and my salvation—whom shall I fear? The LORD is the stronghold of my life—of whom shall I be afraid?'"

In this life we experience disappointments, uncertainties, and sadness. God's light of grace and love shines on us every day. He is constantly watching over us. We know He is! His gift of forgiveness in Christ guarantees that no matter what happens to us in this life, we will live forever with Him in heaven.

——Let's talk: What are some fears God has helped you overcome? What are some you still struggle with? How could a candle or a picture of a candle remind you of today's Scripture passage?

——Let's pray: Dear Lord Jesus, You are my light and my salvation. I know that You will always be there to calm my fears. Thanks, Lord. Amen.

J. C. T.

Give Praise to the King!

The huge doors of the ballroom opened. A large gathering of people stood motionless in quiet excitement. Two messengers stepped into the room, raised their long-stemmed trumpets, and blew loudly. Another messenger joined them and announced, "Ladies and gentlemen, your king has arrived!"

Before another word could be spoken, a royally dressed man appeared in the doorway. It was the king. Instantly the people sprang to their feet. There were cries of joy, cheers of triumph, and thundering applause. The king, the mighty warrior, the conqueror, had returned to his people. What a glorious day it was in that kingdom!

Isaiah, the prophet, speaks of another King, the King of light. Our Lord Jesus Christ is that King, and He greets us as members of His kingdom. Christ is our mighty warrior. He fought Satan on our behalf and conquered sin. Without His help, we would be crushed by the foe—sin—and forced to live eternally in hell.

But Christ's glorious victory leads us through this life to our eternal home in heaven. We rejoice and give praise to the light that shines in us. "Arise, shine, for your light has come, and the glory of the Lord rises upon you."

_____Let's do: Explain to a friend what kind of battle Christ the King fought for you and how His death was a victory. How does confession/absolution bring praise to Jesus?

_____Let's pray: "O God of God, O Light of light, O Prince of Peace and King of kings: To You in heaven's glory bright The song of praise forever rings. To Him who shares the Father's throne, The Lamb once slain but raised again, Be all the glory He has won, All thanks and praise! Amen, amen." (*LW* 83:1)

J. C. T.

Jesus Took Our Place

The pastor said, "Belinda, I baptize you in the name of the Father and of the Son and of the Holy Spirit. Amen."

Belinda and her entire family were being baptized. They had never known Jesus before. After taking some classes at church, Belinda's family learned about their sin and their need for the Savior. Now they were receiving the gift of forgiveness and salvation through the water and the Word of Holy Baptism.

In today's Bible reading, John is baptizing Jesus. But why did Jesus want to be baptized? Was He sinful? No. Jesus said that He wanted to be baptized "to fulfill all righteousness."

God desires that we be perfectly sinless and keep His commandments. Those are requirements that we cannot achieve so Jesus did it all for us. He took our place under God's Law and fulfilled that Law so He could give us the righteousness of God.

Read from God's Word

Then Jesus came from Galilee to the Jordan to be baptized by John. But John tried to deter Him, saying, "I need to be baptized by you, and do you come to me?" Jesus replied, "Let it be so now; it is proper for us to do this to fulfill all righteousness." Then John consented. As soon as Jesus was baptized, He went up out of the water. At that moment heaven was opened, and He saw the Spirit of God descending like a dove and lighting on Him. And a voice from heaven said, "This is My Son, whom I love; with Him I am well pleased." Matthew 3:13–17 ✍

When Jesus was baptized, He also sealed His commitment to go to the cross for our sins. He died in our place and rose victoriously. As Paul said in Romans 6:4, "We were ... buried with Him through Baptism into death in order that, just as Christ was raised from the dead through the glory of the Father, we too may live a new life."

_____Let's talk: What are some ways you celebrate your Baptism birthday?

_____Let's pray: Heavenly Father, remind me of my Baptism, and help me grow in grace each day. Keep my faith in You strong and firm until that great day when You call me home. In Jesus' name. Amen.

J. C. T.

Christmas Every Day

"Mom, please?" Regina pleaded. "Can't we wait another day?"

Although it was almost the end of January, Regina's family still had their Christmas tree up. The tree was drying out and the needles were falling off but Regina didn't want it to be gone. She wanted to leave the tree up all year.

"Why would you want to do that?" Regina's mom asked.

"Because Christmas is so wonderful. Everyone is nice. There are presents, and we eat the best food. I just hate when it's over."

"You know, Christmas isn't over just because we take down the tree."

"It's not?"

Her mother smiled. "No. Remember on Christmas Day when we read from the Bible about what Christmas really means?"

"Sure. Jesus was born to be our Savior."

"That's right," her mother answered. "At Christmas we celebrate the love God shows us by sending His Son into the world. And that love doesn't go away after Christmas."

"You're right, Mom. No matter what day it is, God's Christmas gift is always with us, whether we have the tree up or not."

"So can we take the tree down now?" her mother asked.

"Sure!" Then Regina added with a smile, "But can we put it up early next year?"

‑‑‑‑‑Let's talk: We can share the gift of God's love all year round. What are some ways you can share His love with others?

‑‑‑‑‑Let's pray: Dear heavenly Father, thank You for loving us so much that You gave us the gift of Your Son to be our Savior. Help me to share Your love with others today. Amen.

J. A.

Promises, Promises

"I'll clean my room later. I promise!" "I'll take out the trash later. I promise!"

Have you made promises like these? Most of us make promises we intend to keep, but don't. Thankfully God is not like us. He keeps His promises, even if it does not always seem like it.

God promised Abraham that he would have a son. That promise did not make sense because Abraham and Sarah were very old. But God kept that promise and Isaac was born. Through Isaac, Abraham became the father of all nations and an ancestor of Jesus.

After Adam and Eve sinned in the Garden of Eden, God promised He would send a Savior for all people. Many years went by. God waited until just the right time for Jesus to be born. Some people may have given up on God, but His promise was kept through Jesus, who would suffer, die, and rise again.

Read from God's Word

First of all, you must understand that in the last days scoffers will come, scoffing and following their own evil desires. They will say, "Where is this 'coming' He promised? Ever since our fathers died, everything goes on as it has since the beginning of creation." But they deliberately forget that long ago by God's word the heavens existed and the earth was formed out of water and by water. By these waters also the world of that time was deluged and destroyed. By the same word the present heavens and earth are reserved for fire, being kept for the day of judgment and destruction of ungodly men. 2 Peter 3:3–7

God also promises to come again on the Last Day. Some people may laugh at the thought of the Lord coming again. Some people may doubt because it is taking Him so long. When is He coming? We don't know, but we are sure it will happen. The Bible reminds us that God keeps His promises at just the right time.

_____Let's do: What is one of your favorite promises from God? Tell someone about it.

_____Let's pray: Dear God, thank You for always keeping Your promises. Amen.

J. A.

God Takes Care of Us

In the 1980s, leg warmers were popular. Everybody who was anybody had a pair.

One day Jennifer's mom bought her a pair of gray leg warmers. She was thrilled! Now Jennifer felt like she would fit in and be like all the popular girls.

Do you know what? It didn't make a bit of difference. The people that hadn't noticed her before didn't pay any more attention to her. The only thing that changed was her legs. They were actually warmer.

Sometimes we get too caught up in outward appearances. It's fun to dress up, but it can be dangerous if it becomes more important than what we think or feel.

John the Baptist was not a "cool" guy. He didn't wear the normal clothes of his day. The Bible says his clothes were made of camel's hair tied with a leather belt. John had an important mission. He told people the Savior was coming. He baptized hundreds—even Jesus Himself. John's message was more important than the way he looked.

God promises that He will always take care of us. We have what counts the most—the love of God and salvation through Jesus.

_____Let's talk: What are some ways God has provided for you or your family?

_____Let's pray: Lord, thank You for all the ways You have provided for me. Amen.

J. A.

Every Piece Is Important

Read from God's Word

"But you will receive power when the Holy Spirit comes on you; and you will be My witnesses in Jerusalem, and in all Judea and Samaria, and to the ends of the earth." Acts 1:8

Mrs. Andrews made quilts. She took fabric in different colors, patterns, and textures and cut them into small pieces. Some pieces had polka dots, some had stripes. The pieces were all so different that it might seem that putting them together could never make something beautiful! But Mrs. Andrews followed her plan and sewed the pieces together with thread. Eventually the pieces ended up as a beautiful quilt.

The God who made the world made different kinds of people. Men and women, old and young, short and tall—with different colors of hair, eyes, and skin. People are different on the inside too. Some are funny; others are serious. Some like to read, and others prefer sports. People like different kinds of food, music, and games. Sometimes, it seems like there's no way a world of so many types of people can have something in common!

But we do have something in common—we are all sinful people. And all people need Jesus. God's plan for our salvation included the suffering, death, and resurrection of Jesus. Only Jesus brings us forgiveness and makes us beautiful inside and out.

This is wonderful news. We want to share it with everyone! That's why Jesus told His disciples to go into the world and teach the Gospel to everyone.

_____Let's do: Is there someone in your neighborhood that you haven't been able to get along with? Remind yourself how much God loves them, and try to see them in a different way.

_____Let's pray: Dear Lord, thank You for all the different types of people You made. Please help me to show Your love to others today. Amen.

J. A.

Read from God's Word

Finally, brothers, whatever is true, whatever is noble, whatever is right, whatever is pure, whatever is lovely, whatever is admirable —if anything is excellent or praiseworthy—think about such things. Philippians 4:8

What Are You Thinking?

"You must have stayed up all night at the sleepover," Alex's dad said. "Your eyes look droopy."

Alex shrugged. "We didn't stay up that late. I just couldn't sleep."

His dad was surprised. "Why?"

Alex hesitated, but said, "We really did have a great time. But Dwayne's got this video game called 'House of the Dead.' It's kinda creepy—you've got to kill zombies."

His dad nodded. "Sounds like you didn't like it."

"No. But the other guys thought it was cool, so I played it. Then I couldn't fall asleep. I couldn't stop thinking about it."

"In a way, Alex, it's good that it disturbs you. When we see things like that, the Spirit of God living in us reacts, and our conscience is bothered. This bothering guards our hearts and minds that were claimed in Baptism."

Alex looked up at him. "It does?"

"Yep," his dad said. "You know, those kinds of games and movies give me nightmares too. Jesus is the resurrection and the life. He helps us focus on more positive things we have heard, received, and learned from Him. Let's pray together and ask God to wash those bad thoughts from your head."

"Okay," Alex answered with a smile, "and then I'm going to take a long nap!"

_____Let's talk: Are there any movies or games you know that contradict the Spirit of God?

_____Let's pray: Dear heavenly Father, help me to focus my thoughts on things that are good and pure and pleasing to You. Amen.

J. A

More Than Diamonds

Read from God's Word

"Before I formed you in the womb I knew you, before you were born I set you apart; I appointed you as a prophet to the nations." Jeremiah 1:5

The most precious gem is the diamond, known as a symbol of something very special. This is why diamonds are often used in wedding rings.

Diamonds are worth so much because they are rare and difficult to find. When a diamond starts out, it's just a piece of carbon, like charcoal. After many years of extreme heat and pressure, the carbon turns into a diamond. After it is dug out of a diamond mine, it is carefully cut and polished. Finally, it is set into a piece of jewelry.

Did you know that you are worth more than any diamond? You are more rare than the most beautiful diamond in the world because there's only one of you. Only you act the way you do or look the way you do. No one else has the same talents, makes the same mistakes, or feels the same feelings as you do. Even if you're a twin, you're still uniquely special.

When God created the first people, He made them in His own image, unlike any other thing. The Bible reading for today says, "Before I formed you in the womb I knew you." Isn't it awesome to think that before you were even born, God knew you, loved you, and already had a plan for your life?

_____Let's do: List the many ways God made you different from everybody else.

_____Let's pray: Dear heavenly Father, thank You for creating me in Your image. Help me to remember that You made me special and unique. Amen.

J. A.

Happy Me

There are lots of people in Jennifer's life who make her smile when she thinks of them.

One of them is a teacher who goes out of his way to help students. He even buys classroom supplies with his own money when the school budget is used up.

Another one is her junior high youth-group leader. By example she shows what young Christians can be like. She always forgives people although no one can ever be perfect.

Jennifer and her best friend go through some great times and tough times. They are always able to talk about their faith and share what God is doing in their lives.

These people share God's love. It is a love she counts on in tough times and good times.

Just as God freely gives us His love, He helps us to love others— happy or unhappy people—in the same way. With His help we love others in good and bad times.

Jesus came to earth to eliminate the sadness of our sin and death and the devil. He lived perfectly, died, and rose victorious so we can live with Him in heaven. Knowing that gives deep-down happiness, which we call joy.

_____Let's do: On a piece of paper, write the names of some of the happy people in your life. Choose one (or all) of them to thank God for in the prayer below.

_____Let's pray: Dear Lord, thank You for _____ . Thank You for the way he/she always _____ . Help me to share Your love with someone today. Amen.

J. A.

The Temple of God

Some churches have tall, graceful steeples. Others have enormous stained-glass windows. Pews made of dark wood are polished until they shine. Altars are covered with linen, and candlesticks are bright and clean. A church building is the house of God. Out of love and respect for God, we work hard to keep it clean, beautiful, and in good repair.

The Bible says that our body is the temple of God. Because Jesus atoned for our sins, God's Spirit lives inside each of us.

There are some children who say, "It's okay if I smoke (or drink or take drugs) because it's my body; I'm not hurting anybody." But that's not true. They are hurting themselves and tempting others to do wrong. When we do anything wrong, it's like painting graffiti on the walls of a church. When we swear or gossip about others, we pollute the temple of God. When we cheat or watch bad television, we hurt God's temple.

Read from God's Word

Don't you know that you yourselves are God's temple and that God's Spirit lives in you? If anyone destroys God's temple, God will destroy him; for God's temple is sacred, and you are that temple. 1 Corinthians 3:16–17

We are all guilty. God's Holy Spirit helps us live in baptismal grace. We need God's forgiveness, bought with the perfect life and blood of Jesus, which covers our mistakes better than any fresh coat of paint. His grace abounds, and by His sacrifice we are made clean! By grace, He chooses to live in us always.

_____Let's talk: Think of your body as the temple of God. Is there anything you've been doing that you should change?

_____Let's pray: Dear heavenly Father, thank You for loving me so much that Your Spirit lives in me. Forgive me when I haven't treated my body as Your temple. Help me to remember that You are always with me. Amen.

J. A.

Only God Knows

Sarah's dad was sick. Sarah prayed to God that he would be healed. One day the miracle they'd been praying for happened. The doctor said that Sarah's father was fine!

Janice also prayed for her father. But sadly, the doctor said there wasn't much hope. The next day Janice's father died.

Both men were Christians. Both had families praying for them. Why did God save only one? This is one of the hardest questions to answer because we don't know why.

We do know that when God created the world, it was perfect. Adam and Eve had everything they needed. But then they sinned. Since then we live in a sinful world of sickness and death.

Jesus healed many people. But not everybody who gets sick is healed. How confusing! We know God loves us, and we think He wants everyone to be healthy. However, we don't see the entire picture. God has a reason for everything, but we can't always understand what that reason is. Sometimes sickness helps people trust God more.

We can take comfort in the fact that Jesus came to be our Savior, and He took the sting out of sickness and death. No matter how long or short our physical life is, with Jesus as our Savior we have eternal life with God in heaven!

_____Let's do: Do you know someone who has been very sick and God has healed? What about someone who has died? Give thanks to God that those who believe in Him will live forever.

_____Let's pray: Dear Lord, thank You for sending Jesus to be my Savior and for giving me the gift of eternal life. Amen.

J. A.

Lots of Love

"Tamales for dinner!" exclaimed Mario. "I love tamales!"

His little sister, Patti, walked up behind him and asked, "Mario, do you really love tamales?"

"Yep," Mario answered, "I sure do."

Patti laughed. "Then why don't you marry them?"

It's pretty silly to think that someone would marry food! We use the word *love* in many different ways. There's the love you have for your family. There's the love your parents have for each other. Sometimes, like Mario, we say we love something when we just mean that we like it very much.

As you get older and start dating, you may feel a different kind of love. When you really love someone, you put his or her interests before your own.

The best example of unconditional love comes from God. He loves us so much that He sent us a Savior. He wanted to make sure we would be with Him throughout eternity.

Throughout the Bible, Jesus gives examples of how we should treat each other: with honor, dignity, and respect. Although we can never love perfectly like God does, He is always willing to send us help—lots of help—through the Holy Spirit. With that help we have lots of love to share!

_____Let's talk: What are some ways you can show God's love today?

_____Let's pray: Dear Father, thank You for the love You've shown me. Help me to let Your love shine through me today. Amen.

J. A.

february

Contributors for this month:

Jennifer AlLee

Kim Bejot

Jeanette A. Dall

Ruth Geisler

Jeanette Groth

Who's Calling?

When the phone rings, others often ask, "Who called?"

In today's Bible reading Samuel heard a voice calling him. The voice was God's. At first Samuel did not recognize who it was. Eli helped him identify that God was calling him. Eli told Samuel to say, "Speak, Lord, for Your servant is listening." God had a job and a message for Samuel to deliver. Samuel answered with these words, "Here I am."

Samuel's story helps explain the following devotions based on missionary experiences in Accra, Ghana, West Africa. Why would a teacher enjoying her work leave Lexington, Kentucky, and live in West Africa? The answer is simple. God still calls people today. He calls them to serve Him in many ways as He moves His church.

Are you listening for God's Word? What is God leading you to do? It is doubtful that you will leave today for some far-off place to tell others about Jesus, but with His help you are able to do that right where you are. You can invite your friend to church, where Christ's action through the Sacraments, absolution, forgiveness, and His Word changes lives. These are the kind of opportunities He gives—right in front of us—in the place God has put us.

Read from God's Word

The LORD called Samuel a third time, and Samuel got up and went to Eli and said, "Here I am; You called me." Then Eli realized that the LORD was calling the boy. So Eli told Samuel, "Go and lie down, and if He calls you, say, 'Speak, LORD, for Your servant is listening.'" So Samuel went and lay down in his place. The LORD came and stood there, calling as at the other times, "Samuel! Samuel!" Then Samuel said, "Speak, for Your servant is listening." 1 Samuel 3:8–10 ᔕ

_____Let's talk: What opportunities has God given you to invite others to hear Christ's Word in church?

_____Let's pray: Dear heavenly Father, help me to serve You in wonderful ways in my life. Let me lead others to hear Your Gospel message. Make me bold to speak the marvelous words of Your love and salvation. Amen.

J. G.

Read from God's Word

So I say, live by the Spirit, and you will not gratify the desires of the sinful nature. For the sinful nature desires what is contrary to the Spirit. ... But if you are led by the Spirit, you are not under law. The acts of the sinful nature are obvious: sexual immorality, impurity and debauchery; idolatry and witchcraft; hatred, discord, jealousy, fits of rage, selfish ambition, dissensions, factions and envy; drunkenness, orgies, and the like. I warn you, as I did before, that those who live like this will not inherit the kingdom of God. But the fruit of the Spirit is love, joy, peace, patience, kindness, goodness, faithfulness, gentleness and self-control. Against such things there is no law. Those who belong to Christ Jesus have crucified the sinful nature with its passions and desires. Since we live by the Spirit, let us keep in step with the Spirit. Galatians 5:16–25

Rescued

In Accra, a city in Ghana, West Africa, there is a smelly, polluted lagoon. One day a policeman saw a boy playing in the water. He called out, "Get out of that water!"

The boy yelled, "Help! I'm drowning!" The policeman jumped into the lagoon and rescued the boy.

Today's Bible reading includes a long list of sins that are part of everyday life of people around the world. If the world is like a lagoon, sins are like weights that drown us. Sins make our world into a smelly and dangerous place. We cannot do anything on our own to get out of the polluted pit of sin. We are as helpless to save ourselves as the drowning boy in the lagoon. We need a rescuer.

Jesus is that rescuer. He knew before we did that we needed a Savior—hopeless and helpless. He jumped into the lagoon stinking from sin, death, and evil to rescue us. He came to earth to suffer, die, and win the victory over sin and death for us. His victory gives us heaven as a free gift.

We hear this wonderful message proclaimed by the pastor in the Divine Service at church. Through the confession and absolution, the sermon, the words of the liturgy, and the Sacraments, God announces His rescue.

_____Let's do: Share the message of salvation with a world that is stinking and drowning in sin. What good news you have to share!

_____Let's pray: Thank You, Jesus, for plunging into the world of sin to save the world. Help me share this wonderful news of life and salvation. Amen.

J. G.

Most Important

In Ghana, market day comes once a week. It is nothing like a trip to the grocery store. Marketing takes a great deal of time. You might go to the woman selling oranges. But you don't just buy oranges. You ask about her family; you talk about the crops; you rejoice over the arrival of a baby. Finally you make your purchase. Next you purchase palm nut oil. A whole new conversation takes place. As the day unfolds, you have not only made all your purchases but also renewed friendships and found out a week's worth of news. There is no polite way to hurry this shopping and chatting process. Friendships take time.

The Bible reading explains our relationship with Christ. Christ took time to be our friend—He suffered, died, and was buried. He rose from the dead and grants new life to us now and forever through His promise in Baptism. With His Spirit we have the strength to share Christ-like love.

The friendship we have with God, who daily gives us the richest treasures of heaven and earth, is the most precious friendship of all. We are led to share that love of Christ with others.

Good friends share time, rejoice with each other, and share sorrows. Good friends also share the news of their Savior.

Read from God's Word

Do nothing out of selfish ambition or vain conceit, but in humility consider others better than yourselves. Each of you should look not only to your own interests, but also to the interests of others. Your attitude should be the same as that of Christ Jesus: Who, being in very nature God, did not consider equality with God something to be grasped, but made Himself nothing, taking the very nature of a servant, being made in human likeness. And being found in appearance as a man, He humbled himself and became obedient to death—even death on a cross! Therefore God exalted Him to the highest place and gave Him the name that is above every name, that at the name of Jesus every knee should bow, in heaven and on earth and under the earth, and every tongue confess that Jesus Christ is Lord, to the glory of God the Father. Philippians 2:1–11 ✍

_____Let's do: Spend time listing the names of some of your friends and thanking God for them. Then write a note to each of them.

_____Let's pray: Dear Jesus, thank You for calling me Your friend. Thank You for not counting the cost when You came into the world to make us friends through all eternity. Amen.

J. G.

Read from God's Word

When Jesus spoke again to the people, He said, "I am the light of the world. Whoever follows Me will never walk in darkness, but will have the light of life." John 8:12

Power Source

It is often unbelievably dark in Ghana because of power shortages, especially at night. With no streetlights, a quiet, eerie stillness sets in.

There is no way to work or help anyone. Activity stops. Everyone waits for the power to come back on. Then the shout goes up, "The power is on!" Lights go on, and motors hum. Activity resumes.

Jesus is the light of the world. He gets rid of the eerie darkness of sin, the world, and Satan. Without Him we would be powerless to find our way. Jesus not only frees us from the punishment of our sins but also guides us on earth. He gives us the light of His Word and the gift of the Holy Spirit.

Read also Matthew 5:14–16. How does God's light shine in and reflect onto others? Through His Word He strengthens your faith. "Baptism is a life-giving water, rich in grace, and a washing of the new birth in the Holy Spirit" (Small Catechism IV, 3). God's light leads you to help with the dishes when your mom is tired. He gives you courage to forgive your best friend after a disagreement. Jesus is the light of the world, who powers you to reflect His light.

_____Let's talk: How can Jesus' light make a difference in your family, your classroom, or your neighborhood?

_____Let's pray: Dear Jesus, thank You for being the light of the world. Help me reflect that light to people sitting in the darkness of sin. Give me the power of Your Spirit. Amen.

J. G.

A Real Tangle

One of the routes in the city of Accra, Ghana, has a traffic circle. Passing through this circle can take a few minutes or a couple of hours. The first time you get in the circle tangle, you sense no plan. When you are in the tangle, where horns beep and cars cut you off, you feel uneasy and wonder if you will get out safely.

As you pass through this circle more often, you begin to understand it more. You recognize honking is not expressions of anger but ways of giving messages. Often ordinary citizens get out of their vehicles to help direct traffic so it moves more smoothly. You may even notice a system of give-and-take that makes travel possible along this busy route.

Is your life ever like that circle? Do you see it tangled or in a mess? Have you wondered whether there is any kind of plan for your life? God has the answer. In His Word He tells us about His marvelous plan of salvation. Through the frustrations we have, God reminds us that He is our shepherd and guide—through all the tangles of life. With eyes of faith we are able to see His hand at work.

Read from God's Word

And we know that in all things God works for the good of those who love Him, who have been called according to His purpose. ... What, then, shall we say in response to this? If God is for us, who can be against us? He who did not spare His own Son, but gave Him up for us all—how will He not also, along with Him, graciously give us all things? Who will bring any charge against those whom God has chosen? It is God who justifies. Who is he that condemns? Christ Jesus, who died—more than that, who was raised to life—is at the right hand of God and is also interceding for us. Who shall separate us from the love of Christ? Shall trouble or hardship or persecution or famine or nakedness or danger or sword? ... No, in all these things we are more than conquerors through Him who loved us. Romans 8:28, 31–37 ✐

———Let's talk: What are some of the tangles and problems in your life today? How can God's Word help you with these problems?

———Let's pray: Dear Jesus, I know that even when my life seems snarled and tangled, You have a plan for me. Thank You for always working things out for my eternal good. Amen.

J. G.

Read from God's Word

Now faith is being sure of what we hope for and certain of what we do not see. This is what the ancients were commended for. ... These were all commended for their faith, yet none of them received what had been promised. God had planned something better for us so that only together with us would they be made perfect. Hebrews 11:1–2, 39–40

Sankofa

Jeannette was a missionary in Ghana. One of her favorite mementos is a *Sankofa*—a bird with its head turned backward holding an egg in its mouth.

A friend gave her a *Sankofa* pin as a going-away present. The friend said, "This symbolizes change in your life." Sankofa is a symbol of your past. It reminds you to take the best from the past and go forward into your future, filled with hope and promise.

Jeannette thought about that symbol and about her own life. In her past she was blessed to hear God's Word from her parents. She could apply many of the lessons she learned to life in Ghana. She remembered the wonderful words that brought the news about her Savior. She thought about her own adult children. From their support of mission work in Ghana, Jeannette could support other Christians. She also thought about her congregation in Kentucky supporting her work with money and prayers. What a lesson!

Hebrews 11 lists a number of Bible characters. We read about Christ making them His people. It isn't a detailed account of the things they did, but it shares the most important witness they gave—through faith in the promised Savior, Jesus Christ. Christ is the best part for today and every day in the future.

_____Let's talk: In what ways might baptismal contrition, repentance, and grace bring certainty to your future?

_____Let's pray: Dear Jesus, thank You for Your past acts—Your death on the cross and resurrection from the grave—which secure my future and remain with me forever. Amen.

J. G.

Shaping an Elephant

Jeannette collected many things during her missionary experience in Ghana, West Africa. One of her favorite pieces is an elephant chair. It started out as a big log. A craftsman began to work with tools. Chip-by-chip a form emerged. When the craftsman was done, the log had become a unique elephant chair. Through his master artist's eyes, he saw an elephant.

Today God is forming you. Perhaps He is teaching you lessons in patience. Maybe He is pushing you to study His Word and learn more about Him. He may be encouraging you to play an instrument or to write devotions. He may be shaping you to share the Good News of His love and salvation with people you meet each day.

There is nothing in a log that turns it into an elephant. There is nothing in us that makes us beautiful or valuable. God alone declares us worthy through the death and resurrection of Jesus. He fashions us into a new shape, a new creation, clothed in His forgiveness and strengthened with His power.

Today is a good day to ask God to continue the shaping and molding that began in Baptism. Ask Him to make you a willing servant, ready for the vocation He has in mind for you. Thank Him for the blessing you receive as His dear child.

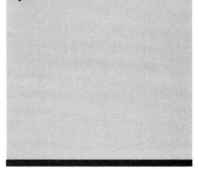

Read from God's Word

"Your hands shaped me and made me. Will You now turn and destroy me? Remember that You molded me like clay. Will You now turn me to dust again? Did You not pour me out like milk and curdle me like cheese, clothe me with skin and flesh and knit me together with bones and sinews? You gave me life and showed me kindness, and in Your providence watched over my spirit." Job 10:8–12 ✑

_____Let's talk: What talents and abilities do you have that give you special chances to share His love with others?

_____Let's pray: Dear Jesus, thank You for making me Your own. Please continue to mold and shape me so I can be a good servant in Your kingdom. Amen.

J. G.

Read from God's Word

Who is going to harm you if you are eager to do good? But even if you should suffer for what is right, you are blessed. "Do not fear what they fear; do not be frightened." But in your hearts set apart Christ as Lord. Always be prepared to give an answer to everyone who asks you to give the reason for the hope that you have. But do this with gentleness and respect, keeping a clear conscience, so that those who speak maliciously against your good behavior in Christ may be ashamed of their slander. It is better, if it is God's will, to suffer for doing good than for doing evil. For Christ died for sins once for all, the righteous for the unrighteous, to bring you to God. He was put to death in the body but made alive by the Spirit. 1 Peter 3:13–18 〜

Prepared

Ghana is known for its wise sayings. As interesting as they are, they are nothing like wisdom that comes from God's Word proclaiming our Savior.

One Ghanaian proverb reads, "The chicken says he does not know when the chief will pass a law that everyone should stand on one leg, and so he is practicing." In Ghana the chief is the absolute source of power. His job is to make decisions and laws for his people. The chicken realizes that the chief might make a law that says to stand on one leg. He often practices to be ready and able to do it.

In the Bible reading God tells us we should always be ready for the Holy Spirit to lead us. We should be ready to share Jesus' love and forgiveness whenever we have a chance. The person who needs to hear may be a friend or someone on the school bus.

You can practice sharing the hope of Jesus. Tell your parents about Jesus' love—although they probably already know it. This isn't so scary! Practice telling a friend who goes to church or Sunday school with you.

Ask the Holy Spirit to give you an opportunity to share the message of Jesus. Be ready! Be alert! You can be prepared—with God's help.

_____Let's do: Plan your sharing. What words will you use in your message?

_____Let's pray: Dear Holy Spirit, make me ready to share the wonderful news of Jesus with anyone I may meet. Amen.

J. G.

How Big Are You?

Show how tall you are. You probably used your hand—palm down—to show your height. In Ghana when you show someone's height that way, it indicates they are done growing. If the palm is up, then they are still growing.

How would Christians show their size? Paul would say they should always be palm up. St. Paul told the Colossian Christians that he had been praying for their spiritual growth. He asked the Lord to fill them with knowledge of God's will to help them grow. Paul was talking about a heart-changing and life-renewing knowledge of Christ to see through all the false claims.

Growing a healthy body means eating good food, resting, and exercising. To grow in Christ means hearing God's Word at church, at home, and in Sunday school. God wants us to always grow spiritually. The Lord helps us through His Word to gain spiritual muscles—to give us courage, to help us fight temptations, and to give us patience for our whole life.

Read from God's Word

For this reason, since the day we heard about you, we have not stopped praying for you and asking God to fill you with the knowledge of His will through all spiritual wisdom and understanding. And we pray this in order that you may live a life worthy of the Lord and may please Him in every way: bearing fruit in every good work, growing in the knowledge of God, being strengthened with all power according to His glorious might so that you may have great endurance and patience, and joyfully giving thanks to the Father, who has qualified you to share in the inheritance of the saints in the kingdom of light. For He has rescued us from the dominion of darkness and brought us into the kingdom of the Son He loves, in whom we have redemption, the forgiveness of sins. Colossians 1:9–14 ✍

Every day is a chance for you to have God's power as you share His love, especially to the recess bully; His joy, even when you can't play video games; His forgiveness, to your brother; and much more. God, through His Word, says, "I will make you grow."

_____Let's talk: What is God's plan for growing in His Word?

_____Let's pray: Dear Jesus, keep me growing in my knowledge of Your greatness and love. Amen.

J. G.

Read from God's Word

In His great mercy He has given us new birth into a living hope through the resurrection of Jesus Christ from the dead, and into an inheritance that can never perish, spoil or fade. ... In this you greatly rejoice, though now for a little while you may have had to suffer grief in all kinds of trials. These have come so that your faith—of greater worth than gold, which perishes even though refined by fire—may be proved genuine and may result in praise, glory and honor when Jesus Christ is revealed. Though you have not seen Him, you love Him; and even though you do not see Him now, you believe in Him and are filled with an inexpressible and glorious joy, for you are receiving the goal of your faith, the salvation of your souls. 1 Peter 1:3–9

A Source of Joy

What gives you joy? Is it winning a game? new clothes? time with your friends? All these things give us joy, but only for a while. You may lose the next game, stain your clothes, or lose your friends.

The joy that Jesus gives is quite different. The joy that Jesus gives does not depend on things or life conditions. In Ghana, many of the people singing about joy do not have televisions or computers. How can they sing about joy? They are singing about Jesus' joy—true, lasting joy built on knowing Him as their Lord and Savior. That joy stays with you no matter what.

A favorite chorus in Ghana is the following:

I have joy in my heart,
  deep, deep down in my heart.
I have joy in my heart,
  deep, deep down in my heart.
Jesus gave it to me.
  And nothing can destroy it.
I have joy in my heart.
Deep, deep down in my heart

The joy that Jesus gives is eternal—nothing can destroy it. You have the joy of knowing you will be in heaven with Jesus with all sins forgiven. God gives this joy to you freely because Jesus won it for you through His perfect life, suffering, death, and resurrection. Rejoice!

———Let's talk: What gives you joy? List three qualities you know about God that give you joy.

———Let's pray: Dear Jesus, let me grow in knowledge of You and of Your Word that I may know the joy of Your salvation and never doubt Your great love and mercy for me. Amen.

J. G.

What to Pray

I t had surprised Shawn-Paul when his parents allowed him to travel as drummer with the young members of the Christian pop group, His Song. Having Pastor Tom as their chaperone helped his parents feel comfortable. And, really, how dangerous was it to perform in shopping malls?

Shawn-Paul said thank you to the last fan and packed up his drum set. The rest of the band had already walked across the street to their hotel.

The smell of alcohol made Shawn-Paul feel sick as he walked into his room. He didn't know how his underage roommate managed to sneak in a bottle of gin, but Kenny did it everyday. Shawn-Paul lay on his bed and began to pray.

What is filling your prayer life? Are you worried about someone who smokes, uses drugs, or drinks too much? Are you afraid you won't get on the basketball team? Are you asking God to give you one good friend?

Read from God's Word

In the same way, the Spirit helps us in our weakness. We do not know what we ought to pray for, but the Spirit Himself intercedes for us with groans that words cannot express. Romans 8:26

God promises that nothing is too big or small to bring to Him in prayer. He knew how to solve your biggest problem—by sending His Son to die to take the punishment for your sins. Talk to God right now. God promises that His Holy Spirit will pray for you even when you don't know what to say.

‗‗‗‗Let's do: Try reading and praying through a psalm each day for the rest of the week.

‗‗‗‗Let's pray: Father, when I don't know what to do, or even how to pray, please help me. In Jesus' name. Amen.

R. G.

Read from God's Word

For just as through the disobedience of the one man the many were made sinners, so also through the obedience of the one man the many will be made righteous. Romans 5:19 ✑

Everybody Does It

Shontae watched her friend slip some earrings into her pocket. "Take something," Rene whispered. Shontae saw that the clerk wasn't looking. However, Shontae wasn't going to steal. She pushed her friend out of the store.

"You can get arrested for shoplifting," Shontae said.

"Everybody shoplifts," Rene said. "Stores price everything higher to cover what gets taken. If you're going to be a snob about it, maybe we shouldn't hang out."

Have you ever been in a situation where a friend tempts you to do something you know is wrong?

Ever since Adam tried to blame his sin on Eve and Eve tried to blame her sin on the serpent, we've lived in a world filled with the temptation to sin. But just as sin came to us through one man, Adam, one man, Jesus, takes our sin away. Jesus has faced every temptation you face. He has also been surrounded by others who tried to get Him to do wrong. His friends deserted Him.

Jesus resisted temptation; He lived a perfect life. Still, He was condemned to die, but not for His sin—for yours and mine.

Think of Jesus the next time you're in a difficult situation. Ask Him to help you handle it. He will help you endure any difficulty, for He has endured all things for us.

_____Let's do: Do you have any friends who might tempt you to do wrong? Ask Jesus to help you figure out what to do in that situation.

_____Let's pray: Jesus, when I'm tempted to do the wrong thing, help me stick up for You. Amen.

R. G.

It's Time to Give Up

During Lent we remember how Jesus suffered and died for us. Some people give up something they enjoy during Lent to remind them, in a small way, of how much Jesus suffered for them on the cross.

If you want, give up something you like—homework doesn't count—during Lent because it is a good and beneficial Christian practice. But God's prophet Joel suggests you give up other things as well.

In biblical times God's people sometimes wore rough cloth made from goat or camel hair. They felt wearing the scratchy cloth, called "sackcloth," would show God how sorry they were for their sins. Sometimes they even tore their clothing to show how sorry they were. But Joel says, "Rend your heart and not your garments. Return to the Lord your God, for He is gracious and compassionate, slow to anger and abounding in love" (Joel 2:13).

God doesn't look at the clothes we wear. He doesn't want us to act sad—giving up things we like just to show how sorry we are. God looks at our heart. He turns our heart away from sin. He tells us to leave our sins at the cross, where Jesus died to take the punishment for them.

Read from God's Word

Rend your heart and not your garments. Return to the LORD your God, for He is gracious and compassionate, slow to anger and abounding in love, and He relents from sending calamity. Joel 2:13

_____Let's do: On a scrap of paper write a sin that's been bothering you. Throw the scrap in the trash. This activity can remind you of Christ's Word of forgiveness spoken and received in the Divine Service. Thank God for taking all your sin away because of Jesus.

_____Let's pray: Dear God, during this Lenten season help me to turn my heart to You. Forgive my sin and fill me with Your peace so I don't feel guilty or worried. In Jesus' name. Amen.

R. G.

Read from God's Word

"Greater love has no one than this, that he lay down his life for his friends." John 15:13 ✍

Loving Names

oa had moved from Vietnam a few weeks earlier. The first time Hoa walked through a mall she wondered why hearts were everywhere. Her dad suggested she look up "valentine" at the school library.

Hoa read that a priest named Valentine was killed in Rome on February 14, in the year 270 because of his love for Jesus. Nobody knew much about St. Valentine or why people started sending each other cards on February 14.

Juliann walked over to Hoa's desk and handed her a card. "Happy Valentine's Day, Hoa. Do you want to walk to the bus with me?" Hoa smiled. This Valentine Day stuff was all right.

The meaning of the name Valentine is something of a mystery, but there's no mystery about Jesus' name. God sent an angel to tell Joseph, "Do not be afraid to take Mary home as your wife, because what is conceived in her is from the Holy Spirit. She will give birth to a son, and you are to give Him the name Jesus, because He will save His people from their sins" (Matthew 1:20–21). Jesus saves us from punishment for our sins, fear of death, and fear of the devil.

As you trade valentines today, remember Jesus. His love is so great that He was willing to suffer and die for us.

———Let's do: Look up St. Valentine on the Internet. Look through the valentines you get today. Find words that remind you of the great love Jesus has for you.

———Let's pray: Dear God, thank You for sending Jesus as my greatest valentine. In His name. Amen.

R. G.

Would You Change?

Ian pushed the wheels of his chair and rolled himself center stage. Pastor Bob noticed the disgusted look on his face. "What's the problem, Ian?" the young pastor asked. "I'm thrilled that you volunteered to be master of ceremonies for the talent show."

"Well, I didn't actually volunteer. After you 'suggested' to Aaron that he'd be a good emcee, he paid me $8.50 and a large candy bar to take his place. It seemed like a good deal at the time, but now I'm not sure. Whoever heard of an emcee in a wheelchair?"

Pastor Bob laughed. "I've never seen that stop you before, Ian. I've seen you wheeling around a basketball court and a dance floor. You've got a fantastic sense of humor—that's what is important."

Ian would probably pay a lot more than $8.50 and a candy bar to be able to leave his wheelchair behind and stand up and walk. Do you ever find yourself wishing you were different in some way—taller, thinner, funnier, more athletic, prettier? Don't worry about it! God made you and loves you exactly the way you are. You are such a special kid that God sent His own Son to die for you.

Read from God's Word

I praise You because I am fearfully and wonderfully made; Your works are wonderful. I know that full well. Psalm 139:14 ᑐ

_____Let's do: When you are discouraged or confused, heed the words of Christ's absolution. These words of God never change no matter what you go through or feel. What a relief that God's love, mercy, and forgiveness remain for us.

_____Let's pray: Dear God, forgive me when I worry about fitting in in ways that aren't important. Thank You for loving me so much. In Jesus' name. Amen.

R. G.

Read from God's Word

So do not fear, for I am with you; do not be dismayed, for I am your God. I will strengthen you and help you; I will uphold you with My righteous right hand. Isaiah 41:10

Home Alone

Chad had sat in the recliner in the family room. *WHIR-R-R-R!* He jumped as the refrigerator motor in the kitchen kicked on. *Click. Click. Click.* He clutched the arms of the chair as tree branches tapped against the window.

Chad's friends thought it was cool to be home alone. It seemed to make them feel grown-up. They talked about how fun it was to microwave a bag of popcorn all for themselves and pick their own video to watch. Chad just couldn't see it. He'd rather have the house full of people and happy, familiar noises.

Mom knew how Chad felt. She'd promised to run to the store and hurry right back. Chad knew she was trying to help him become more independent.

"Help me not be afraid, God," Chad whispered. He jumped out of the chair and marched to the kitchen. He emptied the dishwasher and began to set the table for dinner. If Mom thought he was mature enough to stay alone, he'd show her she was right.

What makes you feel afraid? God tells us that whenever we feel afraid, we can call on Him. He will help us with whatever is bothering us and help us to trust in Him. Call on Him the next time you feel afraid.

_____Let's do: In a journal or on a piece of paper, describe the last time you felt afraid. How did the situation turn out? How did God help you?

_____Let's pray: Dear God, I'm glad that when I feel afraid, I can call on You. In Jesus' name. Amen.

R. G.

Learning to Pray

J ason said, "Nilp, Mommy." Mom replied, "Can you say *milk*, Jason?" But she gave him a glass of milk anyway.

When Jason was playing outside, he pointed to the sky and said, "Heh-di-dod-er." "That's a *helicopter*, Jason," his sister said. Everyone tried to teach Jason what to say.

As Jason got older he learned to pronounce *milk* and *helicopter*. He heard his mom and his teachers and friends and people on television say many words, and he learned to say them too.

One time, when Jesus lived on earth, His disciples asked Him to help them say some special words. "Jesus, teach us to pray," they said. Jesus taught them a prayer you have heard. Because Jesus taught it to us we call it the Lord's Prayer.

When we listen to the Lord's Prayer, Jesus is showing us how to pray. In the Lord's Prayer we call God "our Father" because He made us and loves us. We can talk to Him about all the things we need. We ask Him to forgive our sins and to help us whenever we have trouble. We thank Him for being such a wonderful God.

We have many teachers who help us learn new words. Our best Teacher teaches us how to pray!

Read from God's Word

One day Jesus was praying in a certain place. When He finished, one of His disciples said to Him, "Lord, teach us to pray, just as John taught his disciples." He said to them, "When you pray, say: 'Father, hallowed be Your name. Your kingdom come. Give us each day our daily bread. Forgive us our sins, for we also forgive everyone who sins against us. And lead us not into temptation."' Luke 11:1–4

_____Let's do: Review Luther's Morning or Evening Prayer from your catechism with your family or class.

_____Let's pray: Thank You, Father, for continuing to teach me how to pray from the riches of Your Word. In Jesus' name. Amen.

R. G.

Read from God's Word

Then Jesus went through the towns and villages, teaching as He made His way to Jerusalem. Someone asked Him, "Lord, are only a few people going to be saved?" He said to them, "Make every effort to enter through the narrow door, because many, I tell you, will try to enter and will not be able to." Luke 13:22–24

The Door to Heaven

irls, come see the neighbors' car," Mom called, rushing out the front door. Karen and Karla flew outside. Mr. MacIntyre took them for a ride. They all declared the car awesome.

"Thanks," said Dad. "I'd better get back to work." Karen turned the front doorknob and nothing happened. "Uh-oh," she said. "I locked the door when we ran out. I'll go through the back door and let you guys in."

In a moment Karen was back with their dog, Cindy, barking happily behind her. "We've got a problem," Karen said. "The back door is locked too."

"Oh, fine," Dad laughed. "Locked out of our own house—that could only happen to a family like ours."

"Hold everything!" Karla cried. "I have an idea." Karla led her family to the door and got down on her hands and knees. Slowly she squeezed through the little doggy door, with Cindy wiggling behind her. Everyone cheered as Karla opened the back door.

Heaven doesn't really have a door, but Jesus once said that going to heaven is like going through a narrow door. Only certain people can go through it—people who by faith believe that Jesus is their Savior. Karla opened the door for her family. Jesus opened the door to heaven by dying on the cross for us.

——Let's do: Make a sign for your bedroom door. It might say, "Someone who God loves lives here."

——Let's pray: Jesus, thank You for shepherding me through the door to heaven by Your Word and Sacraments. Help me to tell others the Good News that You died for them and rose again. Amen.

R. G.

"I Am the Resurrection and the Life"

Pastor Lopez was talking, but Jared didn't listen. He felt like crying. Almost all of his Sunday school class was here for Mr. Sawyer's funeral. Jared could see their teacher, Mrs. Sawyer, in the front row. She looked as if she was crying.

Mr. Sawyer visited Jared's class almost every week. Last summer he drove them to the park for their lesson. Another time he'd worn his uniform and told them about being a policeman. Now Jared would never see him again.

Mrs. Sawyer was listening to the pastor. Pastor Lopez was talking about a story she had taught them in Sunday school.

"When Jesus saw Lazarus' grave, He cried," Pastor Lopez said. "But He told Lazarus's sister Martha, 'I am the resurrection and the life. He who believes in Me will live, even though he dies.'" Pastor Lopez looked right at Mrs. Sawyer. "Jesus was with Mr. Sawyer while he was alive, and he is with Jesus now. The dead in Christ are alive in Christ." Mrs. Sawyer nodded and almost smiled.

Jared felt better. When Lazarus died, he didn't stay in the grave. Jesus called, "Lazarus, come out!" and Lazarus walked out. One day Jesus will take Mrs. Sawyer, Jared, and all Christians to live with Him in heaven.

_____ Let's do: Think of someone you know who is sad because a friend or relative died. Send them a card telling them Jesus loves them.

_____ Let's pray: Jesus, thank You for Your promise to take me to heaven. Amen.

R. G.

Read from God's Word

The LORD was with Joseph and he prospered, and he lived in the house of his Egyptian master. ... The LORD was with him; He showed him kindness and granted him favor in the eyes of the prison warden. So the warden put Joseph in charge of all those held in the prison, and he was made responsible for all that was done there. The warden paid no attention to anything under Joseph's care, because the LORD was with Joseph and gave him success in whatever he did. Genesis 39:2, 21–23

Roller-Coaster Living

A roller coaster ride can be exciting, but scary. First you slowly go up to the very top. Then you zoom down—screaming all the way.

Just as you catch your breath, you're on the top again, higher than before. Then it's screaming down to the bottom once more.

The life of Joseph in the Old Testament can be compared to a roller coaster. It seems like Joseph was either way up or he was down in the pits. Here's a summary of Joseph's life:

Favorite son of Jacob/UP
Hated by his brothers/DOWN
Had prophetic dreams/UP
Sold as a slave by his brothers/DOWN
Manager of Potiphar's house/UP
Falsely accused and
    imprisoned/DOWN
Put in charge of prisoners/UP
In prison more than two year/DOWN
Interprets Pharaoh's dreams and is made second in command of Egypt and saves the lives of his father and brothers by providing them with food during the famine/UP

Through all the ups and downs of his life, Joseph trusted God. He obeyed God and gave Him credit for his ability to interpret dreams. All through Joseph's life, God was with him.

Just like Joseph, we can trust the Lord to love us and help us. God redeemed us through the sacrifice of His Son. He promises to be with us always—now and forever.

_____Let's talk: One of Joseph's brothers who was saved from death during the famine was Judah. By saving Judah, how did God use Joseph to bring His salvation to the whole world? (Check out Jesus' "family tree" in Matthew 1:2,16.)

_____Let's pray: God, thank You for loving me and being with me always. Help me trust You and live as You want me to live, through the power of Your Spirit. Amen.

J. A. D.

What Kayla Knows

Pastor Nunes had just announced that it was time for the offering when everyone laughed. A three-year-old girl had walked up and put her nickel right on the altar.

Kayla knew what to do with her money. There was no point in waiting for the ushers. She wanted to give her money right to Jesus.

Pastor Nunes smiled and picked Kayla up. He said, "Let the children come to Me, for to such belongs the kingdom of God."

Kayla reminded everyone of the day that some mothers brought their children to see Jesus. The disciples told them, "Jesus is too busy. Take your children home." But Jesus said, "Let the children come to Me."

Kayla knows that Jesus is her best friend. He died on a cross for her so she can go to heaven and talk and play with Him.

Sometimes we worry about school or our friends. We might worry when our parents have problems or someone we know gets sick. We know Jesus is there, but we may start to wonder whether He can really help.

Kayla would tell you, "Yes, He can." The next time you have a problem, go right to Jesus in His Word and Sacraments and ask Him to help you. He will.

Read from God's Word

People were bringing little children to Jesus to have Him touch them, but the disciples rebuked them. When Jesus saw this, He was indignant. He said to them, "Let the little children come to me, and do not hinder them, for the kingdom of God belongs to such as these. I tell you the truth, anyone who will not receive the kingdom of God like a little child will never enter it." And He took the children in His arms, put His hands on them and blessed them. Mark 10:13–16

———Let's do: Look at your family's Baptism certificates.
Talk about how you learned about Jesus
when you were very small.

———Let's pray: Jesus, thank You for always having the time
to listen to me and help me. I love You. Amen.

R. G.

Read from God's Word

He Himself bore our sins in His body on the tree, so that we might die to sins and live for righteousness; by His wounds you have been healed. For you were like sheep going astray, but now you have returned to the Shepherd and Overseer of your souls. 1 Peter 2:24–25 ✎

Joshua's Side Trip

"Always stay on the trail," said the scoutmaster. "And never wander off alone."

There were lots of neat things to see along the way, including plants, trees, and birds. When they went around a bend, Joshua saw a deer!

He tried to follow it, but he scared the animal away. Joshua turned, expecting to see his troop going up the trail, but they weren't there. In fact, the trail wasn't there.

Joshua was upset with himself. Without meaning to, he had done both things that the scoutmaster had told them *not* to do. He was scared that he might not be able to find the troop. Then he heard someone calling his name. In a moment the scoutmaster was standing in front of him. Joshua had never been so happy!

After sin came into the world, people were separated from God—lost. But God brought them back to Himself by sending His only Son, Jesus, to earth. Jesus came to rescue us. Jesus brings us back to God. We're not lost anymore.

Sometimes we make "side-trips" of our own, going a different direction. But God sends the Holy Spirit in the Divine Service. There the Law leads us to know our wrong path and to confess our sinful "side-trips," and the Gospel proclaims forgiveness in Christ.

———Let's talk: Have you ever been lost? How did you feel when you were found again?

———Let's pray: Dear Lord, forgive me when I decide to go my own way. Thank You for Your Spirit, who leads me back to You. Amen.

J. A.

Everyone's Important

Dwight was excited about the school play. For weeks he practiced reading lines. When the day of the auditions came, Dwight tried his best.

The next day his teacher posted the results on the board. Next to Dwight's name it said "Stage Crew—Curtain."

His mother could see that he was in a bad mood as soon as he walked in the front door. "What's wrong, honey?" she asked.

He told her, "I'm just the stupid old curtain-boy."

"I know you're disappointed," his mother said. "But there's nothing stupid about your job. Working on a play is like being part of a big team. It's like baseball. What would happen if the catcher left? Or what if the person who runs the scoreboard doesn't want to do it anymore?"

Read from God's Word

For by the grace given me I say to every one of you: Do not think of yourself more highly than you ought, but rather think of yourself with sober judgment, in accordance with the measure of faith God has given you. Just as each of us has one body with many members, and these members do not all have the same function, so in Christ we who are many form one body, and each member belongs to all the others. Romans 12:3–5

Dwight answered, "I guess my job is important, after all. Besides," he added with a grin, "they can't start the play until I open the curtain!"

Sometimes we get depressed because we think we're not doing anything important. But to God, everyone is special. He sent His own Son, Jesus Christ, to live and die for us.

Baptized Christians are united to Christ—one body with Him. That makes us one with other believers in Christ. Every believer has an important part to play in life.

_____Let's talk: How does God use an ordinary person like you or other Christians for "extra" ordinary things?

_____Let's pray: Dear God, thank You for creating me as a member of Your body through Holy Baptism. Help me live out my calling in the place You have put me. Amen.

J. A.

Read from God's Word

God is our refuge and strength, an ever-present help in trouble. Therefore we will not fear, though the earth give way and the mountains fall into the heart of the sea, though its waters roar and foam and the mountains quake with their surging. Psalm 46:1–3

Nature Out of Control

In *The Wizard of Oz* a tornado picks up the house where Dorothy Gale lives with her aunt and uncle, and when it lands, she discovers that she's in a place called Oz. This is just the beginning of Dorothy's adventure. But in the end, she finds that it was only a dream and she is really safe at home.

Real-life disasters are much different. Fires, floods, earthquakes, tornadoes, and hurricanes are all called "natural disasters." They are very scary, and when they're over, you don't find yourself in an enchanted land somewhere over the rainbow.

Sometimes people blame God for these disasters. But God is not to blame. When God created the earth, it was perfect. When sin came into the world, it affected everything, not just the people. The earth itself was corrupted by sin.

Jesus Christ came to save God's children from sin. He is the offering that shielded us from God's punishment. But as long as sin exists in the world, there will be natural disasters.

There's no need to be afraid. In Psalm 46 we learn that "God is our refuge and strength, an ever-present help in trouble." God will always protect us and keep us safe.

_____Let's talk: What if a Christian friend or loved one were to die in a natural disaster? How is God still a refuge and strength?

_____Let's pray: Heavenly Father, thank You for all Your promises to guard and keep Your children. Help me remember that no matter what the situation, You are always there to help and protect me. Amen.

J. A.

Seek and You Will Find

C an you find the words *ASK*, *SEEK*, and *KNOCK* in the puzzle below?

S	T	A	S	K	Y
E	I	B	P	N	G
E	Y	O	L	O	Q
K	H	B	V	C	R
C	L	Y	N	K	W
H	X	K	F	B	G

Read from God's Word

"Ask and it will be given to you; seek and you will find; knock and the door will be opened to you. For everyone who asks receives; he who seeks finds; and to him who knocks, the door will be opened." Matthew 7:7–8

God's Word tells us to seek and we will find. Just as you had to look through the puzzle, sometimes you need to search God's Word for help.

To explain to a friend how much God loves them, you could show them John 3:16: "God so loved the world that He gave His one and only Son, that whoever believes in Him shall not perish but have eternal life."

The Scriptures point us to Jesus. When we attend church, God is there in the preaching of the Word and the Sacraments. Only in Him do we have the life that never ends.

There may be a time when you want to find something in the Bible but you're not sure where to look. You can ask a parent, pastor, or teacher to help you. When you ask and seek, God will give you the answer to your need. Paul says in Philippians 4:19, "My God will meet all your needs according to His glorious riches in Christ Jesus."

_____Let's do: Make up a word search of your own. Give it to a friend to see if he or she can find the words.

_____Let's pray: Dear God, thank You for Your Word. May it always be a light for my path through life, until I'm with You in heaven. Amen.

J. A.

Garbage In, Garbage Out

Have you ever used a computer to write a report or to play games? Computers must really be smart.

But a computer knows only what somebody tells it. If you want to print the phrase "Jesus saves," but you type "Sejus vases," what do you think will print out? That's right—just a couple of misspelled words.

Your mind is the most complex thinking machine ever created. It is even more amazing than a computer. It was made by the Creator of all— God! But when sin entered the world, our bodies and minds became corrupt, that is, filled with thoughts that were not what God intended. Jesus Christ died on a cross to save us from sin. Through faith in Him, our minds are renewed.

As with the computer, your thoughts and actions are a direct result of what you feed your mind. Our sinful nature is attracted to the "garbage in" from evil in the world. Unless something wonderful goes into your heart and mind, only garbage will come out. So God rescues you; He feeds you when you read and study His Word and worship Him. Through the Divine Service He offers you His means of grace through which your mind and body are renewed.

_____Let's talk: How does God work through public or private confession and absolution to renew your mind and whole self?

_____Let's pray: Lord God, please forgive me for sometimes feeding my mind garbage. Thank You for renewing my mind through Your Son, Jesus Christ. Help me concentrate on what is good and pure and holy. Amen.

J. A.

God Never Forgets

When Billy first got his puppy, Goldie, they were the best of friends. They played together, and Billy made sure to feed and brush her. But after a while Billy started to forget about Goldie. One day he forgot to take her for a walk. The next day he forgot to feed her. Before long, Billy's parents were doing more to care for Goldie than he was.

Finally his father told him that they needed to have a talk. "Billy," he said, "I think that you've forgotten the promise you made to take care of Goldie. She's your dog, and it's your responsibility to take care of her."

Billy was sad when he realized how badly he'd been treating Goldie. "I'm sorry," he told his father. "I'll try to do better."

Sometimes we all forget to keep promises. But there is someone who never breaks a promise. That someone is God. In the Bible He promises to be with us always and to take care of us (Matthew 28:20). God loves us so much that He gave His only Son, Jesus, to be crucified and to rise again to save us from our sins.

It's wonderful to know that our heavenly Father will never forget to take care of us!

Read from God's Word

"Therefore I tell you, do not worry about your life, what you will eat or drink; or about your body, what you will wear. Is not life more important than food, and the body more important than clothes? Look at the birds of the air; they do not sow or reap or store away in barns, and yet your heavenly Father feeds them. Are you not much more valuable than they? Who of you by worrying can add a single hour to his life? And why do you worry about clothes? See how the lilies of the field grow. They do not labor or spin. Yet I tell you that not even Solomon in all his splendor was dressed like one of these. If that is how God clothes the grass of the field, which is here today and tomorrow is thrown into the fire, will He not much more clothe you, O you of little faith?" Matthew 6:25–30 ✐

_____Let's do: Do you have a pet that you promised to take care of? If not, think of a promise you made recently. Ask the Holy Spirit to give you the strength to keep your promise.

_____Let's pray: Dear Father, forgive me for not keeping my promises. Help me do better to keep my word. Thank You for being a loving Father who never forgets His children. Thanks for sending Jesus to save us. Amen.

J. A.

Read from God's Word

"Come now, let us reason together," says the LORD. "Though your sins are like scarlet, they shall be as white as snow; though they are red as crimson, they shall be like wool." Isaiah 1:18 ✍

Stain Remover

On laundry day we put all the dirty clothes in one big pile. Then they are sorted into different piles according to color. If a shirt or a pair of pants has a stain on them, they need to be pre-treated with a stain remover.

We go through all this work so that after our clothes are washed, they will look clean and new.

Sin is like a great big stain on our life. There is no way we can presoak ourselves to get rid of it or spray a pre-treatment on ourselves. But Jesus Christ is the great "stain remover." He left His home in heaven and gave up His own life to remove the stain of sin from our lives.

Unlike laundry, where some stains are harder to remove than others, all sins are the same. Every sin is paid for by the blood of Jesus applied to our lives in baptismal grace.

Through the goodness and love of Jesus, all our sins are washed away. Isn't it wonderful to know that our Savior has washed away everything wrong we have ever said, thought, or done? Through faith in Jesus that comes to us in Baptism, we are new, clean creatures!

_____Let's do: Talk with whoever does laundry at your house about how Jesus forgives and daily removes the stain of sin from your life.

_____Let's pray: Dear Jesus, thank You for giving Your life to save me from my sins. Forgive me all my sins—those I know and do not know. Thank You for the cleansing of my sins in Baptism and for making me a new creature. Amen.

J. A.

We Count!

Twelve-year-old Brent loves long bike rides with his mom. One day, as they were out riding, they saw a dead bird. "How do you suppose that bird died?" he asked.

"I suppose it was hit by a car," said his mother.

"Why would it fly in front of a car?" Brent wanted to know.

"Well, Brent. It probably didn't mean to, but sometimes bad things just happen."

As they rode along the bike path, they counted more dead animals by the side of the path.

"Four dead birds and one dead snake," said Brent.

Mom added, "Don't forget one live turtle."

"It makes me sad that no one cares about all the dead animals," Brent said when they got home and put their bicycles away.

"God cares." Mom reminded him. "The Bible says that God knows when one little sparrow falls."

"Oh, yeah," Brent remembered. "He knows the number of hairs on our heads too."

"That's right," Mom said and ruffled his hair. "If God cares about sparrows, just think how much more He cares about you. You're so important that He gave His Son for you."

Brent smiled and said, "That makes me really special!"

Read from God's Word

"Are not two sparrows sold for a penny? Yet not one of them will fall to the ground apart from the will of your Father. And even the very hairs of your head are all numbered. So don't be afraid; you are worth more than many sparrows." Matthew 10:29–31

_____Let's talk: Is there anything God doesn't care about? Tell about a time that you felt unimportant. What promises does God give to help you get over that feeling?

_____Let's pray: Dear God, when I'm feeling low and unimportant, remind me that You gave Your Son, Jesus, for me. Help me remember how special I am to You. In Jesus' name. Amen.

K. B.

march

Contributors for this month:

Jacqueline L. Loontjer

Kristine M. Moulds

Christine Ross

Susan Waterman Voss

The Potter's Wheel

Read from God's Word

Yet, O LORD, You are our Father. We are the clay. You are the potter: we are all the work of Your hand. Isaiah 64:8

Madison's father looked at his gift box. "Just open it, Dad. But be careful. It's breakable!" Madison said. Dad removed a beautiful pencil holder.

"The container looks very special, Madison. Did you make it?" Madison explained how she used a potter's wheel to make the gift.

A potter's wheel looks like a round table in the middle of a wheel that turns around and around. The clay sits on the tabletop. The potter forms the clay while turning the wheel.

You are like clay. God is your potter. He is forming you. Unlike clay that just sits there, people have feelings and might not like the way they are being formed. They may even rebel against God and try to remake themselves.

God wanted to make Moses a spokesperson to Pharaoh, the ruler of Egypt. "I'm not a very good speaker," Moses argued. "I don't want to be what You want me to be." But God, the potter, was patient with Moses. Finally Moses, with God's help, agreed to be what God wanted him to be.

God knows it is easy for us to rebel against His plan too. That's why He sent Jesus to forgive us for our rebellion and why He gives us His Holy Spirit in Baptism to help form us in His way.

_____Let's talk: Describe two ways God is forming you.

_____Let's pray: God, my Creator and my Potter, thank You
for forming me into the person You want me to be.
Help me to rejoice in Your plan for my life. Amen.

C. R.

Growing in God

Read from God's Word

And Jesus grew in wisdom and stature, and in favor with God and men. Luke 2:52 ✐

Was Jesus ever a toddler? a teenager? Sure, He was. Jesus went through the same stages of growth you are experiencing. He lost His baby teeth. His voice changed. He even felt clumsy as His body grew faster than His motor skills.

We know very little about Jesus during the years He was growing up. From Luke 2:41–52 we know that when Jesus was 12 years old, He sat in the temple listening and talking to the teachers. He enjoyed being in His Father's house.

You may have questions about the Bible. You may be curious to learn more about God's Word than you were as a young child. The temple was a wonderful place for Jesus to listen, learn, and respond. You will find that your church is a wonderful place to hear and respond to God's Word. Through His Word you will grow in your understanding of who God is and the work of Jesus while He was on earth.

God loves you and wants your body, mind, and heart to be healthy. Through His Word and the living power of Baptism, God works to make sure that you grow in wisdom as your body matures and that you relate with God and with other people.

_____Let's talk: Where or when do you learn about God? Talk about one way that God taught you about Himself this week.

_____Let's pray: Dear Lord Jesus, I pray that You would help me see how I am growing in wisdom, how my body is maturing, and how I can be more like You. Thank You for caring about the way I grow up. Amen.

C. R.

A Sad Celebration

Read from God's Word

I cry aloud to the LORD; I lift up my voice to the LORD for mercy. I pour out my complaint before Him; before Him I tell my trouble. Psalm 142:1–2 ✍

e don't decorate or shop for Easter like we do for Christmas. We don't celebrate Lent by decorating trees or buying gifts. During Advent we think about Jesus' birth. During Lent we think about Jesus' death on the cross. We think about ourselves too.

Lent is a time to think about our sins and our sinful condition—the reason for Jesus' death. We ask God to have mercy on us and to show us the kindness that we do not deserve. Some people read the psalms during Lent, noting the many prayers about sin and sadness. Other people give up something they like: soda pop, an extra hour of sleep to read the Bible more, or video games. When they miss the thing they gave up, they are reminded of how much Jesus gave up for them.

These Lenten preparations help us get ready to celebrate Easter. Why do we celebrate? Because Jesus died on our behalf, we are forgiven of our sins. And because Jesus rose from the dead on Easter, we will live forever with Him in heaven. So go ahead—spend a little time this Lent thinking about yourself—about your sins and your need for a Savior. Then think about Jesus and what He won for you on Easter!

_____Let's do: Plan a little extra time between now and Easter
                  to tell God about your sin and sadness.

_____Let's pray: Dear God, sometimes I am so happy that I don't
                  see my sin. Show me my sin. Show me my Savior.
                  Help me receive Your forgiveness with thanksgiving.
                  In Jesus' name. Amen.

C. R.

No Punishment

Read from God's Word

As He went along, He saw a man blind from birth. His disciples asked Him, "Rabbi, who sinned, this man or his parents, that he was born blind?" "Neither this man nor his parents sinned," said Jesus, "but this happened so that the work of God might be displayed in his life. As long as it is day, we must do the work of Him who sent Me. Night is coming, when no one can work." John 9:1–4 ✑

M om, is Dad sick because he did something wrong?"

Mom turned toward Kimberly. "What makes you ask that?"

"Betsy told me her family was praying that Dad will get well and learn whatever God wants from this sickness. Did God give him cancer for a reason?"

Mom answered gently. "The effects of sin cause sickness in our world. Do you remember the story of the man born blind?" she asked. "The disciples thought he was blind because of sin, but what did Jesus say?"

Kimberly said, "I think Jesus told the disciples the man wasn't blind because of sin but so God would be glorified. Jesus wanted to show His power as God."

"That's right," Mom answered. "Yes, Dad sins and has a sinful nature; we all do. But God doesn't send bad things to punish us. Jesus took the punishment for our sins when He died on the cross. However, God uses hard times to teach others about Himself. That is not the same as God causing the cancer. Does this help you understand?"

"It does. I'm not going to stop praying that God heals Dad from cancer, but I'm going to start praying that we would all see God working in our lives."

_____Let's talk: Think about a hard time in your life. How did God help you? How does knowing this help you face the future?

_____Let's pray: Dear Jesus, thank You for taking the punishment for my sins and earning forgiveness for me. Amen.

C. R.

Gotcha

As Isabelle moved toward the kitchen, out jumped her brother from the corner. "Gotcha!" yelled Juan. Isabelle stepped back quickly. She glared at Juan. He offered Isabelle some cookies to get out of trouble. As she looked at Juan's smiling face, she began to smile back.

She thought about the story of Cain and Abel she had just learned. God had warned Cain about sin "crouching at your door." Sinful thoughts can become like living creatures waiting to jump on us at just the right time, leading us into sinful acts.

In today's Bible passage sin did take over. Cain was angry and killed his brother. God warned Cain that sin "desires to have you" and he must "master" sin. Cain does not listen to God. Sin takes control of him.

God gives us His Spirit through His Word and Sacraments to take our eyes off of sin and put them on our Savior. Sometimes we act like Cain—giving in to our sinful nature, doing sinful acts. But thanks to Jesus' victory over sin on the cross and the open tomb, sin has no full power over us. Our loving Lord God invites us back, forgiving our sins, and giving us eternal life. Through His victory won on Easter, Jesus says, "Gotcha forever!"

Read from God's Word

But Abel brought fat portions from some of the firstborn of his flock. The LORD looked with favor on Abel and his offering, but on Cain and his offering He did not look with favor. So Cain was very angry, and his face was downcast. Then the LORD said to Cain, "Why are you angry? Why is your face downcast? If you do what is right, will you not be accepted? But if you do not do what is right, sin is crouching at your door; it desires to have you, but you must master it." Now Cain said to his brother Abel, "Let's go out to the field." And while they were in the field, Cain attacked his brother Abel and killed him. Genesis 4:4–8

_____Let's talk: Jesus is there for you when you are angry or afraid. How does He help you live for Him?

_____Let's pray: Dear God, help me to keep my eyes on Jesus instead of the sin that is crouching at my door. When I do sin, help me to turn back to You for forgiveness. Amen.

C. R.

Read from God's Word

"Surely God is my salvation; I will trust and not be afraid. The LORD, the LORD, is my strength and my song; He has become my salvation." With joy you will draw water from the wells of salvation. Isaiah 12:2–3

A Trust Walk

In 1859 Charles Blondin, a famous tightrope walker, strung a 1,100-foot tightrope across Niagara Falls and began walking across. The crowd cheered him on. He raised his arms to quiet the crowd. "Do you believe I can walk across with a person on my back?" he asked.

"We believe!" the crowd responded.

"Which one of you will be that person?" Blondin asked.

It took awhile, but finally one man did trust Blondin. The two men inched safely across the falls, one clinging to the other.

The sin of all people separated God and man like the river that separates the banks of Niagara Falls. Jesus, as true God and true man, came to carry us across that wide river of sin. By ourselves we were helpless. Only Jesus, God in human form, can carry us across that river of separation. Because of His perfect life and His death on Calvary, a wire was strung from the bank of us to the bank of eternal life. He offers His Easter victory as our victory. Jesus holds us in His loving arms and carries us through all of life to Himself in heaven. Now we can go wild and shout with all the company of heaven, "Jesus! Jesus!"

_____Let's talk: When has God helped you trust Him to help you?

_____Let's pray: Lord, You helped me begin to believe in You
and to trust You. Help me to grow in faith. Amen.

C. R.

His Plan

M om, I can't believe you're making me spend the day with that little kid!" Jeremy yelled. His mom planned to go shopping and had asked Jeremy to spend the day playing with Peter, her friend's fourth-grade son.

Playing, yeah right, Jeremy thought, *more like baby-sitting. What's a ninth grader supposed to do with a fourth grader who can barely walk without tripping over his feet?*

Jeremy needed to think of a plan to get out of staying with Peter. While he paced in his room, he noticed a paper taped to his mirror. His mom had put it there two years ago, just after he had gotten braces. It was a time when Jeremy didn't like his appearance at all. Jeremy looked at the note and reread the Bible verse.

Then Jeremy realized that his heart was leading him the wrong way. He had become bitter and selfish.

Read from God's Word

So from now on we regard no one from a worldly point of view. Though we once regarded Christ in this way, we do so no longer. Therefore, if anyone is in Christ, he is a new creation; the old has gone, the new has come!
2 Corinthians 5:16–17

Jeremy felt ashamed and prayed, "God, forgive me for yelling at Mom and for thinking mean things about Peter. Change my heart so I can be a friend to him."

God had a plan—to send Jesus to rescue Jeremy, Peter, and all people from bitterness, rejection, and sin. He planned to send the Holy Spirit to save Jeremy and help change his heart and actions.

_____ Let's talk: Is there a person you don't like because of the way they look or act? How might God see him or her?

_____ Let's pray: Father in heaven, You know that I often judge people by how they look. Please help me to see each person through Your eyes. In Jesus' name. Amen.

C. R.

Read from God's Word

If you make the Most High your dwelling—even the LORD, who is my refuge—then no harm will befall you, no disaster will come near your tent. For He will command His angels concerning you to guard you in all your ways; they will lift you up in their hands, so that you will not strike your foot against a stone. Psalm 91:9–12 ✍

Angels Watching over Me

Christine's family lived in a bad neighborhood. Sometimes they were scared they might have things stolen or be harmed. A family friend sent a coffee mug with a picture of an angel and this verse: "He will command His angels concerning you to guard you in all your ways." This brought comfort to Christine's family. God helped take away many of their fears.

You might see pictures of angels in many places—on calendars, Christmas ornaments, and coffee mugs. Many people want to learn about angels: What do they look like? Do they really have wings? Are they among us on earth?

God made angels to praise and worship Him. Think of the angels who told the shepherds about the birth of Jesus. "Glory to God in the highest," they sang.

God made angels to protect His servants. An angel shut the mouths of lions so Daniel wouldn't be harmed. An angel opened the doors of a prison and set Paul free so he could keep sharing God's Word with others.

Angels do wonderful things—but we do not worship them. We worship only God and thank Him for the many ways He shows love and concern for us. He sent Jesus to suffer and die for us, saving us from sin and eternal death.

_____Let's do: Think of three Bible stories with angels in them. Write these stories in your own words.

_____Let's pray: Dear Lord God, thank You for the many ways You protect me every day—especially through Your angels. Amen.

C. R.

Dear Dad

"Who will close with prayer?" Mrs. Mack asked. There was no response. She asked Michael why it seemed so hard for the kids to pray out loud. Michael said, "I don't know what to say."

Mrs. Mack decided to teach the class more about prayer. She started with a silly example. "Imagine saying to your dad, 'My dearest father, please allow your child to be seated at your dinner table to eat this delicious food, which my noble mother hath prepared for me.'"

The students laughed. "My dad would say I was being silly!" said Kendall.

Mrs. Mack continued. "You are God's child. He wants you to talk to Him as easily as you talk to your own parents. Saying 'Abba' is like saying 'Dad.' When Jesus was in need He addressed His heavenly Father in this way." (See Mark 14:36.)

For you did not receive a spirit that makes you a slave again to fear, but you received the Spirit of sonship. And by Him we cry, "Abba, Father." The Spirit Himself testifies with our spirit that we are God's children. Romans 8:15–16

All who believe that Jesus died and rose again for their sin can talk to God as if He were our dad because that's what He is. We don't have to talk to our heavenly Dad so formally. Neither do our prayers need to be long or difficult. Prayers can be one simple sentence or long and formal—any prayer expressed through faith in Jesus, the Savior, is good and acceptable to our heavenly Dad.

_____Let's talk: What are your favorite prayers?

_____Let's pray: This time make up your own prayer from your heart.

C. R.

Read from God's Word

They came to Capernaum. When He was in the house, He asked them, "What were you arguing about on the road?" But they kept quiet because on the way they had argued about who was the greatest. Sitting down, Jesus called the Twelve and said, "If anyone wants to be first, he must be the very last, and the servant of all." He took a little child and had him stand among them. Taking him in His arms, He said to them, "Whoever welcomes one of these little children in My name welcomes Me; and whoever welcomes Me does not welcome Me but the One who sent Me." Mark 9:33–37 〰

You First

She came in *first* place. Who wants to eat *first*? Who has the *first* ticket?

We all like to be first. Although we say that doing our best is more important than being first, we feel excited when we are first. Some people want so much to be first that they may even break God's commandments. Students may cheat on a test. Athletes may use illegal drugs to build their muscles. Someone may lie to gain a prize.

Even the 12 disciples argued about who was first, the greatest, among them. Jesus corrected His disciples. He told them being a servant of others is the greatest position. What a confusing thought—it is a great thing to serve others. Jesus was a perfect example—suffering, dying, and rising for all. He served the world, including us. He is the God-man Savior, the first-born from the dead.

With Jesus' love and servant power we might say, "You go first. I'll wait." Only with God's help can we have a servant heart. When we don't have that attitude, we need the forgiveness of Jesus Christ, our Suffering Servant. His actions in life and death said "you first" as He gave up His own life for our eternal salvation.

_____Let's talk: Think about a time when you realized it was okay not to be first.

_____Let's pray: Dear God, it is very hard not to be first. Teach me what You mean by being last and not first. Help me to be Your servant today. In Jesus' name I pray. Amen.

C. R.

The Winner

"You landed on Atlantic Avenue!" said Glen smugly. "I own that property! Pay $22 rent." His sister counted out the play money.

"Now I passed GO, so give me $200," replied Glen's sister.

They are playing Monopoly, a game where people buy property and houses with play money. When the game ends, the player with the most property and money is the winner.

That's what monopoly means: one having possession or control over many. People in Jesus' day played monopoly games, although they didn't always know it.

For example, the Romans controlled people with weapons and soldiers. They believed they were winning their game with physical power and strength.

The Jewish religious leaders thought they were gaining power by controlling the spiritual lives of others. They made people afraid to disobey hundreds of religious laws.

Read from God's Word

Where is the wise man? Where is the scholar? Where is the philosopher of this age? Has not God made foolish the wisdom of the world? For since in the wisdom of God the world through its wisdom did not know Him, God was pleased through the foolishness of what was preached to save those who believe. Jews demand miraculous signs and Greeks look for wisdom, but we preach Christ crucified: a stumbling block to Jews and foolishness to Gentiles, but to those whom God has called, both Jews and Greeks, Christ the power of God and the wisdom of God. For the foolishness of God is wiser than man's wisdom, and the weakness of God is stronger than man's strength.
1 Corinthians 1:20–25

These leaders didn't want Jesus to be powerful. They were afraid He might win the game. At last, as Jesus died on Calvary's cross, the Romans thought they had won. The priests and scribes laughed and thought they had won.

But Jesus really won. When He rose on Easter, He won over death. He took control of sin and through faith makes us His prized possession in Baptism. Only Jesus Christ has a monopoly on eternal life. By faith in Him we are all winners!

_____Let's talk: What kind of power did Jesus show before His crucifixion? When Christ possesses us, what do we win?

_____Let's pray: Dear Lord, thank You for making me a winner over sin and death. In Your name, Jesus, I pray. Amen.

K. M. M.

Jesus went out to them, walking on the lake. When the disciples saw Him walking on the lake, they were terrified. "It's a ghost," they said, and cried out in fear. But Jesus immediately said to them: "Take courage! It is I. Don't be afraid." "Lord, if it's You," Peter replied, "tell me to come to You on the water." "Come," He said. Then Peter got down out of the boat, walked on the water and came toward Jesus. But when He saw the wind, He was afraid and, beginning to sink, cried out, "Lord, save me!" Immediately Jesus reached out His hand and caught Him. Matthew 14:25–31

Jesus Says, "Come"

The main worship area of a church is called the "nave," which comes from a Latin word meaning "ship."

The next time you're in church, imagine you're in Peter's boat. According to Matthew 14, you might hear the disciples exclaiming, "Watch out for the wind and waves! Who's walking on the water toward us? Come back, Peter! You can't walk on that rough water!"

Peter went anyway. Jesus said to him, "Come." Would you go?

We learn from Peter's example that if we trust Jesus, we don't have to be afraid. Jesus still invites you to come into the "boat" of faith where you receive forgiveness.

When you leave, where does Jesus want you to go? He wants you to come with Him into the world. Think of all the stormy things happening around you. With Jesus by your side, you can help.

Psalm 73:26 says, "God is the strength of my heart and my portion forever." The Holy Spirit helps you think more about Jesus and His wonderful love than about your own worries. That's what it means to keep your eyes on the Lord, just as Peter did. Jesus will not fail you. He is your hope—your Savior from sin.

_____Let's talk: Read Matthew 14:22–33. How can leaving church be like Peter getting out of his boat?

_____Let's pray: Dear Jesus, thank You for staying with me wherever I go. Amen.

K. M. M.

Salvation Symphony

reg covered his ears during the warm-up at the symphony concert. The instruments sounded all mixed up. When the concert finally began, however, Greg heard sounds blending and working together. Beautiful music echoed throughout the symphony hall.

Have you ever considered that Bible stories are like musical instruments? Each story is interesting in its own way. But together, Bible events create one huge symphony message.

Have you noticed in Sunday worship that three Scripture lessons are read each week? They're called the Old Testament Reading, the Epistle, and the Gospel. Together, these three readings focus on the theme of the day to tell of God's love for us. The climax of the Bible concert is the message that God's Son, Jesus Christ, died on the cross and rose from the grave to save us all from eternal death.

Read from God's Word

In Him we have redemption through His blood, the forgiveness of sins, in accordance with the riches of God's grace that He lavished on us with all wisdom and understanding. And He made known to us the mystery of His will according to His good pleasure, which He purposed in Christ, to be put into effect when the times will have reached their fulfillment—to bring all things in heaven and on earth together under one head, even Christ. Ephesians 1:7–10

God wants us to appreciate the whole Bible, not just bits and pieces. As we do this, we learn about God's plan of salvation from the beginning of time to the end of the world. Jesus explained this to two men on the road to Emmaus. "And beginning with Moses and all the Prophets, He explained to them what was said in all the Scriptures concerning Himself" (Luke 24:27).

Clang the cymbals! Strum the harp! Let's hear the salvation symphony!

———Let's talk: What do all Bible stories tell about? What is the most important event in the Bible? What events in the Old Testament remind you of Jesus?

———Let's pray: Heavenly Father, thank You for giving us the whole Bible. Thank You for Your plan of salvation, which gives us eternal life with You through faith in Christ. Amen.

K. M. M.

Read from God's Word

Early on the first day of the week, while it was still dark, Mary Magdalene went to the tomb and saw that the stone had been removed from the entrance. So she came running to Simon Peter and the other disciple, the one Jesus loved, and said, "They have taken the Lord out of the tomb, and we don't know where they have put Him!" So Peter and the other disciple started for the tomb. ... Simon Peter ... arrived and went into the tomb. He saw the strips of linen lying there, as well as the burial cloth that had been around Jesus' head. ... Finally the other disciple ... also went inside. He saw and believed. (They still did not understand from Scripture that Jesus had to rise from the dead.) Then the disciples went back to their homes. John 20:1–10 ✑

Heavy Steps

Samantha was dragging her feet. She had to clean that dirty rabbit cage. Samantha loved the rabbit, but she did not love watering down the smelly cage and scrubbing the mesh.

Do you drag your feet when you have to do something you dread? In the Gospels we learn that Jesus' disciples did some feet dragging too.

The hardest thing the disciples had to do was go to Jerusalem with Jesus. Their steps were heavy as they neared the place of arrest and danger. Mark says, "They were on their way up to Jerusalem, with Jesus leading the way, and the disciples were astonished, while those who followed were afraid" (Mark 10:32).

They remained sad and confused during the Lord's arrest, condemnation, His death, and burial. But on Easter morning, "Peter and the other disciple started for the tomb. Both were running."

Peter and John didn't drag their feet that day. They were beginning to see the miracle of Easter unfold. They realized that Jesus' victory over death would change their lives and give them great joy.

When the Savior lives in our heart, we have much joy and a new outlook on life. We don't have to go around with heavy steps because we know that our Redeemer lives!

_____Let's talk: Why did the disciples drag their feet into Jerusalem? Why were they glad on Easter?

_____Let's pray: Dear Jesus, guide me. Thank You for loving me even though I don't always understand Your plans. Amen.

K. M. M.

Floss Daily

How do you prepare for a dental appointment? Some people brush their teeth and floss every day. If you do these things, your teeth will be protected and you'll be prepared for the day of your checkup.

Easter Day is far more important than a dental appointment. To prepare for Easter, you look to the Lord to strengthen and protect your spiritual life.

Lent is the season of the church year just before Easter. Christians do a lot of preparing during Lent. We think about the things Christ did while on earth. We review events leading up to Jesus' crucifixion. Hearing God's message makes us sorry that our sins caused Him to die. But we are grateful that Jesus went through great pain and suffering to gain forgiveness for us! We prepare for the message of Easter.

When Easter comes, we're ready to jump for joy. We praise God the rest of the year for His Easter blessings to us.

God's children who prepare to celebrate with Him often start every week with a worship service. They may pray often during the day. They may read the Bible daily and attend Sunday school regularly. God uses these things to help us focus on Jesus' love, which carries us through life and into eternity.

Read from God's Word

A voice of one calling: "In the desert prepare the way for the LORD; make straight in the wilderness a highway for our God. Every valley shall be raised up, every mountain and hill made low; the rough ground shall become level, the rugged places a plain. And the glory of the LORD will be revealed, and all mankind together will see it. For the mouth of the LORD has spoken." Isaiah 40:3–5

_____Let's talk: Name a way to prepare for Easter. How is it like a spiritual checkup?

_____Let's pray: Dear Father in heaven, keep me spiritually healthy as I ponder the suffering, death, and resurrection of Your Son. In Jesus' name. Amen.

K. M. M.

God Knows the Answers

Imagine sailing with Christopher Columbus. Day after day passes. You see nothing but sea and sky. Suddenly, you sight land ahead!

What land is it? Since there were no computers or modern charts to record his path, no one, not even historians or mathematicians, can prove where Columbus sailed or landed.

God knows where Columbus landed. God has been keeping track of His world since its beginning. He even knows the future of this earth. Jesus said, "Heaven and earth will pass away, but My words will never pass away" (Mark 13:31).

Jesus lived on earth too. He knew then what was going on, even in far-off places. He knew what His own history would be.

If Jesus knew He would be crucified, why did He allow it to happen? Because of His great love for us. If Jesus hadn't died for our sins, we would have no way to reach heaven. We would be like the *Santa Maria*, rocking up and down on the water without reaching land.

Jesus loves us and wants us to live with Him in heaven. We're glad that our Lord knows all the answers. He needs no charts or computers. With Him leading us every day, we're totally safe and secure.

_____Let's do: Think about what great things God has done.
What words of praise would you write?

_____Let's pray: Dear Lord, thank You for watching over all the people in the world. Help me trust in You throughout my life, until I reach home safely. Amen.

K. M. M.

Never Lost

At some point on every trip the Waterman family took, someone asked if they were lost. Dad's answer was always: "We're not lost. We just don't know where we are." If Dad wasn't concerned, they had no reason to worry.

God sent Abram and his family on a trip. They did not know exactly where they were going, but they knew they weren't lost. Why? God was their travel agent!

Sometimes we may feel like we are lost even when we're not traveling. We may feel lost when we have difficult decisions to make. Perhaps someone we care about is hurting and we feel lost if we can't help.

God reminds His baptized children that we are not lost, even if we don't understand what is going on or know what lies ahead. He knows all our problems, and He cares about us. He also knows how things will work out.

Read from God's Word

The LORD had said to Abram, "Leave your country, your people and your father's household and go to the land I will show you. I will make you into a great nation and I will bless you; I will make your name great, and you will be a blessing. I will bless those who bless you, and whoever curses you I will curse; and all peoples on earth will be blessed through you." So Abram left, as the LORD had told him; and Lot went with him. Abram was seventy-five years old when he set out from Haran. Genesis 12:1–4

Through Christ's death, God set us on the right path, although we sin. Hearing about His love in church and through Bible study can help us find our way at all times.

We may not always know where we are, but we know God has important plans for us as we travel through life. He works hard to keep us from being lost for eternity.

_____Let's talk: When have you felt lost? How did God help you? How does God use you to help other people who are lost?

_____Let's pray: Dear God, You are always with me, even when I feel lost. Thank You for keeping me in Your love and care. Amen.

S. W. V.

Read from God's Word

Jesus knew what they were thinking and asked, "Why are you thinking these things in your hearts? Which is easier: to say, 'Your sins are forgiven,' or to say, 'Get up and walk'? But that you may know that the Son of Man has authority on earth to forgive sins ... ." He said to the paralyzed man, "I tell you, get up, take your mat and go home." Immediately he stood up in front of them, took what he had been lying on and went home praising God. Everyone was amazed and gave praise to God. They were filled with awe and said, "We have seen remarkable things today." Luke 5:22–26 ✍

What Really Matters

The principal asked Katie's mom, "Mrs. Schmidt, can you substitute for a sick teacher? We need you right away." She looked down at her jeans and flannel shirt. "I don't look like a teacher," she said, "but if you need me, I'll do it."

Most of the kids didn't know that Katie's mom was trained to be a teacher. She didn't *look* like a teacher. But when Katie's mom taught them a lesson or gave an assignment, they could tell she *was* a teacher.

While Jesus was on earth, many people didn't recognize His true nature. He didn't look like the Son of God. He didn't look like the King of all creation. But "the crowds were amazed at His teaching, because He taught as one who had authority, and not as their teachers of the law" (Matthew 7:28–29).

There were some people who still didn't believe in Jesus. He loved them anyway and never stopped trying to win them for His kingdom.

It doesn't matter what Jesus looked like. What matters is that He came to earth to be our Savior. We know He really is the Son of God, who forgives our sins and gives us eternal life. So we say with the psalmist, "Praise the LORD, for the LORD is good" (Psalm 135:3).

_____Let's talk: Why didn't some people recognize God's Son, Jesus? What really matters?

_____Let's pray: Heavenly Father, thank You for sending Your Son into the world. Make me always glad to recognize Him as my Savior. Amen.

K. M. M.

Stuck Tight

The wedding reception was okay, Jo thought. She had chocolate cake and little mints. She drank the punch in the tiny glass cup last, enjoying the fruity flavor.

Bored, she began playing with the little punch cup. Suddenly she realized she had a big problem. Her thumb was stuck in the small handle of the cup.

Jo's thumb wouldn't budge. Breaking the cup would cut her hand. She couldn't think of a solution and began to panic.

We often get "stuck" in our sins. We do things against God's will. Then we can't get out—the problem is too great. No solution we can think of can possibly save us. (If you've ever lied to someone, you know how hard it can be to undo that lie.)

Jo finally went to her mom for help. With a little hand lotion the cup slipped right off. The problem was solved.

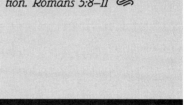

Read from God's Word

But God demonstrates His own love for us in this: While we were still sinners, Christ died for us. Since we have now been justified by His blood, how much more shall we be saved from God's wrath through Him! For if, when we were God's enemies, we were reconciled to Him through the death of His Son, how much more, having been reconciled, shall we be saved through His life! Not only is this so, but we also rejoice in God through our Lord Jesus Christ, through whom we have now received reconciliation. Romans 5:8–11

The solution to our sins isn't so simple. Jesus had to die to save us—a bitter death for our sake. The problem wasn't His; it was ours. But out of love He chose to help us. Through the Savior's death and resurrection, we are free from the punishment we deserve.

How great it feels to be unstuck!

_____Let's talk: What would happen to us if Jesus hadn't died to save us? How does salvation change the way we live?

_____Let's pray: Dear Lord, thank You for freeing us from the punishment of our sins. Help us live each day as Your redeemed children. Amen.

S. W. V.

Tennis, Anyone?

Read from God's Word

Now you are the body of Christ, and each one of you is a part of it. And in the church God has appointed first of all apostles, second prophets, third teachers, then workers of miracles, also those having gifts of healing, those able to help others, those with gifts of administration, and those speaking in different kinds of tongues. Are all apostles? Are all prophets? Are all teachers? Do all work miracles? Do all have gifts of healing? Do all speak in tongues? Do all interpret? But eagerly desire the greater gifts. 1 Corinthians 12:27–31

Susan's older brother and sister used to take her along to play tennis with them. After she hit a few balls, it was her turn to chase the stray balls. Stray balls rolled to the playground or down the hill. After retrieving one ball, she would return, only to chase the next one. Susan never learned to play tennis very well, but she's great at chasing things!

Susan was happy to spend time with her brother and sister because they invited her along and seemed to want her company. Her job was necessary to keep the game going.

God reminds us that there are many different ways to serve Him. Pastors and teachers have important jobs. But God doesn't call everyone to be a pastor or a teacher. He has many jobs that need to be done.

Each time God helps us do something in our church or other places, we are serving the Lord. Each time God helps us show Christian love to another person, we are serving the Lord. We joyfully serve Him because He willingly served us.

Chasing balls is an important job in a tennis game. Raking leaves, sweeping floors, and singing in a choir are important jobs that serve God. What special jobs do you think He has planned for you?

_____Let's do: Make a list of jobs you can do to serve God.

_____Let's pray: Dear Jesus, thank You for helping me serve You each day. Help me be joyful in all I do. Amen.

S. W. V.

Putting the Pieces Together

Seeds

Tiny pieces of paper

Buttons

Small pieces of clay or felt

What do these things have in common? Possibly many things. There is at least one thing, though. They can all be used to make mosaics. If you arrange tiny pieces of something in patterns, you can create a picture called a mosaic. You can arrange and rearrange each colored piece until you have everything just right. When you're happy with the project, you can glue all the pieces together.

You are a kind of mosaic too. There are many little parts of you. Each part of your body works together to make the whole you. You're more than just a body, though. You do a lot of different things each day. You think many different thoughts.

Read from God's Word

For You created my inmost being: You knit me together in my mother's womb. I praise You because I am fearfully and wonderfully made: Your works are wonderful, I know that full well. My frame was not hidden from You when I was made in the secret place. When I was woven together in the depths of the earth, Your eyes saw my unformed body. All the days ordained for me were written in Your book before one of them came to be. How precious to me are Your thoughts, O God! How vast is the sum of them! Were I to count them, they would outnumber the grains of sand. When I awake, I am still with You. Psalm 139:13–18 ✍

God made each part of your body to be uniquely yours. He uses each experience you have to make you a special person. You have a combination of talents and abilities that makes you unique. No one else is exactly like you.

Sometimes we aren't happy with ourselves. But God made us the way He wants us to be. We're each His one-of-a-kind creation. Knowing that, we can give thanks to Him. We can let Him use us in His kingdom, the kingdom we belong to because of Jesus' great sacrifice on the cross.

———Let's do: Design a mosaic that reminds you that God loves you.

———Let's pray: Dear God, thank You for making me special. Use me in Your kingdom. In Jesus' name. Amen.

K. W. V.

Attitudes Show

Read from God's Word

For the LORD God is a sun and shield; the LORD bestows favor and honor; no good thing does He withhold from those whose walk is blameless. O LORD Almighty, blessed is the man who trusts in You. Psalm 84:11–12

"Sunshine is a matter of attitude." This sentence by F. W. Boreham is in a flipbook of "Thoughts for the Day."

"Boy, is that the truth," Jackie muttered as she tried to get ready for another day.

Winter hung on with iron-gray clouds and cold rains. Out came the gloves and the scarf one more time. *Is the sun ever going to shine for a whole day?* she wondered. It would really help her attitude.

Attitudes show on our face and through our actions.

Bad attitudes can show up as pouting after a lost game or a poor grade. They might creep out of a clash between friends as cruel words. Bad attitudes may come from hidden fears or unforgiven sins—disguised as bad tempers or snarling responses.

Good attitudes come to us directly through the faith God gives us in His plan for our life. We know Jesus loved us enough to die in our place. We know He leads us to repent and forgives our sins. Our hearts lighten up and our faces show it.

God's Son will shine in you and through you. He will adjust your attitude and turn the cold chill of sins into the warmth of His loving Son.

———Let's do: Design a picture of the sun, writing the words of Psalm 84:11–12 on the rays you have drawn.

———Let's pray: Dear Jesus, turn my frown upside down. Change my attitude so my forgiven heart shows joy in You. In Your blessed name I pray. Amen.

J. L. L.

Making Music

Play it again. Count that measure over. Practice, practice, practice. Music teachers can be tyrants.

Who was King David's music teacher? Did that person make David wish he had never started playing the harp? Did his brothers tease him about hitting the wrong notes? Maybe that's why he practiced out in the fields with only the sheep listening.

David wasn't just a harpist. He also wrote many of the psalms. His psalms proclaim his belief in the promised Savior, who would die and rise for his sins.

David's gift for music took him to the royal palace, where he tried to soothe Saul's moods. David expressed his deepest emotions through music. Even when he was brought low because of his sins, David composed a song of sincere repentance (Psalm 51). God assured him, like any believer, that he had forgiveness by God's grace.

Read from God's Word

My heart is steadfast, O God, my heart is steadfast; I will sing and make music. Awake, my soul! ... I will awaken the dawn. I will praise You, O LORD, among the nations; I will sing of You among the peoples. For great is Your love, reaching to the heavens; Your faithfulness reaches to the skies. Be exalted, O God, above the heavens; let Your glory be over all the earth. Psalm 57:7–11

But David's most important gift from God was his rock-solid faith. He felt safe with God—from lions and wolves, from Saul and his army, from a traitorous son. He said, "I will take refuge in the shadow of Your wings until the disaster has passed" (Psalm 57:1).

Therefore, David could say with great confidence: "For great is Your love, reaching to the heavens; Your faithfulness reaches to the skies." Now that's music to God's ears.

———Let's talk: What has God done for you? Write your own psalm of trust and love for Him.

———Let's pray: O Father in heaven, fill my heart with faith in the forgiving sacrifice of Your Son. Let me live as a walking psalm of praise to You. In Jesus' name. Amen.

J. L. L.

Read from God's Word

They brought the donkey and the colt, placed their cloaks on them, and Jesus sat on them. A very large crowd spread their cloaks on the road, while others cut branches from the trees and spread them on the road. The crowds that went ahead of Him and those that followed shouted, "Hosanna to the Son of David!" "Blessed is He who comes in the name of the Lord!" "Hosanna in the highest!" Matthew 21:7–9

Heart Hosannas

Gawkers are people who crowd around to stare at something unusual. Gawkers can be found on the highway, where they slow down to look at an accident. Gawkers may crowd around and stare at an injured person.

About two thousand years ago a huge crowd of people in Jerusalem stopped what they were doing to gawk at a man riding into town on a donkey.

They had heard many stories about this carpenter from Nazareth. He healed blindness and leprosy. He chased demons out of people. He even brought dead people back to life! They had big ideas about what they thought He should do next.

But the hosannas on Sunday changed to jeers by Friday. It was clear Jesus wasn't going to chase the Romans out of Israel. Some who said hosanna may have praised Him only when things were going well.

Our shouts of hosanna on Palm Sunday can truly be a heartfelt expression of praise. We know that Jesus is our Savior, who went to the cross to die for our sins and gives us new life through faith. Friday's jeers would turn into Easter Sunday's cheers!

"Blessed is He who comes in the name of the Lord! Hosanna in the highest!" We sing with them through faith.

_____Let's do: Put palm branches on your front door. On Good Friday cover them with a black cloth as a sign of grief that your sins sent Jesus to the cross. Write about the experience.

_____Let's pray: My heart can never express my gratitude to You, Christ, for my soul's salvation. I am thankful for Your innocent death in my place. In Your name. Amen.

J. L. L.

Cover-Ups

Read from God's Word

Now Israel loved Joseph more than any of his other sons, because he had been born to him in his old age; and he made a richly ornamented robe for him. When his brothers saw that their father loved him more than any of them, they hated him and could not speak a kind word to him. Genesis 37:3–4

That must have been *some* coat! To Jacob it was proof of his love for his son Joseph. For Joseph it was another way to needle his brothers. And for the brothers it was a slap in the face from their father.

We've all had times when we've felt that a parent or teacher loved someone more than us. It may not be true, but before long the problem grows bigger in our minds. Eventually this thought can take over our lives.

Joseph's brothers decided they had to get rid of their brother. They sold him as a slave and then soaked his multicolored coat with goat's blood to cover their lie. Word of Joseph's death caused great grief to their father.

But God was working through their deceit. In Egypt God used Joseph to save many lives—including those of his brothers and father.

God, our Father, has given us a beautiful coat also—the righteousness earned by His Son on the cross. Jesus' human brothers gave Him over to Pilate to die a horrible death. God was working through that death and resurrection to save us from our ugliness. God forgives our sins because of Jesus' death. And we can come before God dressed in Jesus' perfection. Now *that* is some coat!

_____Let's do: Do you feel someone is loved more than you?
Ask God to forgive this sin and for help to change
your thinking and behavior. Find new reasons
and ways to love them!

_____Let's pray: Dear God, my heart needs cleansing from my envy
and resentment. Flood my heart with Your love and
forgiveness to fill up those dark holes. In Your Son's
name I pray. Amen.

J. L. L.

Read from God's Word

Hide Your face from my sins and blot out all my iniquity. Create in me a pure heart, O God, and renew a steadfast spirit within me. Do not cast me from Your presence or take Your Holy Spirit from me. Restore to me the joy of Your salvation and grant me a willing spirit, to sustain me. Psalm 51:9–12 ✍

A Poem of Praise

Father,
Our
Redemption
Gives us
Immanuel's
Victory.
Even
Now our
Eternal
Soul
Shouts,
I am
Saved!
My praise
Is
Never
Ending!

Yes, **FORGIVENESS IS MINE** and yours, through Jesus.

_____Let's do: Write an acrostic on REPENTING or CONFESSING.

_____Let's pray: O Lord, help me live as a forgiven and forgiving person. In Jesus' gracious name I pray. Amen.

J. L. L.

Preparations

"Mom, when are we going to dye the eggs?"

"Mom, I still don't have shoes to go with my new outfit."

"Dear, did you pick up my suit from the cleaners?"

About this time, Mom hollers, "I can't do everything!"

Another holiday is coming, along with the stress it brings. Does your house sound this way? If so, it's time for everyone to take a deep breath and focus on the reason for Easter.

Easter Sunday is the anniversary of the most joyful victory in the history of the world! Our Savior proved His power over sin, Satan, and death by rising from the dead. Angels announced that Jesus was alive, His followers raced to the empty tomb, and the risen Jesus appeared to people. *That's* what Easter's about—not fussing about colored eggs or new clothes.

In today's Bible readings, John the Baptist was preparing the way for Jesus' ministry. That was his focus, and when Jesus approached him, John proclaimed Jesus to be the "Lamb of God, who takes away the sin of the world!"

Let your Easter preparations center on the joy you have as a believer in Jesus, the risen Son of God. Then celebrate as you dye eggs or wear new clothes.

> **Read from God's Word**
>
> *In those days John the Baptist came, preaching in the Desert of Judea and saying, "Repent, for the kingdom of heaven is near." This is he who was spoken of through the prophet Isaiah: "A voice of one calling in the desert, 'Prepare the way for the Lord, make straight paths for him.'"* Matthew 3:1–3
>
> *The next day John saw Jesus coming toward him and said, "Look, the Lamb of God, who takes away the sin of the world!"* John 1:29

_____Let's do: When you dye your eggs, decorate them with resurrection symbols and write down what each one means.

_____Let's pray: Victorious Savior, forgive us when we let the world hide Your triumph. Lead us to point others to the empty cross and tomb. May we all praise You only. In Your glorious name. Amen.

J. L. L.

Blood of the Lamb

Read from God's Word

And He said to them, "I have eagerly desired to eat this Passover with you before I suffer. For I tell you, I will not eat it again until it finds fulfillment in the kingdom of God." Luke 22:15–16

"Mom, I cut my hand!" Lindsey screamed. She was peeling potatoes for dinner and the knife slipped.

Her mother quickly checked the cut and went to get the antiseptic and the bandages.

"Why won't it quit bleeding?" Lindsey wailed.

"Bleeding helps clean the wound," Mom answered. "Then we use the antiseptic to kill the rest of the germs."

Later, as Lindsey was studying her confirmation lesson about the Passover, she learned how the blood of perfect lambs saved millions of Israelites from death. But it required many lambs to do this.

On Maundy Thursday, we remember the time Jesus was celebrating the Passover meal with His disciples. They talked of the Old Testament miracle, then Jesus gave the meal a new, more powerful meaning.

Before the disciples' awe-filled eyes, Jesus proclaimed the bread and wine to be His body and blood. Then He told them to eat this meal "in remembrance" of Him, which we still do today in Holy Communion.

Once again, a perfect Lamb was sacrificed to save billions. But this sacrifice required only one Lamb—the perfect Son of God.

Now our heavenly Father sees us with Jesus' blood around the door of our heart. We are set free from the slavery of our sins!

_____Let's do: Write a prayer for those who commune in church. Ask God to forgive your sins too.

_____Let's pray: Father God, when I think of You sacrificing Your only Son for me, I don't know what to say. Thanks for Jesus, my Savior. Help me confess my sins. In the name of Jesus. Amen.

J. L. L.

It Was Good

Read from God's Word

It was now about the sixth hour, and darkness came over the whole land until the ninth hour, for the sun stopped shining. And the curtain of the temple was torn in two. Jesus called out with a loud voice, "Father, into Your hands I commit My spirit." When He had said this, He breathed His last. The centurion, seeing what had happened, praised God and said, "Surely this was a righteous man." Luke 23:44–47

G od's power created our world in six days. Then He pronounced that it was good.

Jackie understood that our world began perfectly. After all, God made it! She also realized that people polluted God's creation with sin. Many years later, we are still polluting this world with our selfish sins.

Jackie is very grateful that God gave us Jesus to remove this sin-pollution. But she couldn't understand how this day could be called *Good* Friday! Jesus suffered so much. Surely it wasn't good for Him.

Jesus was arrested, tried, and mocked numerous times. He was spat upon and whipped. He wasn't allowed to sleep, nor were His wounds bandaged.

His friends betrayed, denied, and deserted Him. The crowds screamed for His death. He was too weak to carry His cross to Calvary, but He went there without a protest.

The nails were pounded in, and the cross was lifted into place. He hung there until His task was finished. God punished His only Son for us; through Him, we are saved.

Now Jackie knows without a doubt why this day is called "good." She believes in the victory of Jesus' death as her salvation. This is Good News. God is so good to Jackie—and to you!

———Let's talk: What are the sins you commit over and over? Those are your own polluters. Ask God to help you confess them and help you to change.

———Let's pray: Lord, forgive my sins that caused Your suffering. Thanks for taking my punishment. Help me live in love for You. In Your name. Amen.

J. L. L.

A Lion or a Lamb?

An old saying goes that March weather begins as a lion and ends as a lamb.

We know that weather is determined by the air conditions God sets in motion. There is no magic formula to the weather. Even weather scientists puzzle over God's weather mysteries.

A lion and a lamb also affect our spiritual weather. In 1 Peter we are warned to be alert, to watch for the devil's approach. The devil is compared to a hungry lion, ready to pull us into his jaws when we sin.

Satan works especially hard on Christians. When we fall into sin, the devil celebrates. He thinks he has a victory over God.

He's wrong! His celebrations are meaningless because our Lamb, Jesus Christ, has totally defeated Satan. Jesus went down into hell, Satan's fortress, and proclaimed His triumph over evil.

Now when Satan whispers tempting thoughts in our minds, Jesus shows His power and victory. Jesus gives us Holy Baptism and the power of His name. When we pray in Jesus' name, the devil runs away.

On the holy day between Good Friday and Easter Sunday, concentrate on the Lamb. He is the *Sonshine* God gives us to send the sin-storms hurrying off our spiritual radar.

_____Let's talk: How is Jesus' defeat over Satan a victory for you?

_____Let's pray: Jesus, give me Your strength to resist Satan. I can't do it alone. Forgive me when I give in to temptation. Cheer me with Your victory. In Your name. Amen.

J. L. L.

Island of Safety

Easter Island is in the South Pacific, between Chile and Tahiti. A Dutch ship reached there on Easter Sunday in 1722. The island was formed by eruptions of three extinct volcanoes. Six hundred huge statues were found there.

Some of these statues, called *moai*, are 40 feet tall and weigh 64 metric tons. How did they get there? Where did they come from? Scientists aren't sure, but Easter Island folklore says they represent the Polynesian explorers who found the island. The folklore also says that this island is the center of the world!

We have our own Easter island, but with only one stone. This stone caused concern to the women believers until they saw it had been moved by an angel in an upheaval, an earthquake.

There is no mystery about this upheaval. God's Son burst forth from the grave. "Don't be alarmed," the angel in the tomb said. "You are looking for Jesus the Nazarene, who was crucified. He has risen! He is not here. See the place where they laid Him."

Read from God's Word

When the Sabbath was over, Mary Magdalene, Mary the mother of James, and Salome bought spices so that they might go to anoint Jesus' body. Very early on the first day of the week, just after sunrise, they were on their way to the tomb and they asked each other, "Who will roll the stone away from the entrance of the tomb?" But when they looked up, they saw that the stone, which was very large, had been rolled away. As they entered the tomb, they saw a young man dressed in a white robe sitting on the right side, and they were alarmed. "Don't be alarmed," he said. "You are looking for Jesus the Nazarene, who was crucified. He has risen! He is not here. See the place where they laid Him. But go, tell His disciples and Peter, 'He is going ahead of you into Galilee. There you will see Him, just as He told you.'" Mark 16:1–7

We see our risen Lord and recognize Him as our rock. He is our island of safety. Only Jesus Christ has the solid strength to bring us forgiveness and salvation.

_____Let's do: Sing the hymn "Rock of Ages." Study the word pictures. Write an Easter verse.

_____Let's pray: Jesus, on this day of Your resurrection, fill our hearts with waves of love and joy. You are our rock and our salvation. Our thanks is not enough, but it is all we have to offer. You are risen indeed! Alleluia! Amen.

J. L. L.

april

Contributors for this month:

Mary Ann Berkesch

Nicole Dryer

Mary Krallmann

Marilyn Sommerer

Don't Be Fooled

Read from God's Word

Jesus said to them, "If God were your Father, you would love Me, for I came from God and now am here. I have not come on My own; but He sent Me. Why is My language not clear to you? Because you are unable to hear what I say. You belong to your father, the devil, and you want to carry out your father's desire. He was a murderer from the beginning, not holding to the truth, for there is no truth in him. When he lies, he speaks his native language, for he is a liar and the father of lies. Yet because I tell the truth, you do not believe Me! Can any of you prove Me guilty of sin? If I am telling the truth, why don't you believe Me? He who belongs to God hears what God says. The reason you do not hear is that you do not belong to God." John 8:42–47 ✍

Antonia remembered when a kind neighbor had given her a baby chick. Antonia dearly loved that chick!

One day her older brother, Alfred, told her that she should plant her chick in the ground and "grow" a whole bunch of chickens. The idea sounded strange, but after all, Alfred was older. She thought she could trust him.

Antonia dug a hole and planted her precious chick. Soon she realized that Alfred had tricked her. With her sister's help, she quickly dug up and revived her pet.

Not everyone will tell you the truth, but Jesus will. He said, "I am the way and the truth" (John 14:6). He also called the devil "the father of lies." The Bible is the truth, pointing us to Jesus alone for our salvation.

No one inside or outside of this world has ever loved and cared for us like Jesus, our Savior. Someone in our family might die for us, but they would not be able to save us from the punishment of our sins. Would any of today's sports or movie stars give up all their treasures and die for us? Could they take us to heaven? *No!* Why should we put much faith in what they say?

Jesus never lies or leads us astray. His Word is truth.

_____Let's do: Think of a foolish idea you have heard recently. Contrast it with a wonderful verse you know from God's Word.

_____Let's pray: Lord, keep our hearts close to You. Don't let us be fooled by the devil or anyone who would lead us away from You. Amen.

M. S.

Read from God's Word

While they were bringing out the money that had been taken into the temple of the LORD, Hilkiah the priest found the Book of the Law of the LORD that had been given through Moses. Hilkiah said to Shaphan the secretary, "I have found the Book of the Law in the temple of the LORD." He gave it to Shaphan. Then Shaphan took the book to the king and reported to him: "Your officials are doing everything that has been committed to them. They have paid out the money that was in the temple of the LORD and have entrusted it to the supervisors and workers." Then Shaphan the secretary informed the king, "Hilkiah the priest has given me a book." And Shaphan read from it in the presence of the king. When the king heard the words of the Law, he tore his robes. 2 Chronicles 34:14–19

Winners

Martina found a game without instructions. She tried to make up her own rules and wrote them down. Then she taught her brother her new rules.

It worked until their neighbor tried to play. He told Martina her rules were wrong, and he went to his house to get the real thing. After Martina read the official rules, she knew she was wrong.

Figuring out the correct way to play is easy once you have the directions. Figuring out God's instructions and plans is impossible without the Bible.

The king and elders of Judah and Jerusalem lost their copy of the Scriptures. Josiah's helpers found it. Josiah had the book read aloud. The Book of the Covenant included instructions for God's people under Josiah's reign. It also told of God's love for His people and how He was working for their salvation.

Do you think these people were able to keep the commands and regulations perfectly? No, they weren't. But they were happy to have a God who loved them so much. Years later He sent the promised Savior, who would die to forgive their sin.

Jesus came to keep the instructions perfectly. He died to pay the penalty for our mistakes, making us all winners through faith in Jesus Christ. What great news to share!

_____Let's talk: What are some ways God is helping you learn about Him?

_____Let's pray: Lord, help me to learn Your Word. In Jesus' name. Amen.

M. S.

Treasure and Trash

Read from God's Word

I have hidden Your word in my heart that I might not sin against You. Psalm 119:11

Before the days of cash and credit cards, people put their gold and silver coins and precious gems in chests then hid the keys to the chests to protect their treasure.

Years ago women had their own kind of "treasure chest." Expensive spices for cooking or medicine were kept in a locked box. Carefully selected herbs were safely tucked away until needed to season food or heal sickness.

Our hearts are like treasure chests. They become filled with our treasured thoughts and dreams, tucked away for later. We treasure memories of a family vacation or dreams for our next birthday party.

God's Word and hymns are more valuable than gold and silver coins. When these treasures are in your heart, God gives you strength from His Word wherever you are.

Our hearts sometimes become like trash cans. Out of them come evil thoughts and desires because we are all sinners. How do we get the trash out of the treasure chest?

Jesus takes away the trash through His death and resurrection. Through His Spirit, He fills our hearts with His peace, forgiveness, and joy. Jesus is the key to a treasure chest of riches—forgiveness of sins and life with Him now and forever. He gives us the treasure, and He Himself is the key.

_____Let's talk: What special things are in your "treasure chest" today?

_____Let's pray: Lord, fill my heart with thoughts of You today, tomorrow, and always. Amen.

M. S.

Read from God's Word

Who gave Himself for our sins to rescue us from the present evil age, according to the will of our God and Father. Galatians 1:4 ✍

To the Rescue

ead the following stories. Are the main characters thinking of themselves or of others?

STORY 1. Twenty-year-old Jake went on a boating trip with his family and friends. During a boating accident Jake panicked, grabbed a child's life preserver, and saved himself.

STORY 2. Eric and Darryl were playing kickball. Eric chased a ball into the street just as a car turned the corner. Darryl saw the danger and pushed Eric out of the way to safety.

STORY 3. Alicia and Jessica were talking at recess about how mean their teacher was. Neither girl did her homework.

STORY 4. Jesus lived a perfect life and died to free all people from sin. He provides a rescue for all people from the punishment of sin. He won eternal life, offering it to all who believe in Him.

It appears that Jake, Alicia, and Jessica were thinking of themselves. We might say their love was selfish; we might say that all people are naturally selfish and need a rescue. Darryl was able to help his friend facing an earthly problem. Jesus went way beyond the actions of Darryl. He provided salvation for all people from all sin—including selfish thoughts and acts. Not only did He rescue us from sin but He also helps us share His love with one another.

_____Let's talk: What unselfish thing have you seen others do?

_____Let's pray: Dear Savior, help us to love one another
as You have loved us. Amen.

M. S.

A-S-K

Jenny looked out the window, hoping to see a friendly face. She didn't see any children. *Where is everybody?* she wondered.

When Jenny's father came home, he found her drawing on a piece of cardboard. It said, "Come out and play with me!"

"What's this?" he asked.

"Dad, I need a friend," Jenny said. "I'm making this sign because I am tired of being alone."

"It's a pretty neat sign, Jenny. It's better than feeling helpless. I wonder if the new family downstairs would like to see your sign. Why don't you go knock on their door?"

Jenny was asking and seeking and knocking, hoping to find a friend, with no guarantee that her efforts would work. She didn't remember that her best Friend, Jesus, was waiting.

The three letters in the word *ask* can remind you of an invitation and promise that Jesus gives in Matthew 7:7–8. Jesus invites you to ask Him anything. Seek or look for your answer through Him. God's Word provides the answer and the opening to all our needs in His salvation. God delights to give His children good things. They might not be exactly what you ask for, but God's response will always be what is best for you. God can help Jenny, and He can help you. What are you waiting for?

Read from God's Word

"Ask and it will be given to you; seek and you will find; knock and the door will be opened to you. For everyone who asks receives; he who seeks finds; and to him who knocks, the door will be opened. Which of you, if his son asks for bread, will give him a stone? Or if he asks for a fish, will give him a snake? If you, then, though you are evil, know how to give good gifts to your children, how much more will your Father in heaven give good gifts to those who ask Him!" Matthew 7:7–12

_____Let's do: Think of a way to be kind to a lonely person.
Try it out.

_____Let's pray: Dear Lord, thank You for answering my prayers.
I love You. Amen.

M. K.

The High Cost

Read from God's Word

So the king gave the order, and they brought Daniel and threw him into the lions' den. ... At the first light of dawn, the king got up and hurried to the lions' den. When he came near the den, he called ... "Daniel, servant of the living God, has your God, whom you serve continually, been able to rescue you from the lions?" Daniel answered, "O king, live forever! My God sent His angel, and He shut the mouths of the lions. They have not hurt me, because I was found innocent in His sight. Nor have I ever done any wrong before you, O king." ... And when Daniel was lifted from the den, no wound was found on him, because he had trusted in his God. Daniel 6:16–23 ✐

Adelaide lived in Germany, a dangerous place during Adolf Hitler's growing power. In the orphanage where she worked, she was expected to greet everyone with "Heil Hitler." Instead she would say, "Grüss Gott." The use of *Gott*, the German word for God, might get Adelaide and the orphanage into trouble.

Adelaide left Germany to volunteer in the United States. Three days later, Hitler's dreaded Gestapo came to the orphanage to question, and possibly arrest, her. Adelaide's faith nearly cost her her life.

The Bible tells many stories of God helping His people face danger. God strengthened Daniel to remain faithful and to give an amazing witness. In response to God's rescue of Daniel, King Darius called on a whole nation to revere the true God. Queen Esther was brave as she decided to act on behalf of her people. God used her to help save His people.

God sent His Son, Jesus Christ, to rescue us from sin, death, and the devil. His perfect life was given on the cross. What was the gain? Forgiveness of sins and life everlasting are given to all who believe in Jesus as the Savior. What is the cost to you? Nothing. God gives you His gifts freely—including strength in times of trouble—so that along with Adelaide you can trust in *Gott*.

_____Let's talk: Do you know any country where Christians are in danger today? What are some ways that God shows His power in your life?

_____Let's pray: Dear Holy Spirit, fill me with joy and courage to not conceal my faith before others. Amen.

M .S.

Trading Places

Read from God's Word

When God saw what they did and how they turned from their evil ways, He had compassion and did not bring upon them the destruction He had threatened. But Jonah was greatly displeased and became angry. He prayed to the LORD, "O LORD, is this not what I said when I was still at home? That is why I was so quick to flee to Tarshish. I knew that You are a gracious and compassionate God, slow to anger and abounding in love, a God who relents from sending calamity. Now, O LORD, take away my life, for it is better for me to die than to live." But the LORD replied, "Have you any right to be angry?" Jonah 3:10–4:4 ✍

An Indian proverb says that before judging another person you should "walk in his moccasins for two moons." If you were to change places with someone, you would be able to understand the actions of that person.

Jonah praised God for rescuing him but he was not happy when Nineveh was shown mercy. Jonah was more concerned about his reputation than the souls of the Ninevites.

Jonah is not so different from us. We have two standards of judgment. One standard is for ourself, finding excuses for bad behavior and happily accepting God's forgiveness offered in Jesus. We have a different standard for others—especially our enemies. When we see bad behavior in them, we quickly find fault. We want punishment to be swift and certain.

If we traded places with that unkind girl or tough-talking bully, we might see a need for compassion or understanding. We might see how God could use us to help them.

Jesus came to change places with us. He took our sins and gives us His victory. He showed His loving compassion for all—lovely or unlovely, friend or enemy, neighbor or stranger. With Jonah we can sing a song of thanksgiving for the Lord's salvation and share His goodness day after day.

_____Let's do: Think of two ways God has shown compassion to you.

_____Let's pray: Dear Father, thank You for Your compassion and understanding. Forgive our sins for Jesus' sake. Amen.

M. S.

Read from God's Word

For we know in part and we prophesy in part, but when perfection comes, the imperfect disappears. When I was a child, I talked like a child, I thought like a child, I reasoned like a child. When I became a man, I put childish ways behind me. Now we see but a poor reflection as in a mirror; then we shall see face to face. Now I know in part; then I shall know fully, even as I am fully known. 1 Corinthians 13:9–12 ✍

Gaps

"I wish my teeth would hurry up and grow in," Aaron said. "It's hard to eat."

"Let's see," said Aaron's dad, checking out the problem.

Aaron had gaps between his teeth on the top and the bottom and a big space in the center.

"You're right, Aaron," said Dad, "but your teeth will come in before long."

Are you troubled by "spiritual gaps"—empty spaces in your understanding of God? We all have questions about God's actions or plans. The prophet Isaiah said long ago that God's thoughts are much higher than ours. That gap of understanding between God and us is as wide as the space between heaven and earth.

Are information gaps a problem for us? No. The Holy Spirit works in our hearts through God's Word and the Sacraments so what is important for salvation is provided for us. God makes it clear that we are sinners. He tells us we have a Savior who lived and died for us. Jesus' resurrection promises us we will rise from death.

We can trust God to take care of what we need and what we don't understand. Someday we will see Him face-to-face. For now He stands in the gap and gives us Himself as our salvation.

_____Let's talk: What question do you have about God or His will in your life?

_____Let's pray: All-knowing God, we trust You with our lives. Thank You for giving us the Bible and telling us how You have saved us. In Jesus' name we pray. Amen.

M. K.

Words of Value

Lizzie Charlton, a teenager in 1866, would have never expected that her diary would become a historic treasure. Lizzie's words describe her overland journey from Iowa to Oregon. Her diary was found in a tin box in a California dump. It was a treasure in the trash.

It takes time to write in a diary, but it is a valuable exercise. In a few sentences you can recapture your day for reflection in the future.

The Bible is a kind of diary. It is the story of God's love for His people. Without the Bible we wouldn't know the Gospel and the epistles (letters) of the New Testament. We wouldn't have the Law, psalms, history, and the prophecies of the Old Testament.

All these Scriptures are ours because God wants us to have His message. God led Luke to write an account of Jesus' life, death, and resurrection and the growth of the early church. God led Luke to gather words from eyewitnesses and servants of the Word. God worked through Luke to provide an orderly record so "you may know the certainty of the things you have been taught."

Thanks be to God for His written Word. The Bible is more valuable than silver, more precious than gold.

Read from God's Word

Many have undertaken to draw up an account of the things that have been fulfilled among us, just as they were handed down to us by those who from the first were eyewitnesses and servants of the word. Therefore, since I myself have carefully investigated everything from the beginning, it seemed good also to me to write an orderly account for you, most excellent Theophilus, so that you may know the certainty of the things you have been taught. Luke 1:1–4 ✐

_____Let's talk: How is God working in your life? How has God worked in your family's life?

_____Let's pray: Lord, thank You for Your Word. Help me to tell about You and Your love in my life. Amen.

M. S.

Tall Grass

Read from God's Word

Then the LORD said, "I will surely return to you about this time next year, and Sarah your wife will have a son." Now Sarah was listening at the entrance to the tent, which was behind him. Abraham and Sarah were already old and well advanced in years, and Sarah was past the age of childbearing. So Sarah laughed to herself as she thought, "After I am worn out and my master is old, will I now have this pleasure?" Then the LORD said to Abraham, "Why did Sarah laugh and say, 'Will I really have a child, now that I am old?' Is anything too hard for the LORD? I will return to you at the appointed time next year and Sarah will have a son." Genesis 18:10–14 ✎

"While on vacation," Neal said, "I discovered I'd lost my wallet while horseback riding.

"My mother got everybody together. We prayed that God would help us find it. Someone said, 'But the grass is awfully high.' My mom said, 'The grass isn't too high for God. He knows where it is.'"

Did they find it?

"Yes, we did," Neal said.

For Abraham and Sarah the "grass was awfully high" too. God said they were to have a child, but Sarah was past the age of childbearing. This was not too hard for God. He provided a son, Isaac, just as He had promised.

Are you going through a difficult time? You may think your problem is not important enough for God. You may wonder if God can solve the problem or if He cares enough to help you. You may see no solution to your problem, but God does. Nothing is too difficult for Him. God knows all about you. He saved you, sending His only Son to live, die, and rise again. He saved you from your greatest problem—sin. Now you are able to celebrate even more than if you had found a lost wallet. You have a God who won't forget about you—now or ever.

_____Let's do: Memorize Philippians 4:13 so the next time you're feeling uncertain, you can rely on God's Word for you.

_____Let's pray: Lord, strengthen my faith. Help me to know that You always know my needs and will answer my prayers. Amen.

M. S.

Pocket Cross

Read from God's Word

Your attitude should be the same as that of Christ Jesus: Who, being in very nature God, did not consider equality with God something to be grasped, but made Himself nothing, taking the very nature of a servant, being made in human likeness. And being found in appearance as a man, He humbled Himself and became obedient to death— even death on a cross! Therefore God exalted Him to the highest place and gave Him the name that is above every name, that at the name of Jesus every knee should bow, in heaven and on earth and under the earth, and every tongue confess that Jesus Christ is Lord, to the glory of God the Father. Philippians 2:5–11 ᔓ

"What a day this has been, Ryan!" said George. "First I get your kite stuck in a tree, and now I lose your favorite coin."

"Oh, it's okay, George. You'll find it. Look in your pocket."

George emptied his pockets. Some old movie ticket stubs, a gum wrapper, a matchbox car, colored stones, and a cross wrapped in paper came tumbling out. "Nope. It's not here."

"Hey, what's this for?" Ryan asked, unwrapping the paper.

"It's my pocket cross," said George. "My Sunday school teacher gave it to me. When I see the cross, I remember that Jesus is with me and will help me. Here's the poem that goes with it."

> I carry a cross in my pocket,
> A simple reminder to me
> Of the fact that I am a Christian,
> No matter where I may be.
> When I put my hand in my pocket
> To bring out a coin or key,
> The cross is there to remind me
> Of the price He paid for me.
> (Author unknown)

May the cross be a reminder to you of the great love Jesus has for you. God's love makes every day perfect.

_____Let's do: Make your own cross. Keep it in your pocket. Write about it.

_____Let's pray: Dear Jesus, help me tell others that You came to save all people. Amen.

M. A. B.

Read from God's Word

Jesus and His disciples went on to the villages around Caesarea Philippi. On the way He asked them, "Who do people say I am?" They replied, "Some say John the Baptist; others say Elijah; and still others, one of the prophets." "But what about you?" He asked. "Who do you say I am?" Peter answered, "You are the Christ." Mark 8:27–29 ∽

Looking for Answers

In the line of capital letters below the four statements, cross out the correct letters to solve the problem. Follow each step carefully.

1. If Noah built the ark, cross out all the *A*'s. If not, cross out the *T*'s.

2. If Joshua parted the Red Sea, cross out all the *O*'s. If not, cross out the *I*'s.

3. If God created the sun, moon, and stars on the fourth day, cross out the *B*'s and *U*'s. If not, cross out the *C*'s.

4. If Pontius Pilate washed his hands in front of the crowd, cross out the *D*'s. If not, cross out the *E*'s.

D C A A O I I A B U R R I A U E I B D B C I A U T

The remaining letters will tell you if you had the correct answers. If you didn't, keep trying.

It's fun to solve a puzzle or find a correct answer. Jesus asked His disciples a question. "Who do you say I am?"

Where would you look for the answer?

A sure place to look is in the Bible. It tells us that Jesus is God's only Son, sent to earth to save all people from their sins. He lived, died, and rose again from the dead. On our behalf He defeated death and gives us the gift of heaven.

Who do you say Jesus is? The right answer is in His Word!

_____Let's talk: Who do you say Jesus is?
         Why is this an important question?

_____Let's pray: Dear Jesus, thank You for being our Lord
         and our Savior. Amen.

M. A. B.

Secret Pal, Best Friend

The first thing Rachel did after running home was to check the mailbox. Yes! There was a letter addressed to her.

> *Dear Rachel,*
>
> *I think you are really neat. I hope you can come to my house sometime. I want to be your friend.*
>
> *Your Secret Pal*

Rachel was so pleased. Someone really liked her and wrote her a letter! For several days Rachel received letters just like the first one.

Finally the day came for the secret pals to meet. Becky was her secret pal. They became friends.

God has written you many letters. They are in the Bible. The letters say that you belong to God and are special and dear to Him. They tell you that He loves you and forgives you because Jesus paid for all you've done wrong.

The letters also show that God has good plans for your life (see Jeremiah 29:11). They tell you that you can trust in Him and not be afraid (see Isaiah 12:2). The letters tell you that Jesus is with you every day of your life (see Matthew 28:20).

Look through the Bible. You will discover many other letters that God has written. These letters tell us that a day will come when God will take us and all who believe in Him to heaven.

_____Let's do: Write a letter to yourself, telling about the promises of God.

_____Let's pray: Dear Lord, thank You for the many letters You have written to me in the Bible. Bless me as I read them. Amen.

M. A. B.

Read from God's Word

But you are a chosen people, a royal priesthood, a holy nation, a people belonging to God, that you may declare the praises of Him who called you out of darkness into His wonderful light. Once you were not a people, but now you are the people of God; once you had not received mercy, but now you have received mercy. 1 Peter 2:9–10

Read from God's Word

Listen, I tell you a mystery: We will not all sleep, but we will all be changed—in a flash, in the twinkling of an eye, at the last trumpet. For the trumpet will sound, the dead will be raised imperishable, and we will be changed. For the perishable must clothe itself with the imperishable, and the mortal with immortality. When the perishable has been clothed with the imperishable, and the mortal with immortality, then the saying that is written will come true: "Death has been swallowed up in victory." "Where, O death, is your victory? Where, O death, is your sting?" The sting of death is sin, and the power of sin is the law. But thanks be to God! He gives us the victory through our Lord Jesus Christ.
1 Corinthians 15:51–57 ✍

A Lily, Trumpet, and Flag

This Easter lily looks nice," said Mom. "Let's take it to the cemetery."

"You put a lily by Uncle Paul's gravestone last spring too," said Ruthie.

"They remind me of Paul," Mom replied. "The flowers look like trumpets, and he played the trumpet. He would stand in the church balcony and play along with some of the hymns."

"Uncle Paul didn't live very long, did he?" asked Ruthie.

"No," Mom answered, "he was only 21 when he died in Iraq."

At the cemetery they followed a narrow road to Uncle Paul's grave. Soon Ruthie saw the American flag that marked the place.

Ruthie and her mom put the lily by the gravestone. They watched the flag and the flowers move in the breeze. "Although lilies have a short life, like your uncle's, they bring us joy at Easter," Mom said.

Lilies and trumpets and flags reminded Ruthie and her mom of life and death. Jesus does too. He died after living a perfect life, but He came back to life at Easter. He fought our battle against sin, death, and the devil. Jesus won a victory for everyone, for all time. We look forward to living triumphantly with the Lord forever. Now we can blow the trumpet and wave the flag! Thanks be to God!

_____Let's do: Look for Christian messages on gravestones. You might see crosses and Bible verses. What did you find?

_____Let's pray: Thank You, Lord, for the victory You won for us. Amen.

M. K.

Favorite Days

Today isn't Easter or Christmas or Valentine's Day. For students it's a day to go to school. For many adults in the United States it's a deadline for income tax forms.

Today sounds like work. One tax deadline ends, but another one will come. The weekend is over, and another workweek begins. Most people would rather think about days of fun, gifts, and relaxing. But sometimes they have to think about other things. Most people have been planning for today's deadline, even if they don't like it.

For Jesus' followers the time after Easter was a time of change. Jesus had finished His work of winning salvation for all people when He died and rose again. The big events of Good Friday and Easter were past.

When Jesus returned to heaven, the disciples had to go back to work. They weren't traveling around with Jesus anymore. They had a new job: telling people what had happened. They had new excitement because they had seen for themselves that Jesus was alive again.

Believers in Jesus share in that new excitement all the time. We're living after Easter every day. We rejoice to know and tell how Jesus has saved us. Sharing the good news of sins forgiven and life eternal can make every day a favorite day.

Read from God's Word

Then He opened their minds so they could understand the Scriptures. He told them, "This is what is written: The Christ will suffer and rise from the dead on the third day, and repentance and forgiveness of sins will be preached in His name to all nations, beginning at Jerusalem. You are witnesses of these things. I am going to send you what My Father has promised; but stay in the city until you have been clothed with power from on high." When He had led them out to the vicinity of Bethany, He lifted up His hands and blessed them. While He was blessing them, He left them and was taken up into heaven. Then they worshiped Him and returned to Jerusalem with great joy. And they stayed continually at the temple, praising God. Luke 24:45–53

_____Let's do: How can you share your Easter excitement today?
How would you tell someone the good news of Easter?

_____Let's pray: O Lord Jesus, You have freed us from the power of
sin and given us eternal life. We praise You. Amen.

M. K.

Read from God's Word

The LORD said to Moses, "Tell Aaron and his sons, 'This is how you are to bless the Israelites. Say to them: "The LORD bless you and keep you; the LORD make His face shine upon you and be gracious to you; the LORD turn His face toward you and give you peace."' So they will put my name on the Israelites, and I will bless them."
Numbers 6:22–27

The "I Love You" Sign

What happens after worship services at your church? In many churches the pastor walks to the door and greets people. He shakes hands, making the greeting personal.

In Mary's church the pastor's little girls, Karen and Connie, started to shake hands with people.

Instead of shaking hands one Sunday, Karen surprised Mary by sharing "I love you" in sign language. "I love you" can be formed with a special hand shape. Three letters of the sign language alphabet are put together. The letters are *I, L,* and *Y*—the first letters in each word.

Karen and Connie were interested in sign language. They discovered that Mary knew some of the hand signs. Very few people at church would have understood the "I love you" sign. It was a message she liked to get.

The cross of Jesus is another "I love you" sign. It's a personal message from God to each of us. Out of love for us Jesus died on the cross. We have forgiveness because He took the punishment we deserved for our sins. The Holy Spirit gives us a new heart that loves and trusts in God. With God's love in our hearts, we leave every church service with the sign of the cross, a sign that says "I love you."

____Let's do: How can you show love to someone at your church?

____Let's pray: Dear God, thank You for loving me so much that You saved me from sin. Help me grow in love for other people. In Jesus' name. Amen.

M. K.

Flying High

M ary and her brother were visiting relatives in the country and decided to fly a kite.

They let the kite sail over an open field. Air currents made the kite dip and soar without any warning. Although we don't see the air currents that carry the kite, we know they are there because we see how the kite reacts.

The life of a Christian is beautiful. Christians can always have hope, courage, peace, and joy through the dips and soars of life. The Spirit of God reminds us that our ugly sins are forgiven because Jesus died and rose again. Nothing can separate us from the love of God.

The Holy Spirit comes to us in Baptism and through the Bible's message of God's grace and love in Jesus. People can't see the Holy Spirit in our hearts. But people do see how we act. They watch how we live using God's Law and rejoicing in His Gospel. They notice how God helps us respond to joys and to sin's sadness. Our life is a witness that the Holy Spirit guides and nurtures.

Read from God's Word

Jesus answered, "I tell you the truth, no one can enter the kingdom of God unless he is born of water and the Spirit. Flesh gives birth to flesh, but the Spirit gives birth to spirit. You should not be surprised at My saying, 'You must be born again.' The wind blows wherever it pleases. You hear its sound, but you cannot tell where it comes from or where it is going. So it is with everyone born of the Spirit." John 3:5–8

_____Let's talk: What might the dips and soars of faith look like?

_____Let's pray: O Holy Spirit, please keep our faith flying high. Let our lives reflect Your love. Amen.

M. K

Read from God's Word

LORD, you have assigned me my portion and my cup; You have made my lot secure. The boundary lines have fallen for me in pleasant places; surely I have a delightful inheritance. I will praise the LORD, who counsels me; even at night my heart instructs me. I have set the LORD always before me. Because He is at my right hand, I will not be shaken. Therefore my heart is glad and my tongue rejoices; my body also will rest secure, because You will not abandon me to the grave, nor will You let your Holy One see decay. You have made known to me the path of life; You will fill me with joy in Your presence, with eternal pleasures at Your right hand. Psalm 16:5–11 ✍

An Afternoon to Remember

Beth walked over to visit Ann, who was sitting on her porch swing.

"I'm reading a diary," said Ann. "I found something I wrote years ago on this date."

"That's neat," said Beth. "Was it a special day?"

"I'll read you what this says. 'Warm sun on the concrete step; a good talk with friend Carrie; mint tea and old-fashioned oatmeal cookies; robins along the fence; magnolias and tulips in bloom; green in the tree branches; a song in my mind.'

"I still remember the song," Ann explained. "It was the Johnny Appleseed song."

After Ann sang it to Beth, they sang the song together, rocking in the porch swing. "The Lord is good to me," fit that gorgeous April day.

The Lord fills our lives with blessings. All our happiness comes from Him. He gives us everything we need. Our greatest need is to be saved from sin and death. Our most important blessing is the forgiveness Jesus earned for us. Without that blessing we couldn't really be happy, even if we had everything else we wanted.

Every day is another day to live for Jesus, even when there are no cookies baking or tulips blooming. Because our Savior rose from the dead, we look forward to perfect happiness in heaven. That is something to sing about.

_____Let's do: Write about good things God puts into your life.
Save what you write and look at it next year.

_____Let's pray: Thank You, Lord, for all the beauties and pleasures of life. You are so good to me. Amen.

M. K.

Promises Kept

Making an afghan takes a lot of time and work. Thomas asked his grandma to make one for him. He picked out his favorite colors and pattern.

Grandma worked and worked to make the afghan for Thomas. "But, Grandma," Thomas said, "it's not right." He wanted the colors arranged a different way.

So Grandma ripped out the many rows of stitches. She rolled the different colors of yarn into big balls. Then Grandma made the afghan all over again.

Grandpa thought it was foolish to do everything over. But Grandma said she had promised to make an afghan just as Thomas wanted it. She intended to keep her promise, and she did.

Long ago God promised a Savior from sin. At the right time God sent His only Son to earth. Jesus lived a perfect life for us, died for all, and rose to life again as He said He would.

Read from God's Word

Let us draw near to God with a sincere heart in full assurance of faith, having our hearts sprinkled to cleanse us from a guilty conscience and having our bodies washed with pure water. Let us hold unswervingly to the hope we profess, for He who promised is faithful. Hebrews 10:22–23

God didn't stop there. He promised and sent His Spirit. The Holy Spirit works in people's hearts through Baptism and God's Word. That's how we become His children.

God promises that when our earthly life is over, we will live with Him in heaven. We know He will give us eternal life because He has promised us this wonderful treasure.

_____Let's talk: What sacrifice made us right with our heavenly Father? Why are you glad it happened?

_____Let's pray: Heavenly Father, it's wonderful to know that You keep Your promises. Help me trust in You all my life. In Jesus' name. Amen.

M. K.

Read from God's Word

Kings of the earth and all nations, you princes and all rulers on earth, young men and maidens, old men and children. Let them praise the name of the LORD, for His name alone is exalted; His splendor is above the earth and the heavens. He has raised up for His people a horn, the praise of all His saints, of Israel, the people close to His heart. Praise the LORD. Psalm 148:11–14 ✑

A Press Run

The Press Run is a foot race sponsored by a local newspaper each April. The Press Run is a race for everyone to try.

Each runner receives a T-shirt, a map, and a tag with a number. Some runners have gray or white hair or not much hair at all. Other runners are so young that the T-shirt goes down to their ankles. There are people of different heights and weights. They wear running shoes of many styles and sizes. Some of the runners are strong and fast. Others take a long time to finish the race.

These runners can remind us of Christians. Christians of all ages, sizes, backgrounds, and talents go through life together.

Christians follow a route that has been run before. Over the years many believers in Jesus have already finished their race. The Holy Spirit helps every believer to follow in Jesus' footsteps.

Jesus paid the registration fee for everyone. He ran His life's race perfectly. He died and rose again for us. Otherwise sin, death, and the devil would keep us from finishing the race.

Believers in Jesus receive a new heart and life instead of a new T-shirt. The Holy Spirit gives us the strength we need to run the race. For God's children heaven is at the finish line.

_____Let's talk: How does God help a person become a better runner in the race of the Christian life?

_____Let's pray: Dear Jesus, thank You for being our path and prize. Help me run a straight race through Your grace. (*LW* 299:2)

M. K.

Jesus, Our Good Shepherd

K imi keeps baseball cards in boxes under her bed. Some of them are valuable so she puts them in special cases. Kimi's favorite card is not autographed or valuable. The player isn't even famous, but Kimi likes him because once he threw her a ball.

One day Kimi realized her special card was gone. She looked everywhere for it.

"Look what I found in Scruffy's dog bed," said Mom. It was her card, messy and missing a corner, but Kimi didn't care. She was so happy she did a little dance around the room!

Jesus told a story about a shepherd who had a problem like Kimi. The shepherd had 100 sheep, but one of them was lost. He was so worried that he left the 99 sheep and searched everywhere until he found the little lost lamb.

Jesus told this story because the people were lost sheep and He was the Shepherd who had come to save them.

Read from God's Word

Now the tax collectors and "sinners" were all gathering around to hear Him. But the Pharisees and the teachers of the law muttered, "This man welcomes sinners and eats with them." Then Jesus told them this parable: "Suppose one of you has a hundred sheep and loses one of them. Does he not leave the ninety-nine in the open country and go after the lost sheep until he finds it? And when he finds it, he joyfully puts it on his shoulders and goes home. Then he calls his friends and neighbors together and says, 'Rejoice with me; I have found my lost sheep.' I tell you that in the same way there will be more rejoicing in heaven over one sinner who repents than over ninety-nine righteous persons who do not need to repent." Luke 15:1–7 ✐

Jesus saved us from being lost in our sins when He died on the cross. When He rose from the dead, Jesus promised we would have eternal life through faith in Him. Jesus is our Savior and our loving Good Shepherd, who forgives our sins and watches over us until the day we go to heaven to live with Him forever.

_____Let's do: Today is Good Shepherd Sunday. Read John 10:11–16. What does Jesus say that can make us feel like dancing?

_____Let's pray: Dear Jesus, thank You for loving me so much that You died so I could be safe in Your fold. I love You, Jesus! Amen.

N. D.

Read from God's Word

Rejoice in the Lord always. I will say it again: Rejoice! Philippians 4:4 ✍

Celebrate

April is Nicki's favorite month. She loves to watch baseball. Each spring she eagerly waits for opening day. She loves sitting in the stands, eating peanuts, and cheering for her team.

The weather is another reason Nicki likes April. The days grow longer and the weather gets warm enough to stay outside. Red tulips, yellow daffodils, and purple pansies begin to bloom.

Guess what? Nicki's birthday is also in April! She has her favorite dinner with family and friends. There are games to play, presents to open, and cake and ice cream to eat. Nicki loves birthdays.

But even if there were no baseball games, no flowers, and no birthday presents, spring would still be the best month of the year because it is the time we celebrate Jesus' resurrection, the greatest miracle of all time.

When Jesus died on the cross and rose again, He defeated our worst enemies: sin, death, and the devil. Jesus gave us the greatest gift we could ever receive—eternal life. And that's something to celebrate not just on Easter Sunday, but the whole month of April, all spring long, and every day of the year!

_____Let's do: Make a calendar for the week. Write a sentence prayer to Jesus in the square for each day like "Thank You, Jesus, for the sunshine!" When you go to bed at night, draw a cross over the same day to remind yourself how much Jesus loves you.

_____Let's pray: Every day I want to praise You, Jesus. When it's cold, when it's hot, when it snows, and when it rains, You are my Sonshine. Amen.

N. D.

What a Nightmare!

Jamal had a scary dream that a giant was chasing him. He was glad when he woke up and realized it wasn't true.

After Jesus died, the apostle Peter probably wished that everything were a bad dream. Peter had promised Jesus that he would stay faithful. Only a few hours later Peter told three people that he didn't even know Jesus! When he realized what he'd done, Peter cried, full of sadness.

Three days later, when Peter saw the empty tomb, it was like waking up from a bad dream. Not only was Jesus alive, but Peter's sins were forgiven.

Peter's life of serving Jesus was just beginning. The next time the soldiers came, with God's help Peter didn't deny Jesus. Later Peter was put to death for his faith. But Peter knew that death was just the beginning of a different kind of life in heaven.

Jesus forgave Peter's sins and gave him the courage to preach the Gospel in a dangerous place. You might not preach like Peter, but you can bring a friend to Sunday school. You may never be in a dangerous place like Peter, but you can go to church when everyone else is playing baseball or soccer on Sunday mornings. Jesus will help you, just like He helped Peter.

Read from God's Word

But Christ is faithful as a son over God's house. And we are His house, if we hold on to our courage and the hope of which we boast. Hebrews 3:6

_____Let's do: Invite a friend to Sunday school and church this weekend.

_____Let's pray: Jesus, please help me to make the right choices for You and forgive me when I don't. Thank You, Jesus! Amen.

N. D.

How Embarrassing!

Embarrassing moments was the topic for the assignment. "I'll just write about last Sunday when I was an acolyte at church," said Cory. "I was so nervous I tripped on the steps. Then some of the candles wouldn't light. Everyone was looking at me."

The apostle Peter had an embarrassing moment too. One night the disciples saw Jesus walking toward them on the water! The disciples thought it was a ghost and were afraid. But Peter believed it was Jesus. He called out, "Lord, if it's You, tell me to come to You on the water."

Jesus told him to come, so Peter climbed out of the boat and started to walk on top of the water! But the wind and the waves distracted Peter. He started to sink. Jesus reached out and caught Peter. How embarrassing!

Embarrassing moments happen to everyone, even in church. Like Peter we feel we're sinking with embarrassment. What can we do? For one thing we can remember these things happen to everyone. We can also remember that Jesus comes to us in all our troubles. He is always beside us.

This loving Jesus has rescued us from sin—a problem worse than any other we will ever have. That's a rescue worth writing about!

_____Let's do: What do you do when you're embarrassed?
Read what God said to Joshua in Joshua 1:9.
How do you feel now?

_____Let's pray: Dear God, sometimes I'm so embarrassed.
Help me to remember that You are always
with me, even when my face is red.
Thank You, God! Amen.

N. D.

St. Mark, the Evangelist

Read from God's Word

The beginning of the gospel about Jesus Christ, the Son of God. Mark 1:1

John Mark heard Jesus preach, and he loved the Lord. Some believe John Mark slipped out of his house one night and quietly followed Jesus and the disciples to the Garden of Gethsemane. He saw the soldiers coming with their swords and torches, arrest Jesus, and take Him away. John Mark was really scared and ran away quickly.

After Jesus' death, resurrection, and ascension, John Mark's mother let the believers worship in her house. John Mark traveled with his cousin Barnabas and the apostle Paul on their first missionary journey.

When he got older, John Mark preached the Gospel himself. John Mark preached in Rome, although the Roman government had killed Peter and Paul. John Mark may have been the author of the Gospel of Mark.

John Mark's death didn't stop the Gospel message from spreading all around the world. Why? Because his words from God call us to discover the heart of the Gospel—the Good News "about Jesus Christ, the Son of God."

Isn't it great to know that God uses all kinds of people to spread the Good News of salvation? God may not call you to be a preacher or a writer, like St. Mark, but He has given you, me, and all people special talents and abilities to use as we serve Him.

_____Let's talk: How can you use your gifts to serve the Lord?

_____Let's pray: Thank You, Lord, for St. Mark. Thank You that I am free to worship You. Please watch over missionaries who risk their lives to spread the Gospel in dangerous places. In Jesus' name. Amen.

N. D.

Read from God's Word

For, "Everyone who calls on the name of the Lord will be saved." How, then, can they call on the one they have not believed in? And how can they believe in the one of whom they have not heard? And how can they hear without someone preaching to them? And how can they preach unless they are sent? As it is written, "How beautiful are the feet of those who bring good news!" Romans 10:13–15 ∽

Inca Messenger

The ancient Inca people built an empire high in the Andes Mountains. Roads and buildings were made of stone cut to fit together so perfectly that no mortar was needed.

The Inca also figured out how to cut terraces for farming on the steep sides of the mountain. The Inca farmers were able to grow enough food for the entire empire.

It's amazing that they had no written language. Instead, they had messengers. When the emperor had a message to send, he would tell it to a messenger. He would race along the road as fast as he could until he reached the next messenger. Runner after runner ran until the message was delivered.

Today we can spread God's Word in many ways. We can translate the Bible for people all over the world. We can print lessons that teach children that Jesus died and rose for them. We can make videos to share God's plan to rescue all people from sin. Some churches broadcast worship services on the radio and Internet.

Sometimes the easiest way to spread the Good News is to invite a friend to come to church and Sunday school with you. Your friend will hear the most important message of all: "Everyone who calls on the name of the Lord will be saved."

_____Let's talk: What are two ways you can be a messenger of the Good News?

_____Let's pray: Thank You, God, for all of the ways we can share the Good News. In Jesus' name. Amen.

N. D.

Opening Day

Read from God's Word

To some who were confident of their own righteousness and looked down on everybody else, Jesus told this parable: "Two men went up to the temple to pray, one a Pharisee and the other a tax collector. The Pharisee stood up and prayed about himself: 'God, I thank you that I am not like other men—robbers, evildoers, adulterers—or even like this tax collector. I fast twice a week and give a tenth of all I get.' But the tax collector stood at a distance. He would not even look up to heaven, but beat his breast and said, 'God, have mercy on me, a sinner.' I tell you that this man, rather than the other, went home justified before God. For everyone who exalts himself will be humbled, and he who humbles himself will be exalted." Luke 18:9–14 ✑

D anny was a good baseball player, but he didn't like to practice. He *did* like to tell everyone how good he was. "I'm the best player on the team," Danny bragged.

Taron wasn't as good as Danny. But Taron didn't give up. He practiced every day. Each week Taron was getting better and better.

On opening day the coach told Taron. "I've been watching you practice and you've really improved. You'll be in the game today." During the game Taron's extra practice paid off. He got two hits and made three good catches. His team won!

In Jesus' time the Pharisees acted the same way Danny did. They liked to brag about themselves. The Pharisees wanted everyone to hear them, so they prayed aloud. Instead of praising God, the Pharisees told Him all the good things they had done.

Jesus taught the people that everyone is a sinner, even the Pharisees. Prayer is a chance for sinners to talk to God. Because Jesus paid the price for our sins, believers can ask for God's help and forgiveness. It is also a time to praise and thank God for His loving kindness.

Our talents and abilities come from God. When you do something you're proud of, don't forget to thank Him.

———Let's do: How can you remember to thank God? Make a list of everything you like to do or all the things you are good at. Every day, thank God for one of those things.

———Let's pray: Thank You, God, for everything You have given me— my family and friends, food and clothes, talents and abilities—but best of all, thank You for Jesus! Amen.

N. D.

Read from God's Word

And that is what some of you were. But you were washed, you were sanctified, you were justified in the name of the Lord Jesus Christ and by the Spirit of our God. 1 Corinthians 6:11

That's Exciting!

During colonial times Thomas Jefferson and George Washington served in the government at Williamsburg, Virginia's capital. There were cozy houses and busy shops everywhere. Horse-drawn carriages took guests to the governor's beautiful palace.

After the Revolutionary War, Virginia's capital moved to Richmond. People forgot all of the exciting things that had happened in Williamsburg. The palace and the capitol building burned down. Houses were changed or sold.

Bruton Parish Church was one building that didn't change. Reverend Goodwin wanted everyone to remember how important Williamsburg was, so he came up with a plan to save the city's history. It took a long time, but the governor's palace and the capitol were rebuilt. Houses, shops, and businesses were restored. Hundreds of thousands of people now come to Williamsburg every year to learn more about colonial life.

Reverend Goodwin saw a wonderful city hidden beneath that old city. What does God see when He looks at us? Because of Jesus, God sees the beauty beneath the surface. The blood of Jesus washed the soil of our sins away. His restoration makes our lives a reflection of His goodness. We are alive in Christ! Now that's exciting!

_____Let's do: Do you know how beautiful you are? Read 2 Corinthians 6:16. God has made you His temple. He lives in you, and that makes you more beautiful than silver or gold. Wow!

_____Let's pray: Lord, I want to be Your beautiful temple. Please come into my heart and fill me with Your love. Amen.

N. D.

Unchained

Miranda's class was learning to write a kind of poem called a "chain verse." In a chain verse, the last words of each line are used as the first words of the next line.

Miranda wrote about Easter. Her chain verse ended like this:

Jesus was laid in the tomb.

The tomb was closed with a stone.

A stone couldn't hold Jesus.

Jesus rose from the dead!

Chains can be very hard to break. The apostle Paul was held in prison by chains because he preached about Jesus. Paul knew that his words about Jesus couldn't be locked up. Although Paul was in jail, the Gospel message was spreading. When Paul was put to death, others kept on preaching. Nothing could stop the Word of God, not even death.

Death couldn't stop God's Son. When Jesus was buried in the tomb, the devil thought he had defeated God. The devil was wrong! God is almighty, and no one can defeat Him. Jesus broke the chains that bound us to our sin when He defeated death and rose from the grave. Now the strongest chain of all is the chain of faith that connects God to us. Nothing can separate us from Him.

Read from God's Word

Remember Jesus Christ, raised from the dead, descended from David. This is my gospel, for which I am suffering even to the point of being chained like a criminal. But God's word is not chained. Therefore I endure everything for the sake of the elect, that they too may obtain the salvation that is in Christ Jesus, with eternal glory. Here is a trustworthy saying: If we died with Him, we will also live with Him. 2 Timothy 2:8–11

_____Let's do: Read Romans 8:38–39. See how much God loves you. Then see if you can write a chain verse about your favorite Bible story.

_____Let's pray: Thank You, Jesus, for breaking the chain of sin that was wrapped around me. Thank You for wrapping Your strong arms of love around me instead. Amen.

N. D.

Read from God's Word

So Christ was sacrificed once to take away the sins of many people; and He will appear a second time, not to bear sin, but to bring salvation to those who are waiting for Him. Hebrews 9:28 〰

Counting the Days

In a few weeks it will be summertime! What do you like to do in the summer? Do you swim or play ball? Do you go to vacation Bible school? Summer is a special time.

The people in Jesus' time were also counting the days for the Messiah to come and deliver them. Many thought He would be a warrior who would make the children of Israel into a powerful nation. But Jesus was not coming to save them from their political enemies. He was coming to save them from their spiritual enemies—sin, death, and the devil.

Jesus came to earth to suffer and die for the sins of all people, both Jews and Gentiles. Many turned away from Him. Sadly, there are millions of people today who are still waiting for someone to give them food, safety, and make their nation great. They don't want to believe that Jesus is the promised Savior.

Christians all around the world are also waiting. On the Last Day Jesus will take everyone who believes in Him, both the living and the dead, to heaven. We will live with Jesus forever!

What will heaven be like? No one knows exactly, but we do know there will be no sadness, pain, or tears. Heaven will be better than the best summer vacation.

____Let's do: Read Titus 2:11–14. What does Paul say about waiting?

____Let's pray: Dear Jesus, please forgive me when I forget that Your salvation is the most exciting thing of all. Thank You, Lord! Amen.

N. D.

may

Contributors for this month:

Terri Bentley

Elaine Hoffmann

Mary Krallmann

Jacqueline L. Loontjer

Betty Moser

Mark R. Rhoads

Laura Siegert

Read from God's Word

"Sacrifice thank offerings to God, fulfill your vows to the Most High, and call upon Me in the day of trouble; I will deliver you, and you will honor Me." Psalm 50:14–15

O God!

On the way home from the store Nico's grandmother suddenly became ill and was unable to control the car. Nico grabbed the steering wheel. "O God!" he said.

He unfastened his seat belt and reached over to move her foot from the gas pedal. As the car slowed down, he concentrated on steering to the side of the road. He managed to get his foot on the brake. At first he pushed a little too hard, but soon the car stopped. Then he used the cell phone to call 911 and his parents. The ambulance came and took Grandma and Nico to the hospital.

Nico's story was on the news and he was called a hero. The reporter asked him what made him so brave. Nico said, "God helped me."

Remember the part in the story when Nico said, "O God!"? Sometimes God's name is used for no reason at all. But when Nico called out God's name, it was a prayer for help.

God loves us very much. He knows when we need help. After all, He sent Jesus to help us with our greatest problem—sin. God has the power to help with every problem. Just like Nico, we can call on God's name. We can be sure that He will help us.

_____Let's do: Make a list of every time you hear someone say "O God!" Can you tell if it is used as a prayer?

_____Let's pray: Thank You, God, for helping me in my times of trouble. Help me to remember to ask You for help and then to give You the glory. Amen.

E. H.

Pray for Whom?

Christine and Diane were lining up for a field trip to the planetarium. They wanted to be partners, but Christine sat with Brandi on the bus, so that made them partners at the planetarium.

Diane was jealous. She tried to get Christine away from Brandi by saying mean things. When it was time to line up, she tried to trip Brandi. Diane was miserable, and she cried softly.

The teacher, Mrs. Grayson, sat with Diane. "You didn't have a very good day, did you?" she asked.

"This morning Christine was my best friend," said Diane. "Now she spends all her time with Brandi! I hate them both!"

Mrs. Grayson gently picked up Diane's hand. "I know you're sad, but being jealous and hating are making you unhappy. Did you know that some of Jesus' friends did the same thing to Him?"

Read from God's Word

"You have heard that it was said, 'Love your neighbor and hate your enemy.' But I tell you: Love your enemies and pray for those who persecute you, that you may be sons of your Father in heaven. He causes His sun to rise on the evil and the good, and sends rain on the righteous and the unrighteous. If you love those who love you, what reward will you get? Are not even the tax collectors doing that? And if you greet only your brothers, what are you doing more than others? Do not even pagans do that? Be perfect, therefore, as your heavenly Father is perfect." Matthew 5:43–48 ✍

"No," answered Diane, "not to Jesus!"

"Yes," replied Mrs. Grayson. "Jesus said we should love our enemies and pray for those who persecute us. He loved everyone so much that He died for all sins, even jealousy."

Diane felt badly. "I just want Christine to be my friend."

"Let's pray about this," said Mrs. Grayson.

Together they asked Jesus to forgive their sins of jealousy and hatred. They asked Him to make all three girls friends again.

_____Let's talk: Why does being jealous make us feel miserable?
Why does loving make us feel good?

_____Let's pray: Dear Jesus, forgive me when I am jealous of others. Help me to be a friend to everyone. Amen.

E. H.

Read from God's Word

Therefore, since we are surrounded by such a great cloud of witnesses, let us throw off everything that hinders and the sin that so easily entangles, and let us run with perseverance the race marked out for us. Let us fix our eyes on Jesus, the author and perfecter of our faith, who for the joy set before Him endured the cross, scorning its shame, and sat down at the right hand of the throne of God. Consider Him who endured such opposition from sinful men, so that you will not grow weary and lose heart.
Hebrews 12:1–3 ✍

Running Straight

Greg is pretty good in the 100-meter dash. Although he often comes in first, he doesn't always win. Sometimes Greg goes out of his lane and is disqualified.

Greg got good advice from his grandfather. As a farmer, Grandpa has lots of experience plowing straight rows. He focuses his eyes on a fence post or a tree in the distance and drives his tractor straight toward it. That way he makes very straight rows. Greg plans to keep his head high and his eyes on the finish line while he runs.

In the Bible, our life is sometimes called a race. We are encouraged to run straight and never give up.

Jesus is an example. His whole life was focused on winning salvation for sinners. Jesus ran the race and won the victory through His perfect life, death, and Easter triumph. Jesus is waiting for us at the finish line, cheering us on.

Just as the runner concentrates on the finish line, God will help us keep our eyes on Jesus. His strength and guidance will keep us running. The twists and turns of sin in our life have ruined our try at a perfect race, so Jesus gives us His victory. What a trade! Now we keep running, not burdened by our sins, but sure of winning.

———Let's do: Close your eyes. Imagine Jesus waiting for you at the end of a race. Draw or paint a picture of what you see.

———Let's pray: Dear Jesus, thank You for finishing the race first so I can run straight toward You. Amen.

E. H.

Get the Prize

Next to the Olympics, the most important games to the people of Corinth were the Isthmian games, foot races that occurred every other year.

The winner wore the wreath of laurel vines on his head for everyone to see. It was a great honor. Many runners hoped to win the prize.

St. Paul wrote a letter to the people at Corinth and said, "Run in such a way as to get the prize." The Corinthians understood what was involved in getting the prize. Paul, however, wasn't talking about the prize of a laurel wreath but about the runner's attitude. He was speaking like a coach pumping up his runners before a race.

Paul's words are not only for those who believed in Jesus during his time, but also for us. He wants us to apply the same kind of excitement and focus we would have for running a race to telling the news of Jesus Christ. Paul encourages us to get up each day and put on our running shoes for Christ because we already have His wonderful victory in our lives. We race with Good News because

> we have the best coach—God;
> we have a great race plan—God's Word; and
> we are running with the prize already in our hands.

Read from God's Word

Do you not know that in a race all the runners run, but only one gets the prize? Run in such a way as to get the prize. Everyone who competes in the games goes into strict training. They do it to get a crown that will not last; but we do it to get a crown that will last forever. Therefore I do not run like a man running aimlessly; I do not fight like a man beating the air. No, I beat my body and make it my slave so that after I have preached to others, I myself will not be disqualified for the prize.
1 Corinthians 9:24–27

_____Let's do: See if you can find information on the Isthmian games. How can you share the news of Jesus today?

_____Let's pray: Dear God, we know we have already won the race because of Jesus' victory over sin. Excite us to run with eagerness, sharing Your victory news with others. Amen.

E. H.

Read from God's Word

Remember this: Whoever sows sparingly will also reap sparingly, and whoever sows generously will also reap generously. Each man should give what he has decided in his heart to give, not reluctantly or under compulsion, for God loves a cheerful giver. And God is able to make all grace abound to you, so that in all things at all times, having all that you need, you will abound in every good work. As it is written: "He has scattered abroad His gifts to the poor; His righteousness endures forever." 2 Corinthians 9:6–9

Cheerful or Tearful?

During Sunday school Donny waited for the offering basket. His dad had given him a dollar for his offering and two quarters for ice cream. Donny thought about how a dollar could buy two treats instead of one.

Later when Donny and his dad stopped for ice cream, Donny pulled out the dollar. "Why didn't you put the dollar in the offering?" his father asked.

"Well," Donny replied, "the teacher said God loves a cheerful giver. I could give the quarters more cheerfully than I could give the dollar."

Did Donny sin and disobey his father? Did he misunderstand God's Word? Yes!

"Remember your blessings," said Dad. "God gives you everything you need. That includes the quarters for ice cream. And that is why we can be cheerful about being generous."

Donny began to understand and he confessed to his father. "I was selfish. I'm sorry, Dad. I wasn't thinking about all that God has given me."

"God understands," Dad said as he patted Donny's shoulder. "He loves you very much and wants to shower you with marvelous blessings, including forgiveness, every day."

Right there in the car, Donny and his dad prayed together. Then they went for ice cream. Donny paid for two—one for his dad and one for him.

_____Let's do: List ten gifts God has given you, three that you cannot touch or see.

_____Let's pray: Dear God, thank You for all the ways You bless me every day of my life. Forgive me when I do not give cheerfully back to You. Amen.

E. H.

Other Mothers

Jackie climbed into his mother's lap and asked, "Where was Daddy born?"

"He was born in New York," his mother said.

"Where were you born?"

"In Minnesota," his mother smiled.

"Where was I born?"

"You were born right here in Illinois."

Jackie smiled, "I'm sure glad we all got together!"

There are many ways of coming together and many kinds of families. On certain days we celebrate families or special people in our family—like Mother's Day.

A dictionary says a mother is a female person who cares for another person. If you think about it, you have other "mothers" in your life. How about a grandmother, aunt, or older sister? Maybe you have a teacher, baby-sitter, or coach who cares about you. Sometimes our friends' mothers treat us like their own children. Foster mothers and adopted mothers are very special and loving.

All of these women are gifts God has given to us out of love. Many of these women care for us, teaching us how to love others as Christ first loved us.

God's perfect love for us caused Him to send Jesus to suffer and die on the cross for our sins. This love continues to provide for us every day, including the gift of other mothers.

Read from God's Word

When He was gone, Jesus said, "Now is the Son of Man glorified and God is glorified in Him. If God is glorified in Him, God will glorify the Son in Himself, and will glorify Him at once. "My children, I will be with you only a little longer. You will look for Me, and just as I told the Jews, so I tell you now: Where I am going, you cannot come. A new command I give you: Love one another. As I have loved you, so you must love one another." John 13:31–34

_____Let's do: Find other mothers in these Bible verses: Genesis 3:20; Judges 5:7; John 19:25; 2 Timothy 1:5.

_____Let's pray: Dear God, thank You for the "other mothers" in our lives. Help us to honor them. Amen.

E. H.

Read from God's Word

You will call and I will answer You; you will long for the creature Your hands have made. Surely then You will count my steps but not keep track of my sin. My offenses will be sealed up in a bag; You will cover over my sin.
Job 14:15–17

Keeping Track

Cindy argued with her family. She had trouble getting along with her classmates. Cindy was always angry and ready to fight. Her teacher kept track of the times Cindy caused trouble. She wrote each one on a sticky note, filling a page. The teacher gave all the stickies to the principal. Then Cindy was called to the office.

The principal, Mrs. Yancy, let Cindy talk for a long time about her anger and stress. Cindy didn't think God cared about her problems. Mrs. Yancy shared Job's struggles with Cindy. Job longed for a God who would not keep track of his sins. Although Job didn't realize it at the time, our Father in heaven is like that.

Mrs. Yancy said, "You may not realize it either, Cindy, but God loves you very much. He knows the kind of trouble you have. He sent Jesus to take all our sins away." Then Cindy watched as Mrs. Yancy put all the stickies in a bag, sealed it shut, and put it in the trash.

Cindy couldn't believe it. She was sure Mrs. Yancy was going to keep track of her offenses. Although Cindy had to take the consequences of her actions, she knew her sins were forgiven. The stickies and the sins were sealed up in a bag and gone forever.

_____Let's do: Read the Bible passage again. Design a sticky note of thanks to God for sealing up your offenses.

_____Let's pray: Heavenly Father, thank You for Your great love for me. Help me to pass along the forgiveness You have given me through Jesus. Amen.

E. H.

Save the Bad Guys

ylan uses action figures to act out scenes from his favorite movies. The good guys always win, no matter how powerful the bad guys are. Dylan wishes he were extra powerful so he could defeat the bad guys and save the world.

We all want to be heroes. We desire to have power to beat the bad guys. We would enjoy the praise a hero gets when saving the city.

God wanted Jonah to be a hero. But He didn't give him superhero powers. Instead, He told Jonah to go tell the bad guys that God knew who they were and what they were doing. God didn't like the behavior of the people of Nineveh and He would destroy them if they didn't change. Through His warning, God really wanted the Ninevites to turn from their evil ways and worship Him.

Jonah wanted God to blow up the bad guys—no second chance. But God doesn't work that way. He wants to save everyone, even those who turn away.

Read from God's Word

Then the word of the LORD came to Jonah a second time: "Go to the great city of Nineveh and proclaim to it the message I give you." Jonah obeyed the word of the LORD and went to Nineveh. ... He proclaimed: "Forty more days and Nineveh will be overturned." The Ninevites believed God. ... When the news reached the king of Nineveh ... he issued a proclamation in Nineveh: "Let everyone call urgently on God. Let them give up their evil ways and their violence. Who knows? God may yet relent and with compassion turn from His fierce anger so that we will not perish." When God saw what they did and how they turned from their evil ways, He had compassion and did not bring upon them the destruction He had threatened. Jonah 3:1–10 ✐

We can be thankful that God wants to save the bad guys because we're like them. We turn away from Him many times because of sin. But instead of punishing us, God sent Jesus, the best hero, to suffer and die for our sins.

_____Let's talk: Who are other messengers God used in the Bible? Who are messengers in your church?

_____Let's pray: Lord, thank You for sending Jesus to take the punishment I deserve. Please get my heart ready to be a hero for You when You ask me to. Amen.

L. S.

I Set You Apart

Read from God's Word

"Before I formed you in the womb I knew you, before you were born I set you apart; I appointed you as a prophet to the nations." Jeremiah 1:5

When Laura lived in Colorado, she knew who she was—the principal's kid, the blonde girl who played sports and loved art. Friends knew her and needed her. When Laura's family moved to California, nobody knew her or needed her. She felt alone and unimportant although other kids surrounded her. Laura had lost her identity.

"Before I formed you in the womb I knew you, before you were born I set you apart." Even before Jeremiah was born, God loved him and gave him some very special talents. God had chosen Jeremiah to be His prophet and tell God's message of judgment and love to His people.

God made each of us. He knew us before we were born. He gave each of us a very special identity. He also redeemed us through the life, death, and resurrection of Jesus. Through Baptism God made us His children. With this new identity God helps us use the special gifts He gives us to spread the message of His love and forgiveness—just like He did for Jeremiah.

Laura's new identity in California really wasn't so different. She was still a blonde, sports-loving, artistic daughter. She was still God's forgiven child, able to share with others the new identity He had given her in Jesus.

_____Let's do: List your talents. Pray that the Lord will use these special gifts for His glory.

_____Let's pray: Lord, thank You for creating me and for giving me talents to use for You. Help me to share Your plan of love and salvation with the people in my life. Amen.

L. S.

To Be Continued . . .

People love sitcoms on television. The characters can solve any problem in just 30 minutes. If you lived in sitcom land, math homework would make sense in just half an hour.

Have you sometimes wondered how the TV problem will be solved in 30 minutes? Then the phrase "To be continued" shows up on the screen. Even in sitcom land, a problem can be too big to solve in 30 minutes.

Today's Bible reading is a "to be continued" story in the Bible. After Jesus showed He was God by dying and rising to eternal life, His disciples asked Him to establish a kingdom for Israel. Jesus told them He was leaving and to wait for the Holy Spirit. Then He ascended into a cloud and went to heaven. Is this the end? No! Imagine the phrase, "To be continued." When we tune in next on Pentecost, the Holy Spirit comes, helping the disciples do incredible things. These men boldly tell others about Jesus' death, resurrection, and the kingdom of heaven.

We are part of the second half of the episode. The Holy Spirit comes to us and works through us to share God's loving plan of salvation for the world.

The real end is never-ending—it is the gift of heaven. There we will live forever in God's kingdom.

Read from God's Word

He said to them, "Why are you troubled, and why do doubts rise in your minds? Look at My hands and My feet. It is I Myself! Touch Me and see; a ghost does not have flesh and bones, as you see I have." ... Then he opened their minds so they could understand the Scriptures. He told them, "This is what is written: The Christ will suffer and rise from the dead on the third day, and repentance and forgiveness of sins will be preached in His name to all nations, beginning at Jerusalem. You are witnesses of these things. I am going to send you what My Father has promised; but stay in the city until you have been clothed with power from on high." When He had led them out to the vicinity of Bethany, He lifted up his hands and blessed them. Luke 24:38–50 ✍

_____Let's talk: What is your favorite Bible story to share?
How does it tell about Jesus?

_____Let's pray: Lord, thank You for the second half of the story. Send the Holy Spirit into my heart. I want to tell others about You. Amen.

L. S.

Read from God's Word

Hear, O Israel: The LORD our God, the LORD is one. Love the LORD your God with all your heart and with all your soul and with all your strength. These commandments that I give you today are to be upon your hearts. Impress them on your children. Talk about them when you sit at home and when you walk along the road, when you lie down and when you get up. Tie them as symbols on your hands and bind them on your foreheads. Write them on the doorframes of your houses and on your gates. Deuteronomy 6:4–9*

Spring's Promise

Every evening after dinner my family had devotions. Every Sunday we went to church and Sunday school.

I learned the Bible over and over. I learned that God created the world in six days. I learned about Adam and Eve, who committed the first sin. I learned about God's reaction of anger when His chosen people turned from Him.

I learned about Jesus' birth and ministry and His love for everyone. I learned that He died on the cross to save us from evil and came alive on Easter. I learned that God asks us to love one another as He loves us.

Was learning the same facts over and over good? It definitely was, but at that time I didn't think so. God knows that we forget important things when we haven't heard about them for a while. That's why He reminds us to talk about His words at home and other places, when we lie down and when we get up. We listen and read God's Word over and over as we grow and change.

Every morning God comes to us with His promises. Every evening He offers us forgiveness, hope, and peace. Every day of every week He strengthens us through His Word—over and over and over again.

———Let's do: Next time you find your mind wandering during Bible class or church, try writing down what you think God wants you to learn. Pray about how to share what you learn with someone else.

———Let's pray: Dear Lord, sometimes I think that I know it all. Please enter my heart and mind, opening them to the possibilities that exist in Your Word. Amen.

L. S.

Be Still!

Sometimes Malcom feels like his life is spinning out of control. He gets up in the morning and rushes to school. He goes to basketball practice or music lessons. He does his chores, helps with dinner, and does homework. The next morning Malcom does it again. Every day as he works harder, his life spins faster.

Even on Sunday Malcom might be going in circles—singing in the choir, working in the nursery. Even his worship is too hurried!

Some days he takes a vacation day to rest. Even God took a day and rested when He finished making the world.

God knows we need His refreshment and peace. That's one reason He gave us the commandment "Remember the Sabbath day by keeping it holy" (Exodus 20:8). God wants to renew us with His strength. In Psalm 46:10 He tells us, "Be still, and know that I am God."

He wants us to remember that He has taken care of the one thing that we really need in our lives. He has given us forgiveness and salvation by grace through faith in Jesus, who died on the cross for our sins. We are triumphant with the risen Lord. God used His power to take care of everything that really matters—no more circles without His rest.

Read from God's Word

"Be still, and know that I am God." Psalm 46:10a

_____Let's do: For one week, spend five minutes a day doing nothing but reading God's Word. Write down some of your thoughts.

_____Let's pray: Dear Lord, please enter my mind as I sit quietly. Bring Your peace and wisdom to me. Show me Your will in the stillness of Your presence. Amen.

L. S.

Read from God's Word

*In the same way, count your-
selves dead to sin but alive to
God in Christ Jesus. Therefore do
not let sin reign in your mortal
body so that you obey its evil
desires. Do not offer the parts of
your body to sin, as instruments
of wickedness, but rather offer
yourselves to God, as those who
have been brought from death to
life; and offer the parts of your
body to Him as instruments of
righteousness. For sin shall not
be your master, because you are
not under law, but under grace.*
Romans 6:11–14 ✍

Mom's Love, God's Love

When Megan started middle school, she had three teachers every day. Each teacher had his or her own expectations and ways of teaching. She felt lost and unimportant.

One semester Megan stopped doing her math homework. She didn't like math and couldn't see why she needed to learn it. She got a D on her report card. Megan knew her mom would be really upset. She'd probably make her quit the softball team to have more time for studying, so Megan changed the grade to a B before her mom saw it.

Megan's mom saw the grade and congratulated her on her fine work. She continued to do badly in math and failed the class the next semester. To this day Megan can't add fractions. Not!

This is what really happened: Mom discovered that Megan had changed her grade. She asked why, and Megan told her. Her teacher and a math tutor helped. She had to quit softball until she brought her grade up.

Megan's mom showed love and compassion that allowed her to suffer the consequences of her actions. God does the same thing for us, but He doesn't make us suffer the most serious result of our sins. Jesus took that load to the cross, changing our grade from failure to His perfection.

——Let's talk: If you were Megan's parents, what would you have done? If you were Jesus, what would you have done?

——Let's pray: Lord, thank You for the grace You show me when I sin. Amen.

L. S.

Fear or Trust?

Read from God's Word

"Be strong and courageous. Do not be afraid or terrified because of them, for the LORD your God goes with you; He will never leave you nor forsake you." Deuteronomy 31:6

J ason's pet rabbit was gone. The wire cage had been cut. A neighbor came to help look for her. She had seen kids chasing a rabbit the day before. With that in mind, she went to investigate. She found Jason's rabbit down the street, locked up in a plastic doghouse with no food or water. She rescued the poor thing and brought her back to him.

After that happened, Jason heard more stories about the kids. He heard that the police had been to their house several times. He heard that the kids were often in trouble around the neighborhood.

For the next few days Jason kept thinking about those kids who had stolen his pet. Something kept nudging him to go talk to them. He thought that God wanted him to be kind to them. But Jason was afraid that their parents would yell at him or that no one would appreciate his effort.

Although Jason felt that God wanted him to show them that someone cared, he didn't go. He let his fears stop him from following the Lord's prompting.

Today's Bible verse says, "Do not be afraid ... for the LORD your God goes with you; He will never leave you nor forsake you." Jason had forgotten that the Lord is always there to provide strength when he's afraid and uncertain. He missed a great opportunity to get to know new people.

We can be thankful that God doesn't miss a chance with us. He sent Jesus to rescue us from a pen of sin that locked us in. Now we are free. His Spirit gives us the strength and courage to tell others of His love.

_____Let's do: Think of things that make you afraid. List ways that God helps you.

_____Let's pray: Dear Lord, please enter my heart and give me strength to serve You. Amen.

L. S.

Struggles

But we have this treasure in jars of clay to show that this all-surpassing power is from God and not from us. We are hard pressed on every side, but not crushed; perplexed, but not in despair; persecuted, but not abandoned; struck down, but not destroyed. We always carry around in our body the death of Jesus, so that the life of Jesus may also be revealed in our body. 2 Corinthians 4:7–10

"Oh, Jenna, what a pretty cat!" said Lacey. "What's her name?"

"Struggles," said Jenna.

"Why did you name her Struggles?" asked Lacey.

"Her mother, Fluffy, had four kittens," began Jenna. "The first three were born easily, but Fluffy struggled a long time with the last one. She struggled the first few days just to live. Then she struggled for her place to nurse. Later she had to struggle to learn how to walk and leap. Now," laughed Jenna, "she struggles just to stay out of trouble."

Have you ever thought that your life is something like that? Are you always struggling to make friends, learn something new, or stay out of trouble? Sometimes it seems that no matter how hard we struggle to do what is right, we end up doing wrong. Sometimes the wrong kinds of TV shows, movies, and friends draw us away from Jesus and into trouble.

But Jesus' love is greater than all our struggles. Jesus loved us so much that He was willing to die on the cross and rise again for us. He won the greatest struggle of all time—the battle against the devil, sin, and the world. Jesus also helps us as we struggle against our troubles in this life.

____Let's do: Take your problems to Jesus in prayer.
How can you help others who are facing troubles?

____Let's pray: Dear Jesus, help me give all my troubles to You.
Thank You for always being near to help me. Amen.

B. M.

Bicycles and Freedom

What is it about bike riding that we like? Is it the intense exercise? Is it the excitement of an outing with our family and friends? Is it the surge of power as we steer, brake, and pedal on our way?

With our parents' permission we're free to explore the neighborhoods and parks, to let the wind blow through our hair and the sun shine on our face. What a glorious feeling!

There is a freedom greater than this. In Romans 6:17–18 we read, "You used to be slaves to sin ... [but] you have been set free from sin." Through God's grace Jesus has set us free from sin. Nagging reminders of our unkind ways and our selfish thoughts are silenced by the freedom of confession (to tell God you are sorry for your sins) and forgiveness (God telling you He forgives your sins) that Christ won for us. Now we are free to obey God, to worship Him, to tell others about His love, and to honor Him with our lives.

Read from God's Word

What then? Shall we sin because we are not under law but under grace? By no means! Don't you know that when you offer yourselves to someone to obey him as slaves, you are slaves to the one whom you obey— whether you are slaves to sin, which leads to death, or to obedience, which leads to righteousness? But thanks be to God that, though you used to be slaves to sin, you wholeheartedly obeyed the form of teaching to which you were entrusted. You have been set free from sin and have become slaves to righteousness. Romans 6:15–18

Praise be to God for our freedom every day of the year. What a glorious feeling it is to be free—truly free.

_____Let's do: Compare the freedom you have when you ride your bike with the freedom you have from the slavery of sin. Use the last two paragraphs to help you.

_____Let's pray: Lord God, thank You for the freedom from sin that You have given me through Jesus. Work through me to share this freedom with others. Amen.

B. M.

Read from God's Word

Because of His great love for us, God, who is rich in mercy, made us alive with Christ even when we were dead in transgressions—it is by grace you have been saved. And God raised us up with Christ and seated us with Him in the heavenly realms in Christ Jesus, in order that in the coming ages He might show the incomparable riches of His grace, expressed in His kindness to us in Christ Jesus. Ephesians 2:4–7

Cracked Cement

The next time you take a walk, notice all the cracks in the sidewalks. Some cracks are skinny and barely visible while others are dangerously wide. Even newly paved streets have tiny cracks. Grass, leaves, sticks, paper, bugs, glass, seeds, and even pinecones collect in the cracks. Many things find a home there.

Our daily lives could be compared to a sidewalk. We want to start each day with no cracks. But we have been "cracked" since birth. We were born with a sinful nature. It doesn't take long for new cracks of sinful thoughts and actions to appear on the surface of our day.

Like the sidewalk cracks, our lives fill up with sins of lying, making fun of others, laziness, and more. How do we get rid of the ugly cracks and the nasty debris? We can't. Nothing we do will fill up those cracks. We cannot get enough good grades or behave well enough to save ourselves. There is no sidewalk cement we can use.

The answer comes to us through the salvation work of Jesus Christ. God "who is rich in mercy, made us alive with Christ even when we were dead in transgressions [sins]." God fills our cracks with Christ's perfection and makes us perfect.

_____Let's do: Reread Ephesians 2:1–7. List all the things God has done for His children.

_____Let's pray: Heavenly Father, forgive my sins. Thank You for Your love and mercy, which make me whole again. I pray in the name of Jesus Christ. Amen.

B. M.

An Ocean in Illinois

Read from God's Word

So that Christ may dwell in your hearts through faith. And I pray that you, being rooted and established in love, may have power, together with all the saints, to grasp how wide and long and high and deep is the love of Christ, and to know this love that surpasses knowledge— that you may be filled to the measure of all the fullness of God. Ephesians 3:17–19

My friend invited me to go see an ocean. We would only be gone an hour, and we were in the middle of the United States. That didn't make much sense!

We followed a sign toward a car factory. I started to see something that looked dark and wavy.

I discovered we were looking down on the tops of cars. There were rows and rows—an ocean of brand-new cars! From a distance the car tops looked like dark waves in the sunshine. It was only when we got closer that I saw the different colors.

Sometimes the dark waves in our lives seem to be in control. They may be waves of sickness or loneliness. These troubles all come from sin.

But Jesus came to defeat the power of sin, death, and the devil. Through His wide, long, deep, and high love, Jesus washed our sin away. He lived every day perfectly. He died to pay for all our sins, and He arose victorious on the third day.

Easter brings to us new waves of hope, peace, and joy. God helps us through His Word and Sacraments to find strength and patience in Him. He gives us power to ride the tide as He turns the dark waves of troubles into oceans of blessings.

_____Let's talk: What waves of troubles do you see in your life? What oceans of blessings do you see?

_____Let's pray: Lord Jesus, we thank and praise You for Your oceans of blessings. Amen.

M. K.

Read from God's Word

When the day of Pentecost came, they were all together in one place. Suddenly a sound like the blowing of a violent wind came from heaven and filled the whole house where they were sitting. They saw what seemed to be tongues of fire that separated and came to rest on each of them. All of them were filled with the Holy Spirit and began to speak in other tongues as the Spirit enabled them. ... A crowd came together in bewilderment, because each one heard them speaking in his own language. Utterly amazed, they asked: "Are not all these men who are speaking Galileans? Then how is it that each of us hears them in his own native language? ... We hear them declaring the wonders of God in our own tongues!" Amazed and perplexed, they asked one another, "What does this mean?" Acts 2:1–12 ✍

Power to Speak

B onjour, mesdames et messieurs! Dieu vous aime!

¡Buenos días, damas y caballeros! ¡Dios los ama!

Guten Tag, meine Damen und Herren! Gott hat euch lieb!

Do you understand these sentences? If you don't know French, Spanish, or German, you won't. They say, "Good day, ladies and gentlemen! God loves you!"

When someone speaks in a language different from our own, our faces may look puzzled. That's what happened on the first Pentecost Sunday to Peter and the other disciples. They were with people from all over the world. The disciples wanted to tell everyone that Jesus had died so they could live forever.

The disciples knew only one language. The Holy Spirit took care of that problem in a special way on Pentecost. When Peter and his friends started talking about Jesus, all the listeners understood them in their own language! How exciting!

Through God's power Peter could tell everyone how wonderful God is. He preached a powerful sermon. By the working of the Holy Spirit, 3,000 people believed in Jesus and were baptized.

Those who believe in the Savior through His Word and Sacraments have the Holy Spirit working in them too. He gives believers the amazing, beautiful words about His loving sacrifice to tell all nations.

_____Let's do: Write "Jesus loves you" in other languages.

_____Let's pray: Holy Spirit, help me speak the language of love as I share Your words of love and forgiveness with people I know. Amen.

M. R. R.

Going to Bat for Us

Read from God's Word

What I am saying is that as long as the heir is a child, he is no different from a slave, although he owns the whole estate. He is subject to guardians and trustees until the time set by his father. So also, when we were children, we were in slavery under the basic principles of the world. But when the time had fully come, God sent His Son, born of a woman, born under law, to redeem those under law, that we might receive the full rights of sons. Because you are sons, God sent the Spirit of His Son into our hearts, the Spirit who calls out, "Abba, Father." So you are no longer a slave, but a son; and since you are a son, God has made you also an heir. Galatians 4:1–7

Baseball season is in full swing. Fans shout with joy or moan with disappointment. It all depends on the play.

A game with a close score tests the team. The pitchers must throw their best pitches. The fielders must be alert, preventing an extra base or run. The batter tries to change the outcome with one swing. Once in a while the manager decides the time is right for a pinch hitter. Everyone in the stadium goes wild as the substitute batter steps to the plate—the balance of the game is in the power of his swing.

Jesus was our pinch hitter. By ourselves we could not win the big game—our salvation. The opposing manager, Satan, was relaxing in his dugout, knowing we didn't have a chance by ourselves.

Then Jesus came to earth as a baby, lived a perfect life, and took our place by dying on the cross for our sin. "When the time had fully come, God sent His Son, born of a woman, born under law, to redeem those under law, that we might receive the full rights of sons."

Now whatever Satan throws at us won't work—no tempting thoughts or reminders of our sins or sinful nature. God has made us winners because of Jesus' death and resurrection. Yea, God!

_____Let's do: Write a newspaper article telling how Jesus won the victory for us.

_____Let's pray: Jesus, my Savior, thank You that Your perfect life and innocent death have guaranteed a place for me in heaven. Help me love You and live for You. In Your blessed name. Amen.

J. L. L.

Read from God's Word

Do everything without complaining or arguing, so that you may become blameless and pure, children of God without fault in a crooked and depraved generation, in which you shine like stars in the universe as you hold out the word of life—in order that I may boast on the day of Christ that I did not run or labor for nothing. But even if I am being poured out like a drink offering on the sacrifice and service coming from your faith, I am glad and rejoice with all of you. So you too should be glad and rejoice with me. Philippians 2:14–18 ✍

A New Way

Some people grumble because they have to get up for school in the morning. They grumble because they want pancakes instead of cereal for breakfast. They grumble because it's too hot or too cold.

We all grumble. We think of our crummy situation before thinking of others. We grumble against our parents, friends, and God. Our words rebel against the way we are (against our hair color or athletic ability) or against things that happen in our lives (like rain on our Scout campout or a canceled field trip). Grumble, grumble, grumble.

Throughout the Bible we read about other grumblers. The Israelites complained often during their 40 years in the desert. The disciples grumbled about the costly ointment that Mary of Bethany used to anoint the feet of Jesus. The Pharisees grumbled when Jesus healed the sick and the lame on the Sabbath.

Jesus died for our grumbling sin and offers us His forgiveness. God offers us His Holy Spirit to give us power to fight the temptation to grumble. The Spirit helps us do what God wants us to do. Through the Spirit we become interested in meeting the needs of others instead of our own. We receive a new heart to care for others, new eyes to see their needs, and a whole new way of life.

———Let's do:　List things that might make you grumble.
　　　　　　Ask the Holy Spirit to help you see your
　　　　　　grumbling with a new heart and new eyes.
　　　　　　Write down new ways to look at the listed items.

———Let's pray: Lord God, thank You for giving me life.
　　　　　　Please forgive me for my grumbling.
　　　　　　Help me live each day with You. Amen.

B. M

The Needed Treasure

Read from God's Word

"Do not be afraid, little flock, for your Father has been pleased to give you the kingdom. Sell your possessions and give to the poor. Provide purses for yourselves that will not wear out, a treasure in heaven that will not be exhausted, where no thief comes near and no moth destroys. For where your treasure is, there your heart will be also." Luke 12:32–34

Baseball cards, stamps, hats, coins. People love to collect things.

We also collect things in our hearts. Some of these things are sinful thoughts and beginnings of sinful actions. We remember little problems we have with our parents. Then we bring it up again when our feelings are hurt. We can't seem to forget the mean words we spoke with our friends. Or we may get the idea that "we can't do anything right," and that nagging thought takes over our thinking. What a nasty collection.

Do we really need or want that kind of collection? No. The false treasures we keep in our heart really hurt us. We become so focused on those rights and wrongs that we are not able to see the real treasure. In fact, our false treasure of sins condemns us before a righteous God.

Yet it is this same loving God who brings the real treasure into our hearts and lives. Through the Holy Spirit, God leads us to repent, and He forgives our sins. He does this all because of Jesus, the one treasure we really need. Jesus draws us to Himself through His means of grace—Baptism, the Lord's Supper, and the Word of God. Through these treasures we have the gift of an eternal relationship with Him.

———Let's talk: Why is Jesus your greatest treasure?

———Let's pray: Dear Jesus, help me to keep You as the priceless treasure in my life. Live in me so I might live in You. Amen.

J. L. L.

Problems Ahead

Seth got to touch the hedgehog when the zoo volunteer came to class. He was so excited to tell his mother that he rushed out the school doors. As he sped toward the parking lot, his mother shouted, "Stop!"

Seth was unaware of a car racing down the hill right in front of him. His mother could see it from the parking lot.

Jesus told Simon Peter, "Satan has asked to sift you as wheat. But I have prayed for you, Simon, that your faith may not fail" (Luke 22:31–32). Peter couldn't see the problem coming, but Jesus could.

Our God loves and watches out for us. He cares about the things that happen to us every day and uses them to help us stay close to Him. Jesus is with us today as we go swimming or study. He is with us as we run across the street or are tempted to lie. He knows the problems we will face even if we don't.

God saw our biggest problem coming years before we were born. That problem of sinful disobedience began way back in the Garden of Eden and continues in us today. Right then and there God promised the world a Savior. Our Savior is the best solution to the worst problem we will ever have.

_____Let's talk: How does God use your pastor, teacher, or parents to protect you?

_____Let's pray: Dear Lord Jesus, thank You for being with me in this life and forever. Amen.

T. B.

What a Relief

Read from God's Word

No temptation has seized you except what is common to man. And God is faithful; He will not let you be tempted beyond what you can bear. But when you are tempted, He will also provide a way out so that you can stand up under it. 1 Corinthians 10:13

Jaime didn't know if Tori and Justin saw her watching their game, but they didn't invite her to play. She went back into the house, wishing someone would invite her to play ball.

Later Jaime saw that Tori and Justin had left their ball in the yard and gone off. *Well, if no one will play with me,* Jaime thought, *I'll take the ball and play by myself.* Although she knew it wasn't right, she did it anyway.

As she bent to pick up the ball, a big dog came charging around the corner. Jaime was sure it would attack her. She dropped the ball and ran toward the fence, hoping she could get through the opening before the dog bit her.

As Jaime reached the fence, the dog let out a big yelp! The dog had run out of chain just as Jaime set foot in her own yard. What a relief! The chain saved Jaime.

What saves us when we sneak through the fence of sin? God sent Jesus to put a chain on the consequences of our sinful nature. Through His death and resurrection Jesus has won the battle with the devil against sin and death. He invites us in His Word and Sacraments to be His own and live in safety forever. What a relief!

———Let's do: List temptations that trouble you (lying, stealing, saying bad words). Mark a cross over each one as you take them to Jesus in prayer.

———Let's pray: Thank You, Jesus, for rescuing me from temptation. When I sin, help me run to You for Your forgiveness. Please deliver me from all evil. Amen.

T. B.

Read from God's Word

Rejoice in the Lord always. I will say it again: Rejoice! Let your gentleness be evident to all. The Lord is near. Do not be anxious about anything, but in everything, by prayer and petition, with thanksgiving, present your requests to God. And the peace of God, which transcends all understanding, will guard your hearts and your minds in Christ Jesus. Finally, brothers, whatever is true, whatever is noble, whatever is right, whatever is pure, whatever is lovely, whatever is admirable— if anything is excellent or praise-worthy—think about such things. Philippians 4:4–8

The Great Exchange

Some of Leon's friends were out of school for the summer and he wasn't. They were going bowling and he had to go to school. He got his grumpy self dressed, moaning all the while that life wasn't fair.

At school Leon was asked to be captain of a team in gym, but that didn't help him feel better. Leon also got an A on his final book report. So what! He'd rather be keeping score at the bowling alley.

Leon was finishing up his clay project in art. Using tiny letters, he was imprinting a Bible verse on a molded vase. Just as he finished the words from Philippians, he began to absorb their meaning.

"Do not be anxious about anything, ... present your requests to God. And the peace of God, which transcends all understanding, will guard your hearts and your minds in Christ Jesus."

Leon's hurt could be exchanged for God's peace. Leon took his disappointment to God in prayer.

We know we can take everything to God in prayer. He promises to hear us and to stand guard at the door of our heart, protecting us. The peace of God's Spirit floods our hearts and minds. Our worries are traded for His peace—it's a great exchange for Leon and for us!

_____Let's talk: What sins, worries, and concerns do you need to talk to your Savior about today?

_____Let's pray: Dear Jesus, I know You care about me and will watch over me every day—in good times and in bad. Amen.

M. R. R.

A Big Surprise

Read from God's Word

"See that you do not look down on one of these little ones. For I tell you that their angels in heaven always see the face of My Father in heaven. What do you think? If a man owns a hundred sheep, and one of them wanders away, will he not leave the ninety-nine on the hills and go to look for the one that wandered off? And if he finds it, I tell you the truth, he is happier about that one sheep than about the ninety-nine that did not wander off. In the same way your Father in heaven is not willing that any of these little ones should be lost." Matthew 18:10–14 ✏

Tasmyn was surprised to find a beagle eating from her collie's dog dish one morning. She didn't know to whom the puppy belonged, but it followed her everywhere.

The puppy's collar had a Pocatello, Idaho, phone number on it. Tasmyn's older sister called the number on the other side of the state but no one answered.

Tasmyn named the puppy Pocatello and rigged up an old doghouse for her. She fed her, played with her, and tried to teach her not to wet on the carpet. The new member of the family seemed to be fitting in when suddenly Pocatello was gone!

Tasmyn and her dad were surprised to find that Pocatello was on the next street—over at her *real* home. The owner had lost the wandering puppy just after the moving van emptied out all their family's belongings.

Now Pocatello was happy, just as we will be when Jesus takes us from our earthly home to our real home in heaven. We're visiting that earthly home now, like Pocatello visited Tasmyn.

After Jesus died and rose again, He went ahead of us to heaven to prepare a place for all believers. It's no surprise that the God who made us and redeemed us will return with open arms to take us to our real home with Him.

_____Let's do: Write the words and learn stanza three of the hymn "I'm But a Stranger Here."

_____Let's pray: Thank You, Lord, for finding me when I was lost. I look forward to being home in heaven with You forever. Amen.

T. B.

Read from God's Word

But you, man of God, flee from all this, and pursue righteousness, godliness, faith, love, endurance and gentleness. Fight the good fight of the faith. Take hold of the eternal life to which you were called when you made your good confession in the presence of many witnesses. 1 Timothy 6:11–12 ✎

Onward, Christian Soldiers!

Memorial Day is a special day to remember the men and women who have fought in wars to defend their country and preserve freedom.

The Bible has many stories of soldiers who fought for God. Unscramble the letters to find their names. You can check your answers by looking up the Bible verses below the scrambled names.

H O Y I T T M
1 Timothy 1:18

O M A N S S
Judges 13:24

U P L A
Acts 19:11

V D I A D
1 Samuel 17:32

E E P R T
Acts 4:13

A O H D B R E
Judges 4:4

Now write the letters that are underlined, in order. You will discover who else is a soldier for the Lord.

St. Paul told Timothy, "Fight the good fight of the faith. Take hold of the eternal life to which you were called." We have God's own strength to be Christian soldiers. The victor's crown is a gift from Jesus, who won salvation for us by His valiant suffering to overcome death and hell. So we are given power and purpose to go onward, as Christian soldiers!

_____Let's do: What help has God given His soldiers? Read Ephesians 6:10–17.

_____Let's pray: Lord God, thank You for making me Your soldier. Help me fight the good fight and share Your love with other people. Amen.

M. R. R.

A Psalm for All Seasons

K ing David wrote most of the psalms that believers have used for thousands of years. Whether you are sad, angry, lonely, or happy, you can find a psalm that fits your needs.

All the psalms remind us that God cares about us, loves us, and saves us. Psalm 145 tells God how great and wonderful He is. Use an NIV Bible to fill in the missing words from these verses in Psalm 145. Then find the same words in the puzzle below and circle them.

Verse 1—I will exalt You, my God the

_____.

Verse 3— _____ is the LORD.

Verse 8—The LORD is . . . slow to

_____.

Verse 13—The LORD is _____ to all His promises.

Verse 15—The _____ of all look to You.

Verse 19—He hears their _____ and saves them.

Verse 20—The LORD watches over all who _____ Him.

Verse 21—My mouth will speak in _____ of the LORD.

Read from God's Word

The LORD is righteous in all His ways and loving toward all He has made. The LORD is near to all who call on Him, to all who call on Him in truth. He fulfills the desires of those who fear Him. He hears their cry and saves them. The LORD watches over all who love Him, but all the wicked He will destroy. My mouth will speak in praise of the LORD Let every creature praise His holy name for ever and ever. Psalm 145:17–21

_____Let's talk: What has the Lord done for you today?

_____Let's pray:My God and King, thank You for rescuing me forever through the work of Your Son, my Savior. Amen.

M. R. R.

```
L R Z K G Q B R L X
R U E U I E A A R S
N S F E U N P E U Y
Z K C H P Y G N A K
G R E A T N S Q H L
Y O P R A I S E C O
I W V B X T A I Y V
T O S Y Q X A F K E
```

Read from God's Word

But now a righteousness from God, apart from law, has been made known, to which the Law and the Prophets testify. This righteousness from God comes through faith in Jesus Christ to all who believe. There is no difference, for all have sinned and fall short of the glory of God, and are justified freely by His grace through the redemption that came by Christ Jesus. God presented Him as a sacrifice of atonement, through faith in His blood. He did this to demonstrate His justice, because in His forbearance He had left the sins committed beforehand unpunished—He did it to demonstrate His justice at the present time, so as to be just and the one who justifies those who have faith in Jesus. Romans 3:21–26

Playing the Game

The Bible is like the ball used in baseball.

Defensively, the ball is used to keep a team from scoring. When the ball is caught, the other team is out. Offensively, the same ball is hit past the opponent. If it isn't caught, the team will score runs. The team with the higher score wins.

Defensively, the Bible shows us our sins: "All have sinned and fall short of the glory of God." The Bible lists the Ten Commandments that we're supposed to keep. As we read it, we realize we could never keep them perfectly. Our sinful nature and sinful acts put us out of our relationship with God like the ball in the game gets players out. We can't score a single run by ourselves. We call this part the Law.

Offensively, the Bible shows us our Savior. The words record how Jesus won salvation for us: "[All] are justified freely by His grace through the redemption that came by Christ Jesus."

Jesus, our designated hitter, stepped up to the plate for us. He hit a home run when He died on the cross and rose again. He won forgiveness for all sins and eternal life for all believers.

For children of God, the game is won! Let the crowd rejoice.

_____Let's do: How does it feel to make an out? What sin is "putting you out" today? Confess that sin to God or someone else you trust. How does it feel to score a run? How has Jesus helped you today? Have you told Him thanks?

_____Let's pray: Dear God, thanks for the Bible. Parts of it make me feel bad, and other parts make me glad. I know I need to hear both parts because I know I need You. Thanks for being my helper and Savior. Amen.

M. R. R.

Fix It or Forget It

When something breaks, we can choose to fix it or throw it away and forget about it.

Jesus tells a parable in Luke 13 about a man with a "broken" fig tree in his vineyard. The tree is not bearing figs. At first the owner chooses to forget the tree. He tells the gardener to chop it down. But the gardener wants to save the tree. He tells the owner to give him one more year to fertilize the tree. If the tree doesn't bear fruit next year, then he will chop it down.

The parable is about God. He expects us to bear the fruit of right living. But the bad things we say, think, and do break our relationship with God. The good things we don't say, think, or do also break us apart from God. Our Father in heaven can forget about us or He can fix us.

The good news is that God in His mercy chose to fix us by sending Jesus to earth. Jesus took all our brokenness, all our sin, to the cross. By dying on the cross Jesus paid the price for our repair. He gives us faith to believe in Him so we have a new, right relationship with Him. With God's help we are ready to bear fruit.

Read from God's Word

Then He told this parable: "A man had a fig tree, planted in his vineyard, and he went to look for fruit on it, but did not find any. So he said to the man who took care of the vineyard, 'For three years now I've been coming to look for fruit on this fig tree and haven't found any. Cut it down! Why should it use up the soil?' 'Sir,' the man replied, 'leave it alone for one more year, and I'll dig around it and fertilize it. If it bears fruit next year, fine! If not, then cut it down.'" Luke 13:6–9

_____Let's talk: What is "broken" in your life right now?
How can God fix it?

_____Let's pray: Heavenly Father, thank You for choosing to fix my life through Jesus. In His name I pray. Amen.

M. R. R.

Read from God's Word

To the Jews who had believed Him, Jesus said, "If you hold to My teaching, you are really My disciples. Then you will know the truth, and the truth will set you free." They answered Him, "We are Abraham's descendants and have never been slaves of anyone. How can You say that we shall be set free?" Jesus replied, "I tell you the truth, everyone who sins is a slave to sin. Now a slave has no permanent place in the family, but a son belongs to it forever. So if the Son sets you free, you will be free indeed." John 8:31–36 ᴄᴏ

Liberty for All

The Liberty Memorial is a tall, round tower in Kansas City. It was built to remind people of the struggles of World War I, "the war to end all wars." The people of Kansas City wanted to honor the men and women who fought and to believe that there wouldn't be any more global wars. Sadly, things turned out differently.

According to the dictionary, liberty is "the ability to act, speak, or think the way one pleases." We can do as we please as long as we don't step on someone else's rights. These rights are written down in the laws of each country.

As Christians we have another kind of liberty. Christ has freed us from sin through His suffering and death. Now we are free to be slaves to God. Freedom and slavery seem to be opposite ideas. But they aren't because God's love frees us to love Him and other people.

Christians have their own "liberty memorial." It's the empty tomb of Easter. Jesus has fought the most important war—and won! Now we know that our greatest enemy, Satan, can no longer threaten us with destruction. Jesus will lead us safely through our earthly battles. One day we'll return home to heaven in triumph, full of praise for our Commander.

_____Let's talk: What earthly freedom do you appreciate the most? Why? What spiritual freedom means the most to you? Why?

_____Let's pray: Crowns and thrones may perish, Kingdoms rise and wane, But the Church of Jesus Constant will remain. Gates of hell can never 'Gainst that Church prevail; We have Christ's own promise, And that cannot fail. Onward, Christian soldiers, Marching as to war, With the cross of Jesus Going on before. (*LW* 518:3)

J. L. L.

june

Contributors for this month:

Dorothy J. Haggstrom

Donna L. Koren

Ethel P. Lesh

Diane Maurer

Eileen Ritter

Read from God's Word

The fear of the LORD is the beginning of knowledge, but fools despise wisdom and discipline. Proverbs 1:7

God's Good Advice

Benjamin Franklin was a respected businessman, writer, printer, and publisher who helped form our nation. We can read some of his good advice in *Poor Richard's Almanac*: "A penny saved is a penny earned" and "Early to bed and early to rise, makes a man healthy, wealthy, and wise."

Many years before Benjamin Franklin, God used King Solomon and others to write good advice. This advice is found in the Book of Proverbs. One piece of good advice God gives us is in Proverbs 1:7: "The fear of the LORD is the beginning of knowledge, but fools despise wisdom and discipline." This verse says that if we fear (love and respect) God, it is the start of a wise and godly life for us. The Holy Spirit will work through God's Word to guide and help us in the decisions we make.

There are many times when we won't make wise decisions because we are sinners. Temptations can be great, and we may choose to follow the ways of the world. That is why God made His wise plan to send Jesus to be our Savior. For Jesus' sake, God forgives us when we fail to live as His children, and He enables us to share His love and forgiveness with others.

_____Let's talk: What kind of advice did Benjamin Franklin give to others in *Poor Richard's Almanac*? How does God give us good advice? What has God done for us in Jesus?

_____Let's pray: Dear God, thank You for the words of wisdom You have given us in the Bible. Help us to study Your Word and live a life pleasing to You. In Jesus' name we pray. Amen.

D. M.

A Wonderful Plan

A ndy walked sadly into his Sunday school classroom, dragging his feet.

"What's wrong?" asked Jared.

"My dad just got a new job, and we're moving to Chicago. All my friends are here. My baseball team is here. I'm happy where I am. My life is ruined!"

Miss Walker asked Andy to come up to her desk. "Andy, this Bible story might help you." She continued, "God spoke these words to His people, the Israelites, but He also wants to reassure you with them: 'For I know the plans I have for you, [Andy,] plans to prosper you and not to harm you, plans to give you hope and a future.'"

"God knew the Israelites would be held captive in a strange land. He knew the people would think it was awful, but God had a better plan for them. He promised to return them to their homeland. He wanted them to put their trust in Him. God must have work for you and your family to do in Chicago. Let this verse be of comfort to you. We will certainly miss you. We pray that the Holy Spirit will reassure your heart and help you and your family see how 'in all things God works for the good of those who love Him'" (Romans 8:28).

Read from God's Word

"For I know the plans I have for you," declares the LORD, "plans to prosper you and not to harm you, plans to give you hope and a future." Jeremiah 29:11

_____Let's talk: What happened to the Israelites that made them unhappy? What comfort can we get from Jeremiah 29:11?

_____Let's pray: Dear God, when things happen that disappoint us, help us to remember that You have a plan for our lives. In Jesus' name we pray. Amen.

D. M.

Power and Majesty

Read from God's Word

Your ways, O God, are holy. What god is so great as our God? You are the God who performs miracles; You display your power among the peoples. With Your mighty arm You redeemed Your people, the descendants of Jacob and Joseph. The waters saw You, O God, the waters saw You and writhed; the very depths were convulsed. The clouds poured down water, the skies resounded with thunder; Your arrows flashed back and forth. Your thunder was heard in the whirlwind, Your lightning lit up the world; the earth trembled and quaked. Your path led through the sea, Your way through the mighty waters, though Your footprints were not seen. You led Your people like a flock by the hand of Moses and Aaron. Psalm 77:13–20

Lightning is powerful and awesome. It is important to be careful, even if you like thunderstorms. One day a teacher in Memphis, Tennessee, came home and went out on the porch to watch a storm coming. She was leaning against a steel door when a bolt of lightning struck the door and traveled through her body. As a result, her hair turned from brown to white and she lost part of her sight, hearing, and memory.

Lightning shows the majesty of God. The Bible talks about God's majesty and shows us how He used His power to help His people. For example, He led His people out of Egypt by parting the Red Sea. God shows the same power in His love for us when He sent His Son, Jesus, to die for us. Because of God's powerful love in Jesus, our sins are forgiven, and we will live forever with Him in heaven.

Sometimes we feel that God is not present in our lives, that He is not answering our prayers. God's Word reminds us how awesome God is. Because of His powerful love in Jesus, we can rely on all the promises He gives us in His Word. We can be sure that He will always be there for us too.

_____Let's talk: What are some other ways that God has shown
His power in the past? What is the best way
He has done this for us?

_____Let's pray: Dear God, You are a powerful and majestic God.
Strengthen us with the knowledge that You are there
for Your people. Thank You for the awesome and
powerful gift of forgiveness given to us through the
death of Your Son. In Jesus' name we pray. Amen.

D. M.

Shining like Stars

Find the stars in this story. Steve, Marty, and Chris were in the convenience store one afternoon. Steve said, "Let's get a candy bar."

"I don't have enough money," Marty replied.

"Neither do I!" echoed Chris.

"So?" Steve asked. "This place makes plenty of money—they won't miss three little candy bars!"

Marty said, "No, it's stealing," and quickly left by himself.

Later that day Chris phoned Marty and said, "I've felt awful ever since I took the candy bar. I wish I had been brave like you and stood up to Steve. I just told my mom about it. She was pretty upset, but she forgave me and loaned me the money to pay for the candy bar."

How does God make sinners stars? He gives us Himself, His light. He gives us His Son, Jesus, who died and rose again so our sins could be forgiven. He gives us His Spirit, who creates and strengthens faith in us through Baptism and the Word. The Spirit was "shining" through Marty as he did what was right when he was tempted to steal. The Spirit was "shining" through Chris as he confessed his sin and received forgiveness. We, too, have God's Spirit to empower us to "shine like stars" in a sin-darkened world.

Read from God's Word

So that you may become blameless and pure, children of God without fault in a crooked and depraved generation, in which you shine like stars in the universe. Philippians 2:15

_____Let's talk: How did Marty shine like one of God's stars?
How was he able to do that? How did Chris shine
like one of God's stars? Compare the two starlights.

_____Let's pray: Dear Jesus, in our world there are many temptations. Give us Your Spirit to help us resist.
Forgive us when we fail. In Your name we pray.
Amen.

D. M.

The Winner

Jared stood at home plate. The score was tied; the bases were loaded. If he made an out, the other team would have a chance to win. Jared already had two strikes and three balls. Here comes the next pitch. It's too high—it'll be a walk, he thinks.

"Strike three! You're out!" cried the umpire.

Jared was so angry he yelled at the umpire, "Do you need glasses? You're blind! That was a ball!" Jared took the bat and threw it toward third base. The ump threw him out of the game.

After he had calmed down Jared was ashamed of the way he had acted. "Why did I do that, Dad? I was so angry then, but now I feel sorry for the way I acted. I just wanted my team to win!"

"Jared, your feelings were in control of you," said his dad. "You were caught up in winning the game for the team. Letting our feelings take control of us leaves us wide open for sin."

"God's Spirit led you to be sorry for your sin and to want forgiveness. And God promises to forgive our sins for Jesus' sake because Jesus went to the plate for us and won the game against sin and the devil. Because of Jesus, we're all winners."

_____Let's do: Look up Galatians 5:22–23. What fruit does God's Spirit give us?

_____Let's pray: Dear God, many times my anger gets the best of me and I act foolishly. Please forgive me and help me through Your Spirit. In Jesus' name. Amen.

D. M.

Over and Over

Read from God's Word

There is a time for everything, and a season for every activity under heaven: a time to be born and a time to die, a time to plant and a time to uproot, a time to kill and a time to heal, a time to tear down and a time to build, a time to weep and a time to laugh, a time to mourn and a time to dance, a time to scatter stones and a time to gather them, a time to embrace and a time to refrain, a time to search and a time to give up, a time to keep and a time to throw away, a time to tear and a time to mend, a time to be silent and a time to speak, a time to love and a time to hate, a time for war and a time for peace. Ecclesiastes 3:1–8

The *Ox-Cart Man* by Donald Hall tells how people in eighteenth-century New Hampshire lived. In winter the family made brooms, shingles, and other necessary items. In spring they tapped maple trees and boiled the syrup. They sheared the sheep, spinning the wool into yarn and weaving the yarn into cloth. Summertime found them tending their apple trees and potato plants. Finally in October the farmer loaded his cart and walked to the market. There he sold his produce and bought things his family needed and wanted. Then the next year they would do it all over.

Although we don't live like the ox-cart man, we also have a list of jobs to do almost every day. Each new day means we start over. Each new year means we begin again.

To those who know Christ, every task is an opportunity to give glory to God. Christ gives our work meaning because Christ gives us meaning. He calls us His children in Baptism, showing and telling us that He loves us. He forgives our sins and grants us eternal life. We can mourn and laugh, do social studies and play the flute, pray and tell others about Jesus, live and die. Cleaning our room, doing fractions, and sharing His love over and over have meaning and value.

_____Let's talk: How does God give your everyday tasks meaning?

_____Let's pray: Dear God, thank You for dying on the cross
for me and calling me to be Your child.
Thank You for giving meaning to my jobs
and homework. In Jesus' name. Amen.

D. M.

Surprise

Read from God's Word

When He had finished washing their feet, He put on His clothes and returned to His place. "Do you understand what I have done for you?" He asked them. "You call Me 'Teacher' and 'Lord,' and rightly so, for that is what I am. Now that I, your Lord and Teacher, have washed your feet, you also should wash one another's feet. I have set you an example that you should do as I have done for you. I tell you the truth, no servant is greater than his master, nor is a messenger greater than the one who sent him. Now that you know these things, you will be blessed if you do them." John 13:12–17

"Wow, did you see Victor hit that ball? Maybe he can join our team!" Alejandro exclaimed.

Miguel replied, "Oh, I know Victor. Mrs. Jones wants me to help him with his math. He doesn't even know the facts. And forget fractions. He has no clue."

We all put someone down to lift ourselves up. We try to figure out where we fit in with our friends. Like Miguel, we want others to think we are smart or athletic or musical or popular.

As we just read, Jesus washed the feet of His disciples. Wasn't that a servant's job? His surprising actions showed His disciples that they should serve others instead of worrying about who was the greatest.

Who would think God would become one of us? When we realize how low God went because of the depth of our sin and need, then we realize how deep the love of God is. The great love for sinners that carried Jesus from the cross to the grave is beyond our understanding.

We could be foot-washers. As we are led to follow Jesus' example, we might find endless ways to surprise others with loving service.

_____Let's talk: Read John 13:1–17. What are some surprising ways that God comes to us? What did Jesus promise His disciples if they showed love and concern for other people?

_____Let's pray: Make me a servant, Lord. Amen.

D. M.

Dressed for the Game

Andrew loves to play soccer. He runs quickly and wears shoes with cleats to give him extra traction on the grass. He wears shin guards to protect his legs from other players' kicks.

One day Andrew was in a hurry and left his shin guards in his locker. Since he knew he was a good player, he didn't worry. During practice another player was trying to get the ball away from him, missed the ball, and kicked Andrew right on the shin!

The skin split open and Andrew began to bleed. After one look, his mom knew it was bad. One shot and 11 stitches later, the wound was repaired. A painful experience taught Andrew to protect himself.

Holy Baptism acts as a guard for our souls. In today's Scripture verse God reminds us that we are clothed with Christ in our Baptism. Playing soccer without shin guards is dangerous for our legs; living this life without the blessings of Baptism is dangerous for our souls. Baptism gives forgiveness of sins and rescues us from death and the devil. In Baptism we became God's own—forever.

When the devil tempts you to feel worthless because of your sins, God will give you protection better than shin guards. You can say, "I'm a forgiven child of God."

Read from God's Word

You are all sons of God through faith in Christ Jesus, for all of you who were baptized into Christ have clothed yourselves with Christ. Galatians 3:26–27

———Let's talk: What can you do to protect your body from injury?
What does God do to protect your soul?

———Let's pray: Heavenly Father, thank You for the gift of Baptism, which makes me Your child. In Jesus' name. Amen.

D. L. K.

Read from God's Word

As Jesus and His disciples were on their way, He came to a village where a woman named Martha opened her home to Him. She had a sister called Mary, who sat at the Lord's feet listening to what He said. But Martha was distracted by all the preparations that had to be made. She came to Him and asked, "Lord, don't You care that my sister has left me to do the work by myself? Tell her to help me!" "Martha, Martha," the Lord answered, "you are worried and upset about many things, but only one thing is needed. Mary has chosen what is better, and it will not be taken away from her." Luke 10:38–42

First Things First

Jonathan asked a new friend at pre-school if she wanted to be a farmer. When she said yes, Jonathan said, "I will teach you. First, you have to get up very early in the morning."

Jonathan didn't talk about caring for livestock, planting crops, or driving a tractor. He thought of first things first—getting up early!

What did Mary and Martha think of when entertaining Jesus? Mary was listening to Jesus' words. Martha was frustrated with all the preparations and asked Jesus to send Mary to help her. Jesus told Martha that Mary had chosen what was needed—hearing His Word.

Like Martha, you might get so busy with your daily tasks that you decide you have no time to listen to God's Word. But Jesus is waiting to spend time with you, just like He did with Mary.

God knew you would give in to sinful thoughts and actions. He knew you would be born with a sinful nature. He put you first, planning for your salvation back in the Garden of Eden. He invites people to come and sit at His feet and listen to His wonderful words. In a church service, in class or family devotions, and in personal Bible reading you have the same invitation as Mary—to sit at the feet of Jesus.

_____Let's talk: How did God put you first? When you have an important decision to make, how will God help you?

_____Let's pray: O Lord, I have so many things to think about. Help me put You before all other things. Guide me and bless me. Amen.

D. L. K.

Rabbits and Rescue

I n *The Tale of Peter Rabbit* Peter disobeyed his mother's instructions— "Don't go into Mr. McGregor's garden." He also ignored her warning— "Your father was put in a pie by Mrs. McGregor." Peter went there anyway. In the garden he lost his clothing in a narrow escape!

In *The Tale of Benjamin Bunny*, Peter's cousin Benjamin convinces him to go back to the garden to retrieve his lost clothes. At one point Benjamin and Peter scoot under a basket to hide from a cat. Unfortunately the cat climbs atop the basket and falls asleep, trapping them inside for five hours! Only after Benjamin's father fights the cat are they set free.

Benjamin and Peter's experiences are like ours. We are caught in sin by disobedience of God's instructions. Like the cat atop the basket, the devil wants us to think we will never get free—that no one can forgive what we have done.

Read from God's Word

If we claim to be without sin, we deceive ourselves and the truth is not in us. If we confess our sins, He is faithful and just and will forgive us our sins and purify us from all unrighteousness. 1 John 1:8–9

Someone stronger and braver fought the old cat. For us, someone stronger, braver, and perfect came to defeat Satan. Jesus Christ has rescued us from sin and forgives us. As our Bible reading says (and we often say in Sunday worship), "If we confess our sins, He is faithful and just and will forgive us our sins and purify us from all unrighteousness."

———Let's talk: How does God provide for and help you remember the way out of sin?

———Let's pray: Dear Jesus, thank You for rescuing us from our sins. Help us to see that there is nothing too great to forgive. Amen.

D. L. K.

Read from God's Word

Naaman's servants went to him and said, "My father, if the prophet had told you to do some great thing, would you not have done it? How much more, then, when he tells you, 'Wash and be cleansed'!" So he went down and dipped himself in the Jordan seven times, as the man of God had told him, and his flesh was restored and became clean like that of a young boy. Then Naaman and all his attendants went back to the man of God. He stood before him and said, "Now I know that there is no God in all the world except in Israel. Please accept now a gift from your servant." 2 Kings 5:13–15 ✍

Earthquake!

One summer morning Donna's bedroom started shaking. It was an earthquake! By the time she got to the doorway to brace herself the shaking stopped. The earthquake lasted less than 30 seconds.

Sometimes we have spiritual earthquakes—experiences that shake our faith. A girl from Israel had a big spiritual earthquake. After an army invaded her land she was taken as a slave to the home of Naaman, the commander of the army. Through this "earthquake" the girl remembered God's power. God gave her the courage to tell how Naaman could get help for the terrible disease that afflicted him. The girl sent him to see Elisha, the prophet of the true God. Naaman eagerly went to Elisha, but reluctantly followed God's instructions to dip himself seven times in the Jordan River. After he did, his body healed, and he came to know the true God!

Our greatest spiritual earthquake is sin's grip on us. The ground shaking of Good Friday signaled the completion of our rescue when Jesus died on the cross. The earthquake as the angel rolled the stone away on Easter morning announced our Lord's victorious resurrection.

We are led by God's Spirit to His Word and Sacraments, where we receive complete healing—forgiveness for sin and strength to live through the earthquakes of life.

_____Let's do: Read the complete story of Naaman in 2 Kings 5. Explain how God used the faithful and unfaithful servants.

_____Let's pray: God, You have all power and all knowledge. Help me tell others about You. Amen.

D. L. K.

I Love to Tell the Story

Read from God's Word

The man who saw it has given testimony, and his testimony is true. He knows that he tells the truth, and he testifies so that you also may believe. These things happened so that the scripture would be fulfilled: "Not one of his bones will be broken." John 19:35–36

More than 100 years ago a teenage girl attended a special school for people with blindness. Her name was Mary Ingalls.

Years later, her sister Laura Ingalls Wilder would tell her family's stories—including the one about Mary's travel to the School for the Blind.

Mary was not a ruler, inventor, or author. She lived quietly with her family for most of her life. She was not famous for any reason. But we can know her story because her sister told it.

In the Book of John, the apostle said, "He tells the truth, and he testifies so that you also may believe." John walked, talked, and ate with Jesus. He saw Jesus die at Golgotha. He saw the empty tomb. He saw Jesus alive on Easter. God inspired this man with His Holy Spirit so he could write the words that we might believe in Jesus.

We know Jesus through the Bible. We have not seen Him as John did, but we can tell the story of Jesus to everyone we know. We can tell others how He was born, lived, died, rose, and redeemed us. He has promised that His Word will not return empty when it is shared. Go—tell the news to someone you know.

_____Let's do: Find out more about ministry with people who are blind. Search on the Internet or at the library. What did you learn?

_____Let's pray: Lord, thank You for people like John, who saw the great things You did, and for guiding them to write them down. Amen.

D. L. K.

Homesick

Read from God's Word

Therefore we are always confident and know that as long as we are at home in the body we are away from the Lord. We live by faith, not by sight. We are confident, I say, and would prefer to be away from the body and at home with the Lord.
2 Corinthians 5:6–8

E mily was excited to go to camp for the first time. She made a list of things she needed to bring. As she packed, she also made the following list of the things she was looking forward to:

Her little brother, Nathan, would not be there.

She would learn to ride a horse.

She would swim every day.

She would make new friends.

What she expected to happen at camp didn't happen quite the way she had planned. She missed her brother; the horses were bigger than she imagined; the bottom of the lake was squishy; and although she made new friends, she still missed the ones at home.

She was not in a bad place, but she really wanted to be home. God's Word tells us that our life on earth as Christians is like Emily's time at camp. We and our world are sinful; things don't always work the way we plan. We long for a better, safer place. We want happiness, peace, and love. God reminds us in Philippians 3:20 that "our citizenship is in heaven."

Thanks to Jesus, we will spend eternity there. He suffered, died, and rose to make heaven open to us. One day, our time in this camp will be over. Jesus will welcome us home, where our joy will last forever.

_____Let's do: Write about your heavenly home and the Savior who won that place for you.

_____Let's pray: Dear Jesus, thank You for making a perfect home for me in heaven. Be with me as I tell my friends about Your wonderful plans for them. Amen.

D. L. K.

Whose Fault Is It?

As He went along, He saw a man blind from birth. His disciples asked Him, "Rabbi, who sinned, this man or his parents, that he was born blind?" "Neither this man nor his parents sinned," said Jesus, "but this happened so that the work of God might be displayed in his life. As long as it is day, we must do the work of Him who sent Me. Night is coming, when no one can work. While I am in the world, I am the light of the world." Having said this, He spit on the ground, made some mud with the saliva, and put it on the man's eyes. "Go," He told him, "wash in the Pool of Siloam" (this word means Sent). So the man went and washed, and came home seeing. John 9:1–7 ✎

Charmaine has diabetes and has to check her blood several times a day. Her sister doesn't have diabetes, and neither do her parents. Some people might wonder if God is punishing her.

But God *isn't* punishing her. Her condition is just one of the results of living in a sinful world. Some people need wheelchairs or walkers; some wear glasses or braces. Some have parents who are divorced or abuse alcohol.

Jesus understands the hurts in our lives. When He saw the man born blind, His disciples asked whose fault it was. They did not understand that blindness, sickness, and tragedy were part of being in a sinful world. Jesus replied that God allowed this man to be born blind so when Jesus brought him to faith and healed him, he could tell others about Jesus.

In the Garden of Eden, Adam and Eve's sin wrecked God's perfect world. Out of love for all people our God came up with a plan for our rescue. He decided to sacrifice His one and only Son to pay for our sins.

God uses things that go wrong to show His power and to bring people to faith. Pray that He uses the events of your life to display His glory.

———Let's do: Write about someone you know with a health condition or disability, then pray for this person.

———Let's pray: Dear Lord Jesus, You healed bodies from sickness and souls from sin. Help me to share Your love. Amen.

D. L. K.

Does God Take a Vacation?

When does your school year end and summer vacation begin? Maybe your vacation has already started. Have you made any special plans? Put a check mark by the things you might do:

Play outdoors

Read books

Go to vacation Bible school

Visit grandparents
or other relatives

Help with work at home

Travel by car, bus, train,
or airplane

Go to summer camp

Make a list of your own.

Vacations are fun. We have time to do things we like to do. Do you think Jesus ever took a vacation? The Bible tells us that sometimes Jesus went away by Himself. He spent a lot of time praying to His heavenly Father.

Does Jesus still take vacations? We know that Jesus is with the Father now. The Bible tells us that God is always with us. He doesn't ever go to sleep. He surely never takes a vacation.

God is with us to keep us safe. He's with us to hear us when we pray. He's with us when we're with other people and when we're alone. He's with us to help us grow and learn. He's with us when we work and when we play. He's with us at home or far away. He's with us when we're awake or asleep. God is always with us.

_____Let's talk: What does the name "Immanuel" mean? (See Matthew 1:23.) What does the name "Jesus" mean? (See Matthew 1:21.) Why are both of these names of our Savior important to you?

_____Let's pray: Thank You, Jesus, for offering Your own life to save me from all my sins. Amen.

E. P. L.

God's Wonderful World

Enrique likes to make things with words. He knows how to make a *leaf* from *sand*—change only one letter at a time. Each change must make a real word. Here's how Enrique does it— sand, land, lend, lead, leaf. Now try to change *rock* to *pear*.

What can you make out of nothing? There isn't anyone in the world who can do this. Where did everything in the world come from? God tells us in the Bible that He made the whole universe (our world and all the stars in the sky). He just said the words and whatever He said became real.

God made everything so people can enjoy His gifts. He made food plants so we can eat. He made other plants we can use to make into clothing. He made animals to help us work. He put iron and other minerals in the ground for us to use as raw materials. What did God make so you can have the chair you're sitting on? (Don't forget the people who made the chair!)

How wonderful it is to enjoy and use God's world! We enjoy it even more because we know that the God who loves us gave it to us. He loves us so much that He even gave His Son to pay for our sins.

O LORD, our Lord, how majestic is Your name in all the earth! You have set Your glory above the heavens. From the lips of children and infants You have ordained praise because of Your enemies, to silence the foe and the avenger. When I consider Your heavens, the work of Your fingers, the moon and the stars, which You have set in place, what is man that You are mindful of him, the son of man that You care for him? You made him a little lower than the heavenly beings and crowned him with glory and honor. You made him ruler over the works of Your hands; You put everything under his feet: all flocks and herds, and the beasts of the field, the birds of the air, and the fish of the sea, all that swim the paths of the seas. O LORD, our Lord, how majestic is Your name in all the earth! Psalm 8 ✍

_____Let's talk: What is the most amazing thing in God's creation? How does it cause you to give honor and praise to your Maker?

_____Let's pray: Dear God, thank You for giving us this wonderful world. Help us use it the way You planned. Forgive us when we damage or waste Your gifts. Amen.

E. P. L.

Praise the Lord!

Praise the LORD. Praise God in His sanctuary; praise Him in His mighty heavens. Praise Him for His acts of power; praise Him for His surpassing greatness. Praise Him with the sounding of the trumpet, praise Him with the harp and lyre, praise Him with tambourine and dancing, praise Him with the strings and flute, praise Him with the clash of cymbals, praise Him with resounding cymbals. Let everything that has breath praise the LORD. Praise the LORD. Psalm 150

Mother went grocery shopping. She put the bags of food in the car, but forgot her purse in the shopping cart. Later the store manager called, "Someone has returned your purse to my office." Mother said, "Praise the Lord!"

Thursday night Josie studied extra hard for her test on Friday. When she got her paper back with a big A on it, Josie said, "Praise the Lord!"

Hector's little brother fell off the swing. Hector picked him up and brushed the dirt from his arms and legs. When he saw that his brother wasn't hurt, Hector said, "Praise the Lord!"

God sends so many blessings. He sends sunshine and rain. Praise the Lord! He gives us people who love us and teach us. Praise the Lord! He has given us bodies that can move, sing, laugh, and shout. Praise the Lord! God has given us minds to know what we see, feel, hear, smell, and taste. Praise the Lord! God has given us minds to learn more about Him and His world. Praise the Lord!

Most of all we praise God for giving us His Son, who came to save us. When we do wrong things, we feel bad. But for Jesus' sake God forgives and gives us His joy again. Praise the Lord!

———Let's do: Think about times in your life when things
                could have turned out badly but didn't.
                Make a sign to hang in your room that says,
                "Praise the Lord!"

———Let's pray: Praise God, from whom all blessings flow;
                Praise Him, all creatures here below;
                Praise Him above, O heav'nly host;
                Praise Father, Son, and Holy Ghost. (*LW* 461)

E. P. L.

Of Course Not

Carlos hit the ball over Nancy's head. If she had caught the ball, it would be her turn.

Nancy chased the ball, picked it up, and rolled it toward the bat. Before the ball got to the bat, Carlos put out his foot, stopping the ball.

Nancy shouted, "That's not fair. It would have hit the bat!"

Nancy was upset because Carlos broke the rules. Do you like to play with someone who doesn't play by the rules of the game? Of course not.

Match these games with the penalty for breaking the rules:

1. Football   a. Free throw

2. Basketball   b. Free kick

3. Hockey   c. Ball is moved away from goal

4. Soccer   d. Time in penalty box

Read from God's Word

"O Jerusalem, Jerusalem, you who kill the prophets and stone those sent to you, how often I have longed to gather your children together, as a hen gathers her chicks under her wings, but you were not willing. Look, your house is left to you desolate. For I tell you, you will not see Me again until you say, 'Blessed is He who comes in the name of the Lord.'" Matthew 22:37–39

Are rules made just so penalties can be given? No. They're made so everyone can know how to play the game.

The Bible gives us God's rules for living. What a wonderful world it would be if everyone kept His rules!

Since Adam and Eve broke God's rules, there is only one person who has kept them all. Jesus came to keep the rules, God's Law, for everyone. Did He keep the victory all to Himself? Of course not! He died for us so our rule-breaking would be forgiven and we could always be with Him.

_____Let's talk: What commandment did Jesus give in Matthew 22:37?

_____Let's pray: Thank You, Jesus, for keeping God's Law and paying for my sins. Help me show that I love You. Amen.

E. P. L.

Just Perfect

Read from God's Word

Don't be deceived, my dear brothers. Every good and perfect gift is from above, coming down from the Father of the heavenly lights, who does not change like shifting shadows. He chose to give us birth through the word of truth, that we might be a kind of firstfruits of all He created. James 1:16–18

What if a four-year-old prince wanted to go into the lions' cage at the zoo? Would you let him go in?

What if a three-year-old princess wanted to pick up the pieces of a glass she had dropped? Would you let her?

Would you want that prince or princess to blame you if they got hurt? Probably not, because you were lovingly watching out for each child's safety, not leading him or her into temptation.

Temptations and everything evil in life come from the devil and our sinful nature. James tells us that we should not be deceived into thinking that temptation comes from God. He will not tempt you to cheat or lie.

God gives only good gifts. God loves you, His sons and daughters, so much that He wants you to have perfect gifts. He's the only one who knows what tomorrow will bring. Maybe the gift we want would cause us trouble tomorrow or separate us from Him.

If it seems like God takes care of everything for His children, He does. Besides our everyday needs, He took care of our greatest need—the need for a Savior. He sent Jesus to be the perfect sacrifice for our sins. By grace He also gives us the gift of salvation, making us His prince or princess.

_____Let's do: Compare Acts 10:38 with James 1:16–18.

_____Let's pray: Dear Lord, we thank and praise You for the loving gifts that You provide for us. Thank You especially for Jesus, our Savior. Amen.

E. P. L.

Getting Dressed

H ave you ever been to a wedding? Did you wear your most comfortable clothes or your best clothes?

Often we try to dress like our friends. There are other times we wear special clothes that set us apart from the crowd. Maybe it is when we sing in a choir or go to a Scout meeting or play on a sports team. Sometimes it's important to be wearing the right thing to tell others who we are or what we are doing.

The Bible tells us of some really important clothes that God wants to give us. Isaiah 61:10 says, "He has clothed me with the garments of salvation and arrayed [dressed] me in a robe of righteousness." We wear these clothes with great excitement and joy, like a bride and groom getting dressed for their wedding.

You probably have a robe of righteousness on right now. Jesus is the only one who can give us this robe because He paid for all our sins by dying on the cross and earning salvation for us. Then He gives us the gift of faith. With the gift of faith we are perfectly dressed before God. We can come to our heavenly Father because we are wrapped in the garment of the holiness that Jesus won for us.

Read from God's Word

I delight greatly in the LORD; my soul rejoices in my God. For He has clothed me with garments of salvation and arrayed me in a robe of righteousness, as a bridegroom adorns his head like a priest, and as a bride adorns herself with her jewels. For as the soil makes the sprout come up and a garden causes seeds to grow, so the Sovereign LORD will make righteousness and praise spring up before all nations. Isaiah 61:10–11

——Let's do: Design a robe of righteousness. What makes Christians so joyful to have on the clothing that God provides for us?

——Let's pray: Heavenly Father, thank You for the clothes You give us that claim us as Yours, wrapping us in the holiness of Jesus. Amen.

E. P. L.

The Cover-Up

Read from God's Word

Blessed is he whose transgressions are forgiven, whose sins are covered. Blessed is the man whose sin the LORD does not count against him and in whose spirit is no deceit. When I kept silent, my bones wasted away through my groaning all day long. For day and night Your hand was heavy upon me; my strength was sapped as in the heat of summer. Then I acknowledged my sin to You and did not cover up my iniquity. I said, "I will confess my transgressions to the LORD"— and You forgave the guilt of my sin. Psalm 32:1–5 ᔕ

"What happened at school today Bryan?" asked his mother.

"Well, Josh and this other kid kept whispering all through reading class. They even laughed when Maureen made mistakes reading out loud."

"That was mean," Mom commented. "What happened?"

"Both boys lost their computer time and didn't get to go outside on break."

"I'll bet the boys didn't like that," said Mom.

"They sure didn't. The whole thing was funny at first, but not when Maureen cried."

"Bryan," Mom asked quietly, "who was the other boy?"

Who do you think the other boy was? Right; it was Bryan. What should he do now? How about a cover-up? Psalm 32:1 reads, "Blessed is he ... whose sins are covered." This is a different covering than hiding something or someone else. The covering Bryan needs is God's mercy, which forgives our sins. When we try to cover up our own wrongdoing, we fool no one but ourselves. But when our sins are covered by the blood of Jesus, we walk away clean—a clean conscience and a clean record.

_____Let's talk: What is it about Jesus that leads us to tell Him we're sorry for our sins?

_____Let's pray: Bless me, Lord, with Your forgiveness. Amen.

E. R.

Rejoicing in Suffering

Read from God's Word

Therefore, since we have been justified through faith, we have peace with God through our Lord Jesus Christ, through whom we have gained access by faith into this grace in which we now stand. And we rejoice in the hope of the glory of God. Not only so, but we also rejoice in our sufferings, because we know that suffering produces perseverance; perseverance, character; and character, hope. And hope does not disappoint us, because God has poured out His love into our hearts by the Holy Spirit, whom He has given us. Romans 5:1–5

"We didn't know if Mom would recover from cancer. And if she did, would she be able to take care of us?" Dana told Jill.

Jill couldn't imagine coming home from school and not finding her mother there.

Dana continued, "What if I had to face junior high alone? Who would make sure Lizzie and Pete went to bed on time? I didn't know how to run the washing machine. I told God He just *had* to make Mom well.

"Then Dad called all three of us to the table to give us an update and to pray. He asked God to heal my mother, but he also praised God. He actually thanked God for Mom and all she had done for us. Dad thanked God for making Mom a Christian. He even thanked God for the strength He was giving each of us while Mom was sick.

"I learned that even if life is hard, God is still good. If Dad could thank God now, while Mom was so sick, surely I could too."

Rejoicing when we are suffering is difficult to understand and hard to do, but God promises to help us do this difficult thing. Ask the Holy Spirit to help you more fully understand this truth.

Let's talk: Why do we have peace with God through our Lord Jesus? How does this peace help us rejoice in suffering?

Let's pray: Dear Lord, we praise and thank You for being our God in good times and in bad. Keep us always thankful, no matter what happens to us. In Jesus' name. Amen.

E. R.

Thank God

Read from God's Word

I will praise You, O LORD, with all my heart; I will tell of all Your wonders. I will be glad and rejoice in You; I will sing praise to Your name, O Most High.
Psalm 9:1–2

"Who would want to live in this desolate place?" That's what Star heard a visitor say about the Navajo reservation in the desert where she lived.

Star wondered what the person could have meant. There were so many reasons the reservation was special. She loved watching the sunrise. She loved the small cacti like sea urchin, catclaw, and beavertail. She loved the huge saguaro cactus, with its thick arms.

Star loved the stories of the desert. Her dad told about people who had been saved from dying by drinking the milk of a cactus plant.

Star loved the seasons, especially spring when the cactus flowers bloomed. She loved the clean, dry air and the flatland with tumbleweeds racing across the plain. Wherever she looked, she saw beauty in this spot where God had placed her. Star thought, *I like it here. Thank You, God, for this place.*

Are you happy in the place God has put you? Your home and your life in it are gifts of God's grace. Not only has God given you your beautiful spot, but He also sent Jesus to rescue you from sin and win a better home for you in heaven, a home even more beautiful than your earthly home. What great reasons to give thanks to God every day!

_____Let's talk: What do you like best about the place where you live? Why can you say with Star, "Thank You, God, for this place"?

_____Let's pray: I will praise You, Lord, with all my heart; I will tell of all the wonderful things You have done. Amen.

D. J. H.

Measuring God's Love

Match each of these to a way of measuring it:

1. Weight	a. Numbers
2. Distance	b. Degrees
3. Liquid	c. Ounces (or grams)
4. Game scores	d. Gallons (or liters)
5. Time	e. Minutes
6. Heat	f. Yards (or meters)

Read from God's Word

For this reason I kneel before the Father, from whom His whole family in heaven and on earth derives its name. I pray that out of His glorious riches He may strengthen you with power through His Spirit in your inner being, so that Christ may dwell in your hearts through faith. And I pray that you, being rooted and established in love, may have power, together with all the saints, to grasp how wide and long and high and deep is the love of Christ, and to know this love that surpasses knowledge— that you may be filled to the measure of all the fullness of God. Ephesians 3:14–19 ✍

Scientists can tell us the temperature of the air and the speed of the wind. They know how fast sound and light travel. They know the distance to the sun and moon.

How wide is God's love? It's so wide there isn't a place in the whole universe you can go and be outside of it.

How long is God's love? It is forever. God loved us before we were born. He loves us every day of our lives.

How high is God's love? You might be a king, a prime minister, a president, a TV or sports star, but you can't be higher than God's love.

How deep is God's love? You may be the poorest, weakest, most unknown person in the world. But you can't be farther down than God's love can reach.

How do we measure God's love? By looking at Jesus and remembering how far He went to rescue us. He became poor that we might be rich. He made Himself nothing that we might enjoy everything in God's home eternally.

_____Let's do: Check out 1 John 4:10. What does it tell us about God's love?

_____Let's pray: Heavenly Father, thank You for sending Jesus to show us how great Your love for us is. Please send me Your Holy Spirit so I may show that love to everyone I meet. Amen.

E. P. L.

Be Still and Know

K er-thunk, ker-thunk, ker-thunk ...
When we planned this backpacking trip, we talked about loud sounds—thunder, howling winds, rain. But in our pup tent on top of Mount Cammerer, the smallest sounds became the loudest of all. The great ker-thunking that kept me awake was just a tiny deer mouse.

As we hiked along the Great Smoky Mountain trails, we often sang or told stories. We never heard birds or animals while we were singing or talking. But when we were quiet, we were blessed with bird songs or the rustle of a doe near the trail.

Our walk with God is full of our own noises—noises like worrying, fighting, acting selfish, lazy, or mean. These noises are sin, and sin keeps us from hearing the voice of God.

That's why the psalmist writes, "Be still, and know that I am God." Jesus has taken away sin's racket, bringing peace to our hearts.

Then we can hear what He has to say to us: "Son [or daughter], your sins are forgiven" (Mark 2:5); "I am with you always, to the very end of the age" (Matthew 28:20); "I am going there to prepare a place for you ... that you also may be where I am" (John 14:2–3).

⎯⎯⎯Let's talk: Tell about a sound you can hear when it's very
quiet. What keeps us from hearing what God
has to say to us?

⎯⎯⎯Let's pray: Lord Jesus, take away the sins in my life that
keep me from hearing You. Amen.

E. R.

Friends Make the Difference

Read from God's Word

"My command is this: Love each other as I have loved you. Greater love has no one than this, that he lay down his life for his friends. You are My friends if you do what I command. I no longer call you servants, because a servant does not know his master's business. Instead, I have called you friends, for everything that I learned from My Father I have made known to you. You did not choose Me, but I chose you and appointed you to go and bear fruit—fruit that will last. Then the Father will give you whatever you ask in My name. This is My command: Love each other." John 15:12–17 ✍

Lonely summer days seem to drag on forever. But summer days with your friends overflow with things to do and places to go.

Jesus enjoyed His friends too. Peter, James, and John climbed a mountain with Jesus. They saw Him speak with Moses and Elijah. They heard God call Jesus His beloved Son. On the night before He died, Jesus ate a special Passover meal with His friends.

Sometimes friends hurt each other. We lie, fight, gossip, or tell secrets. We do this because we are sinners. No matter how hard we try, we can't be a perfect friend.

Sometimes Jesus' friends hurt Him too. They argued with each other about their place in His kingdom. One of Jesus' best friends told people he didn't even know Him. When Jesus died on the cross, most of His friends ran away and hid.

But Jesus remained their best friend. He loved them so much that He died and rose again to take away the ways they hurt Him. He showed them that they were still His friends by sending them to tell everyone about Him. He promised to take them to heaven.

Jesus is our best friend too. One day, by His grace, He will take us to be with Him in heaven.

———Let's talk: What's the difference between a good friend
and a bad friend? Why is Jesus our best friend?

———Let's pray: Dear Savior, You are the best friend of all.
Thank You for taking away all my sins. Amen.

E. R.

Because of Jesus

Read from God's Word

God saw all that He had made, and it was very good. And there was evening, and there was morning—the sixth day. Thus the heavens and the earth were completed in all their vast array. By the seventh day God had finished the work He had been doing; so on the seventh day He rested from all His work. And God blessed the seventh day and made it holy, because on it He rested from all the work of creating that He had done. Genesis 1:31–2:3 ✍

Long ago there were green fields with trees and flowers, blue skies, sparkling water, and animals living peacefully together. Adam and Eve lived in harmony with nature and with God. They cared for the garden God had given them.

Our world is more like this: yards filled with garbage, smoky air, dead fish in murky water, birds and animals dying from pesticides, and people hurting each other and God's world.

Sin spoiled the beautiful world God made and the happy relationship Adam and Eve had with God. Every human being born since Adam and Eve has been filled with sin. Day after day we do what we know is wrong.

Sometimes our sin results in carelessness, like leaving litter on the playground. Our greed makes us want more and cheaper possessions, encouraging factories to operate without concern for the environment. Selfishness leads to arguing and fighting with our family members and friends.

This isn't the way God intended the world to be. Sin caused this. But God had the perfect solution for sin. He sent His Son, Jesus, to sacrifice Himself in our place. Because of Jesus, God forgives all our sins. Because of Jesus, we are free to take care of the world God made. Because of Jesus, we look forward to God's perfect world in heaven.

_____Let's talk: How have you seen God's world spoiled? How is all this a result of sin? What is God's solution for sin?

_____Let's pray: Heavenly Father, forgive us for the way we have spoiled Your world. Help us take good care of all You have given us. We ask this for Jesus' sake. Amen.

E. R.

Never Separated

The sign read "Road under Construction." Since we were almost home, we kept driving. We turned onto our street and saw a big trench in front of our driveway.

Life is full of obstacles. Sickness causes us to miss school. Parents may fight or divorce. We may have to move to another town. Other children might make fun of us. Someone we love may die. These obstacles make us wonder if God still loves us.

The apostle Paul traveled 10,000 miles preaching about Jesus. He suffered shipwrecks, a stoning, beatings, and being put in jail. Paul must have known that he would eventually be killed for his faith. He had good reason to think that God didn't love him.

But Paul wrote, "I am convinced that neither death nor life, neither angels nor demons, neither the present nor the future, nor any powers, neither height nor depth, nor anything else in all creation, will be able to separate us from the love of God that is in Christ Jesus our Lord."

Read from God's Word

Who shall separate us from the love of Christ? Shall trouble or hardship or persecution or famine or nakedness or danger or sword? As it is written: "For your sake we face death all day long; we are considered as sheep to be slaughtered." No, in all these things we are more than conquerors through Him who loved us. For I am convinced that neither death nor life, neither angels nor demons, neither the present nor the future, nor any powers, neither height nor depth, nor anything else in all creation, will be able to separate us from the love of God that is in Christ Jesus our Lord. Romans 8:35–39 ✍

God's marvelous love caused Him to send His Son, Jesus, to die for our sins. That love of God gives us forgiveness for Jesus' sake. It keeps us His, even when everything around us seems wrong. For nothing can ever separate us from God's love.

———Let's do: Write about a time when you felt separated from God's love. How does Romans 8:38–39 help?

———Let's pray: Dear God, sometimes our world falls apart around us. It seems like You no longer care. But You showed us Your love by sending Jesus to give Himself for us. Forgive us and help us for His sake. Amen.

E. R.

Read from God's Word

"And if I go and prepare a place for you, I will come back and take you to be with Me that you also may be where I am. You know the way to the place where I am going." Thomas said to Him, "Lord, we don't know where You are going, so how can we know the way?" Jesus answered, "I am the way and the truth and the life. No one comes to the Father except through Me. If you really knew Me, you would know My Father as well. From now on, you do know Him and have seen Him." John 14:3–7 ✍

Many Ways or One Way?

"I'm studying about all the different religions," Kelly told Heather. "That way I'll be able to decide what I want to believe."

"Aren't you worried that you might not get to heaven?" asked Heather.

"All religions lead to some kind of heaven," answered Kelly. "It doesn't really matter *what* you believe—only that you try to live a good life."

Later Heather told her father about her conversation with Kelly. "Is it true, Dad?" asked Heather. "Can a person get to heaven by being a Hindu or Buddhist or Muslim?"

Dad said, "People follow many different religions, Heather. Some of them encourage their followers to do good to their neighbors. Others teach the thoughts and words of someone who lived long ago. Some tell people they must follow certain rules to live in a God-pleasing way."

"But, Dad," interrupted Heather, "are all religions just the same?"

"No, Heather. Christianity is very different. In all other religions, going to heaven depends on what a person does. Christians know that no one can keep God's Law perfectly. That's why God sent His Son, Jesus, to keep it for us and then to die for our sins. Jesus tells us that He is the only way to heaven. Jesus makes all the difference!"

———Let's talk: Can you think of three ways that Christianity is like some other religions? What makes it different?

———Let's pray: Lord Jesus, we believe in You as our Savior. Forgive us for the wrong things we do and say. Help us live in ways that honor You until we live with You in heaven. Amen.

E. R.

Travel Plans

If you plan to travel far from home on your summer vacation, you will see unusual sights. You may meet people whose lives are very different from yours. You may have the opportunity to taste new food. All these experiences wouldn't be much fun if you had to go alone.

King David asks this question in Psalm 139:7: "Where can I go from Your Spirit? Where can I flee from Your presence?" He answers, "If I rise on the wings of the dawn, if I settle on the far side of the sea, even there Your hand will guide me, Your right hand will hold me fast" (Psalm 139:9–10). We can take great comfort in knowing God is always with us.

Because God is always with us, we get travel benefits. It means we receive His forgiveness when we sin because of Jesus' gift of salvation. We receive God's loving care night and day and His help to do what is right. At the end of our earthly life, God takes us to heaven to be with Him.

Read from God's Word

Where can I go from Your Spirit? Where can I flee from Your presence? If I go up to the heavens, You are there; if I make my bed in the depths, You are there. If I rise on the wings of the dawn, if I settle on the far side of the sea, even there Your hand will guide me, Your right hand will hold me fast. Psalm 139:7–10 ✍

As you travel this summer, from largest canyon to highest mountain, remember that God is always with you. He loves you, protects you, and cares for you. He forgives your sins for the sake of His Son, Jesus.

———Let's talk: Read Psalm 139. What were the things God knew about David that amazed the psalm writer?

———Let's pray: God of land and sea, earth and sky, be with me no matter where I go. Help me live as Your child, and when I fail, forgive my sins for Jesus' sake. Amen.

E. R.

july

Contributors for this month:

Jennifer L. AlLee

Phil Lang

Kim D. Marxhausen

Kristine M. Moulds

Hope

Hold your hands with palms facing each other in front of your face to sign the word *hope* in American Sign Language (ASL). Move your right hand so your fingers touch your forehead while the left hand remains still. Bring your right hand slightly away from your forehead—the fingers of each hand bend in a kind of wave to each other.

Have you ever responded, "I hope so" to a friend who asks if you can play? Have you ever hoped your answer to a test question was right? We use the word *hope* to mean we would like something to be true, but we are not sure of it.

The word *hope* as it is used in the Bible means "assurance." We do not wonder *if* God's Word is true or *if* God's promises will happen. Because we have faith in Jesus, which the Holy Spirit gives us in Baptism, we are certain that God's Word is true. We are certain that Jesus rose from the dead to take away our sins. We are certain that we will go to heaven when we die. We are certain that God loves us no matter what.

Using your hands and lips, you, the heir of Christ's blessing, can pass on this sign and message of hope.

Read from God's Word

At one time we too were foolish, disobedient, deceived and enslaved by all kinds of passions and pleasures. We lived in malice and envy, being hated and hating one another. But when the kindness and love of God our Savior appeared, He saved us, not because of righteous things we had done, but because of His mercy. He saved us through the washing of rebirth and renewal by the Holy Spirit, whom He poured out on us generously through Jesus Christ our Savior, so that, having been justified by His grace, we might become heirs having the hope of eternal life. Titus 3:3–7 ✍

—————Let's do: List five truths about God that you know.
Follow each truth with the sign for "hope."

—————Let's pray: Dear Lord Jesus, thank You for the faith that makes our hope in Your Word and promises sure. Amen.

K. D. M.

Mountain

Read from God's Word

I love You, O Lord, my strength. The Lord is my rock, my fortress and my deliverer; my God is my rock, in whom I take refuge. He is my shield and the horn of my salvation, my stronghold. I call to the Lord, who is worthy of praise, and I am saved from my enemies. Psalm 18:1–3

Make both hands into fists to sign the word *mountain* in ASL. Strike the back of the right-hand fist (thumb up) against the back of the left-hand fist (thumb down) two times. Then open both fists and slide your hands (palms down) up the side of the mountain you are drawing in the air. The first part of the sign means "rock." The second part indicates that rock's size.

Mountains are beautiful. God is beautiful too. Think about the beauty of what Jesus Christ did for you when He died for your sins on Calvary's mountain. Mountains are strong, but God is stronger than anything that could hurt us. He offers us the refuge of His fortress. Mountains erode and change, but God is the same yesterday, today, and forever. Mountains change over years, but God's love never changes; it is stronger and bigger than anything.

"Big" things happened on mountains in the Bible. Think of Noah and the ark, Moses and the Ten Commandments, and Jesus' transfiguration and ascension. Noah, Abraham, and Moses met with God up high on mountains.

We don't have to stand on a mountain to be close to God because His love reaches down to us in His Word and in His Sacraments. He is our rock and our salvation—a mountain of a God.

_____Let's do: Mount of Olives, Moriah, Ararat, Sinai, and Horeb are five famous mountains from the Bible. Can you match them with their big events? Check out Genesis 8:4; Genesis 22:2; Exodus 3:1–2; Exodus 19:11; and Acts 1:12.

_____Let's pray: Lord, You are my rock and my salvation. I praise You for Your strength, protection, and love. In Jesus' name. Amen.

K. D. M.

Grace

Touch your heart with the middle finger of your right hand. Next, place both hands in front of your chest, palms in, middle fingers slightly bent. Stroke the air in small circles moving toward your head. The bent finger is the sign for "rain" (turned toward yourself). When the bent finger touches the heart it means *mercy* or *grace*.

Jesus points out that the sun shines and the rain falls on kind people and mean people alike. God does not send rain to fall on one house and not the house next door. Everyone in the neighborhood gets rain—whether they deserve it or not.

We do not get to heaven by being good. Everything we do is stained with sin. Heaven is a gift, freely given to us because of Jesus' death and resurrection. We do good things because we are filled with God's love and thankfulness for what Jesus has done for us. We want His message to shine through us.

We do not deserve the grace that "rains" down on us any more than a neighbor who does not believe in God or a classmate who steals our lunch money. But God's grace falls on us sinners anyway. He showers us with blessings—signs of His love—on earth as well as in heaven.

Read from God's Word

"You have heard that it was said, 'Love your neighbor and hate your enemy.' But I tell you: Love your enemies and pray for those who persecute you, that you may be sons of your Father in heaven. He causes His sun to rise on the evil and the good, and sends rain on the righteous and the unrighteous." Matthew 5:43–45

_____Let's do: Think of a person who has done something mean to you. Plan something kind to do for him or her. Practice grace; do that kind deed!

_____Let's pray: Lord Jesus, I do not deserve Your love and forgiveness. I thank and praise You that You give them to me anyway. Help me to show grace to others. Amen.

K. D. M.

Read from God's Word

When Moses went up on the mountain, the cloud covered it, and the glory of the LORD settled on Mount Sinai. For six days the cloud covered the mountain, and on the seventh day the LORD called to Moses from within the cloud. To the Israelites the glory of the LORD looked like a consuming fire on top of the mountain. Exodus 24:15–17 ✎

Glory

To sign *glory*, lay your hands open, the right hand on top, palms touching. Give a little clap. Now move the right hand away from the left in an arc past your right shoulder. Wiggle your fingers, shaking your hand like a tambourine.

In the United States today many will celebrate the birth of freedom with fireworks. Those who respect the gunpowder's power use caution. They are extra careful, fearing what could happen. But spectators don't think of the danger when they gaze up into the summer sky. They see only the glorious display of sparkling colors.

Those who know God and His power fear and respect Him. Just as the fireworks fill the sky, we praise and honor God with the words and actions that fill our days.

When you see a rocket or missile during fireworks, remember how God sent His Son, Jesus, to this earth to be our Savior from sin. He is our weapon against sin and our sure defense. When you see a fountain, think about God's love in Baptism that flows for you, giving forgiveness of sins, rescue from death and the devil, and eternal salvation. Enjoy the brightness of a sparkler as it reminds you to sparkle like a star, pointing others to Jesus—giving Him the glory.

_____Let's do: Design a fireworks display to the glory of God. Add rockets, missiles, fountains, and sparklers.

_____Let's pray: Lord Jesus, we give honor and glory to You in thanks for the many things You have given to us. Amen.

K. D. M.

Lord

To sign the word *Lord* extend your right thumb and first finger with palm down to make an *L*. Touch your thumb to your left shoulder and bring it down to touch your right hip. You have drawn a ribbon like the kind worn across the chest by royalty.

If you signed *Lord* for your friends, they might doubt that you knew what you are doing. Sometimes we doubt our friends, too, or we have doubts about our future. Will we be able to win the baseball game? Will our Scout trip be filled with fun? Is our aunt really coming for a visit?

Thomas had doubts too. Thomas was sure Jesus was dead. How could all his disciple friends say that Jesus was alive? Thomas wanted proof that Jesus was alive. So Jesus came to him and told Thomas to "stop doubting and believe." Thomas was convinced then, and he exclaimed that Jesus was his Lord and God. The unbelievable is true. Jesus is Lord and ruler of all. Jesus is God and Savior of the world.

God "signs" His love to us in Baptism and through His Word. He blesses us with faith although we cannot see Him. Jesus is the Lord who calms our fears and says to us, "Peace be with you!"

Read from God's Word

Now Thomas (called Didymus), one of the Twelve, was not with the disciples when Jesus came. So the other disciples told him, "We have seen the Lord!" But he said to them, "Unless I see the nail marks in His hands and put my finger where the nails were, and put my hand into His side, I will not believe it." A week later His disciples were in the house again, and Thomas was with them. Though the doors were locked, Jesus came and stood among them and said, "Peace be with you!" Then He said to Thomas, "Put your finger here; see My hands. Reach out your hand and put it into My side. Stop doubting and believe." Thomas said to Him, "My Lord and my God!" Then Jesus told him, "Because you have seen Me, you have believed; blessed are those who have not seen and yet have believed." John 20:24–29 ✍

_____Let's do: Write down three or four things that trouble you. Take them to the Lord in prayer. Remember, He says, "Peace be with you."

_____Let's pray: Lord, thank You for Your mercy and compassion. Remind me that You are the One who makes good things happen in my life. In the name of Jesus. Amen.

K. D. M.

Apple

To sign the word *apple* make a fist with your right hand, extending the thumb up. This is the sign for the letter *A*. Take the *A* hand shape and touch your cheek with your thumb. Use your thumb as a pivot and turn the fist up and down several times. You are chewing the letter *A* to sign the word *apple*.

The "apple of the eye" is the part of your eye that needs protection—like the pupil. If something gets too close to your pupil, your eyelid will automatically close quickly. Blinking protects your pupil and your ability to see and take in information about the world.

You are more important to God than your pupil is to your body. When the world becomes a dangerous place or when our sin causes us harm, God is our refuge and protector. In the blink of an eye He will act to protect us.

The most important thing He protects is our faith. He claimed us as His in our Baptism. The Spirit planted the seed of faith in our hearts and waters it with His Word. As we go through our life, God stays with us and protects our faith from the dangers of unbelief. We are precious to Him. We are the apple of His eye.

——Let's do: Practice the sign for "apple." Write a prayer of thanks the next time God protects you from harm.

——Let's pray: Lord, Your Word tells me that I am the apple of Your eye. Thank You for Your loving care. In Jesus' name I pray. Amen.

K. D. M.

Repent

Cross the first two fingers on each hand to make *R* hand shapes. Put the bottoms of your palms together at a 45-degree angle. Twist the sign—ending with the hands in reverse position. You have made the sign for *change*—the change that means *repentance.*

When we repent, we say we're *sorry.* Often we say it reluctantly because we know we should. Sometimes we only say it because mom wants us to. The word *sorry* does not mean much when we say it that way. Without a change of heart it is not repentance.

How many times have you said "sorry" although you didn't change? Like the twisted fingers, we have twisted the meaning of repentance. But when we are led by God's Spirit to repent, we are sorry for our sin and we ask God to give us a new heart. In Joel 2:13 God tells us to tear our hearts and not our clothes. By this He means that putting on a show of saying we are sorry is not what changes us. God changes us. He turns us away from sin and back to His loving mercy.

When we are sorry for our sin and come to God in repentance, He answers our prayer with comfort, mercy, and forgiveness.

Read from God's Word

"Therefore, O house of Israel, I will judge you, each one according to his ways," declares the Sovereign LORD. "Repent! Turn away from all your offenses; then sin will not be your downfall. Rid yourselves of all the offenses you have committed, and get a new heart and a new spirit. Why will you die, O house of Israel? For I take no pleasure in the death of anyone, declares the Sovereign LORD. Repent and live!" Ezekiel 18:30–32

———Let's do: The next time you say, "I'm sorry," sign the word *repent* and ask God to help you change.

———Let's pray: Jesus, I am sorry for my sins. Give me a new heart that trusts in You. Amen.

K. D. M.

Read from God's Word

The twenty-four elders and the four living creatures fell down and worshiped God, who was seated on the throne. And they cried: "Amen, Hallelujah!" Then a voice came from the throne, saying: "Praise our God, all you His servants, you who fear Him, both small and great!" Then I heard what sounded like a great multitude, like the roar of rushing waters and like loud peals of thunder, shouting: "Hallelujah! For our Lord God Almighty reigns. Let us rejoice and be glad and give Him glory! For the wedding of the Lamb has come, and His bride has made herself ready." Revelation 19:4–7 🖎

Hallelujah!

A way to sign the word *hallelujah* is to combine the signs for *praise* and *victory*. To sign *praise* touch the fingers of your right hand to your lips, then make a small clap. Now make both hands into a fist with your first fingers bent up into a hook or an *X* hand shape. Use this hand shape to make small circles above both shoulders, pretending to wave two flags, to sign *victory*.

The Book of Revelation tells us that *hallelujah* is a word used in heaven. That is one reason we like to use it in church. We want to praise God with the same word the angels use.

The word *victory* is an important part of the meaning of the word *hallelujah*. We praise God because of the victory He provides for us. Jesus died, and death has lost its hold on us. The devil lost the game because Jesus is the victor.

We try to follow all of the rules in our lives, but day after day we fail. The devil wants us to believe he is winning this game.

But we know that we are on God's team. When we serve God, learn about Him, and praise Him, it doesn't matter what the devil tries to make us think. Jesus already won the victory. Hallelujah!

_____Let's do: Write two sentences about how Jesus is a winner and makes us winners too. Then sign "hallelujah" and think about the victory Jesus won for you.

_____Let's pray: Lord, thank You for calling me in my Baptism to be a member of Your winning team. I praise You, Jesus, for Your victory over death and the devil. Amen.

K. D. M.

Bless

Make your hands into fists and touch your thumbs to your lips. As you bring your hands down, open them. The sign ends with your hands extended as if you are holding each hand over someone's head to bless them.

To be blessed means that God thought of you in a special and loving way. The same God who knows our sins, thoughts, fears, and weaknesses, loves us.

The sign for *bless* begins at the mouth, reminding us that God's blessings come from His Word. God only needed to say, "Let there be ..." and the world was created. Every need we have is met as He cares for us. God's Son, Jesus Christ, met our greatest need— our need for forgiveness.

The image of outstretched hands also reminds us that God blesses us with all the things we need to live in this life and His love and forgiveness for our sins, which takes us into eternity.

Psalm 65 is filled with examples of God's blessings, including the blessing of being chosen as God's child. Faith in Jesus as our Savior, which began at our Baptism, grows stronger through the study of God's Word and the Sacraments. And we respond with words and actions of praise.

Read from God's Word

Praise awaits You, O God, in Zion; to You our vows will be fulfilled. O You who hear prayer, to You all men will come. When we were overwhelmed by sins, You forgave our transgressions. Blessed are those You choose and bring near to live in Your courts! We are filled with the good things of Your house, of Your holy temple. You answer us with awesome deeds of righteousness, O God our Savior, the hope of all the ends of the earth and of the farthest seas, who formed the mountains by Your power, having armed Yourself with strength, who stilled the roaring of the seas, the roaring of their waves, and the turmoil of the nations. ... You care for the land and water it; You enrich it abundantly. The streams of God are filled with water to provide the people with grain, for so You have ordained it. You drench its furrows and level its ridges; you soften it with showers and bless its crops. You crown the year with your bounty. Psalm 65

_____Let's do: Read through Psalm 65 and write out the kinds of blessings God provides.

_____Let's pray: Lord Jesus, Your blessings are wonderful and free. Bless my study of Your Word. Amen.

K. D. M.

Read from God's Word

The LORD reigns forever; He has established His throne for judgment. He will judge the world in righteousness; He will govern the peoples with justice. The LORD is a refuge for the oppressed, a stronghold in times of trouble. Those who know Your name will trust in You, for You, LORD, have never forsaken those who seek You. Psalm 9:7–10

Trust

To sign the word *trust,* use the index finger of your right hand to touch your forehead. Then put each hand in a fist and place the right fist on top of the left as if you are tightly grasping a rope.

You are holding on to a rope that connects you to God. You are always connected to God with His rope of trust so you can have confidence during times of trouble.

Think of the shepherd boy, David, as he faced the giant Goliath. David had no shield or weapon. It was just David, God, and the rope that was a sling in David's hand. David knew God would protect him as he walked right up to the laughing Goliath. He trusted that God was bigger than any giant. God blessed the rope of David's slingshot as he flung the stone at Goliath.

What giants do you have to conquer today? Are you starting something new? Remember that God loves you no matter what. He loves you when things are going great, and He loves you when life is full of troubles. God is always there and always ready to help.

After all, if He loved you enough to send Jesus to rescue you from sin, you can also trust your changeless God to solve any problem.

_____Let's do: Think about a change in your life that has been hard for you. Now, think of three ways you have seen God help you with this change.

_____Let's pray: Lord Jesus, when You gave me faith You extended a rope of trust to me. I know I can cling to You. Thank You for Your unconditional love. Amen.

K. D. M.

You're "It"!

"Let's play Add-On Tag," said Bonnie. "How do you play that?" Willie and Susan asked.

"When 'it' tags another person, they both become 'it.' All who are tagged join the 'it' team. Pretty soon everyone is tagged—except the last person. The last one tagged gets to start the new game."

"Let's do it," chimed in all the kids.

Later that evening Bonnie told her dad about the new tag game.

Dad said, "That game reminds me of the way the church spread. The last words Jesus spoke to His disciples in Matthew are often called the Great Commission. Jesus first called and 'tagged' His 11 disciples, giving them a mission. Then they went out and tagged or told others about Jesus and what He had done. Then those people believed and were baptized, then they told even more people how Jesus died on the cross for our sins and rose from the dead to give us eternal life in heaven. Jesus also gives us that mission to tell everyone we know about Him and invite them to church and Sunday school, where they can hear more about their Savior.

"Someone told me Jesus died and rose to save me from my sins. I told you. Now, it is your turn to tag someone new."

Read from God's Word

Then the eleven disciples went to Galilee, to the mountain where Jesus had told them to go. When they saw Him, they worshiped Him; but some doubted. Then Jesus came to them and said, "All authority in heaven and on earth has been given to Me. Therefore go and make disciples of all nations, baptizing them in the name of the Father and of the Son and of the Holy Spirit, and teaching them to obey everything I have commanded you. And surely I am with you always, to the very end of the age." Matthew 28:16–20

_____Let's talk: What are ways God uses to bring people into His church?

_____Let's pray: Dear Jesus, thank You for tagging me and making me part of Your team. Help me bring others to You. Amen.

P. L.

Read from God's Word

In the same way, count your-selves dead to sin but alive to God in Christ Jesus. Romans 6:11 ✍

Two Riddles

There are names of 12 books of the Bible hidden in the paragraph below. Some are made by connecting parts of two words side-by-side. See how many you can find:

Some of you will find this an easy revelation. Others may remark that this is hard. Some just look for the facts. Others get in a jam, especially since the Bible book names are not capitalized. Do a good job, and you will find the truth. This is a most inter-esting puzzle to see what numbers of Bible books can be found. Yes, there can be frustration, just don't cry or go into lamentations. Just admit it usual-ly takes longer than you think it will. So, see how well you can compete. Relax. How did you do?

God wants you to use your Bible often, searching for His truth. As you read, God's Spirit will teach you about God's desire for justice (the Law) and His grace (the Gospel).

Read Romans 6:11. There you will find you are both dead and alive at the same time. How can that be? The sinful child you once were died on Calvary with Christ. The new life you have received from Christ is as real and certain as it can be. You have a whole new life, a fresh start.

―――Let's do: Did you find the Bible books of Revelation, Mark, Acts, James, Job, Ruth, Amos, Numbers, Esther, Lamentations, Titus, and Peter? Write a paragraph, hiding the words "dead to sin but alive to God in Christ Jesus."

―――Let's pray: Dear Jesus, thank You for showing me Your love in Your Word. Amen.

P. L.

Missing and Hitting

"I don't like missing the mark," Matthew muttered. "I wish I could hit the bull's-eye instead of the hay bales. Mr. Jangles says, 'Practice makes perfect,' but I don't seem to be getting any better."

"Don't worry!" Luke said. "Nobody's perfect. Pastor said my archery lessons reminded him of the Bible."

"You mean like all those stories with bows and arrows and sword battles?"

"No, he said it reminded him of sin."

"What does sin have to do with archery?"

"Pastor said that sin means 'missing the mark.' We want to be perfect and obey God, but when we try to shoot our own life's arrows, we miss the mark."

"That's a bigger problem than my archery game," confessed Matthew.

Read from God's Word

Therefore, just as sin entered the world through one man, and death through sin, and in this way death came to all men, because all sinned. ... But the gift is not like the trespass. For if the many died by the trespass of the one man, how much more did God's grace and the gift that came by the grace of the one man, Jesus Christ, overflow to the many! ... For just as through the disobedience of the one man the many were made sinners, so also through the obedience of the one Man the many will be made righteous. Romans 5:12, 15, 19

Mr. Jangles, the archery instructor, came along to give the boys a few pointers. He pulled back the bowstring and took aim. The flying arrow sizzled through the air, hitting the bull's-eye. "Wow!" both boys shouted.

If you had been with Matthew and Luke, you would have heard the end of their conversation. Jesus—like Mr. Jangles at archery—hit the bull's-eye. He kept the Law perfectly. He offers His perfection (His righteousness) to us by grace through faith in Him as our Savior. We are saved; we are winners.

_____Let's talk: What does it mean to be righteous?

_____Let's pray: Dear Jesus, I confess that I "miss the mark." I am so glad You hit the bull's-eye for me. Amen.

P. L.

Read from God's Word

A gentle answer turns away wrath, but a harsh word stirs up anger. Proverbs 15:1

Take It Back; Give It Back

Abbey was sobbing as she rushed to her mother. "Jared called me four-eyes."

"I was just kidding," defended Jared. "I'll take back what I said. I'm sorry. Please forgive me?"

Often people blurt out mean things to one another. As the words slip between their lips, they wish they could stuff them back down their throats.

Words are impossible to get back. Jesus came from heaven to earth, from the cross to the grave, to rescue us from the sin of all the insults we hurl at others. His Spirit leads us to repent and say we are sorry. He offers us a gentle answer: "I forgive you."

Sinful Abbey needs God's help just like sinful Jared. Proverbs 15:1 gives her two options: a gentle answer or a harsh word. The gentle answer stops the hurt but is hard for her to say. Humility to give gentle answers is a gift from God Himself. It comes as we are led to confess our sins and trust Christ's payment for those sins on the cross. When we see ourselves as a forgiven sinner, like Jared or Abbey, gentle answers, which come from God, help us speak kind words.

Only God can take back sin, only He can give us His grace.

_____Let's do: Read other proverbs in Chapter 15. Write about one of your favorites, or draw a picture to illustrate one.

_____Let's pray: Dear Jesus, help me to give gentle answers. Forgive me when I don't. Amen.

P. L.

Proverbs

Which proverb is from the Bible? A stitch in time saves nine.

Many hands make light work.

The fear of the Lord is the beginning of wisdom.

Ben Franklin is said to have written the first two sayings. He knew from experience that it is easier to solve a problem when it is small than later when it has gotten bigger—like a hole in a sock. And it is more fun to do a job with your friends than doing it by yourself—like collecting canned goods for the food pantry. Ben Franklin learned a lot from observing things.

But nothing is as true as the wonderful wisdom and knowledge of God. Colossians 2:3 tells us that the treasures of wisdom and knowledge are hidden in Christ. The way of the Lord is the beginning of wisdom. There are times when following the way of the Lord will be easy, like when you agree with your friends. There are other times when it will seem hard. But we can be sure our Lord only wants what is best for us. He proved that when He sent Jesus to die for our sins, bringing us forgiveness and eternal life. The very best wisdom of all is knowing that Jesus is our Savior and friend.

Read from God's Word

The proverbs of Solomon son of David, king of Israel: for attaining wisdom and discipline; for understanding words of insight; for acquiring a disciplined and prudent life, doing what is right and just and fair; for giving prudence to the simple, knowledge and discretion to the young—let the wise listen and add to their learning, and let the discerning get guidance—for understanding proverbs and parables, the sayings and riddles of the wise. The fear of the LORD is the beginning of knowledge, but fools despise wisdom and discipline. Proverbs 1:1–7 ✐

_____Let's talk: Which proverbs in this chapter do you like? Why?

_____Let's pray: Dear Jesus, give me wisdom to look to You for the answers to all of my problems. Amen.

P. L.

Farmyard Gifts

One day three farmyard animals were comparing their gifts.

The speckled hen boasted, saying, "I'm important to the farmer! I give him an egg every morning for breakfast."

"What about me?" mooed the black cow proudly. "I give a full pail of milk for the family to drink every day."

The fat pig thought about his gift and said, "Each of you gives a small sacrifice daily, but when I give my ham and bacon, I die and give my all."

Christians also have many gifts to share with God's people around them. Some give part of their money to help people in need. Some people give their time as a way to help others—like mowing lawns, picking up litter, or visiting a lonely neighbor. Both time and money, given with a thankful and cheerful heart, are gifts that please God.

Every day God gives us gifts, like the hen and the cow gave the farmer. We have families, homes, clothing, food, drink, and lots of extras. God also gave us the gift of His Son, Jesus. His perfect life gives us victory over sin, death, and the devil. God has redeemed, restored, and forgiven us in Jesus, giving His all. Now we have so much to share—each day and forever.

____Let's do: What other gifts has God given you? Make a list, then thank God for His generous love.

____Let's pray: Dear Jesus, thank You for giving Your all for me. Help me to share my gifts with others. Amen.

P. L.

The Last Piece;
The Lasting Peace

Jigsaw puzzles can have 10 pieces, 100 pieces, or 1,000 pieces. The goal is always the same: Fit all the pieces together to make a complete picture. No matter how many pieces you put in, the picture isn't done—the puzzle isn't complete—until the last piece is in place.

Some people try to put pieces together in their lives so they can complete a chance to go to heaven. They try to have good behavior, pray regularly, worship God often, and help others whenever they can. These pieces seem to fit together, and certainly they are wonderful things to do. But they will never make a complete picture. There are never enough pieces of our goodness to overcome the sin in our lives.

Jesus is the One who brings heaven to us. He offers us the piece we could never come up with—a perfect life. His perfect love offers it as a gift to us. His sacrifice made peace with the Father for the sin of the world. That means we don't have to worry about our sin puzzle. And of course we want to go on with good behavior, prayer, worship, and helping others because they show our love for the Lord. We are free to do all these things because we have Jesus—the lasting peace!

Read from God's Word

"All this I have spoken while still with you. But the Counselor, the Holy Spirit, whom the Father will send in My name, will teach you all things and will remind you of everything I have said to you. Peace I leave with you; My peace I give you. I do not give to you as the world gives. Do not let your hearts be troubled and do not be afraid. You heard Me say, 'I am going away and I am coming back to you.' If you loved Me, you would be glad that I am going to the Father, for the Father is greater than I. I have told you now before it happens, so that when it does happen you will believe. I will not speak with you much longer, for the prince of this world is coming. He has no hold on Me." John 14:25–30 ✐

_____Let's do: What are ways you like to serve others? Draw a puzzle and fill the puzzle pieces with fun ways to serve the Lord.

_____Let's pray: Dear Jesus, thank You that I have lasting peace in heaven because of You. Amen.

P. L.

Praise be to the God and Father of our Lord Jesus Christ, who has blessed us in the heavenly realms with every spiritual blessing in Christ. For He chose us in Him before the creation of the world to be holy and blameless in His sight. In love He predestined us to be adopted as His sons through Jesus Christ, in accordance with His pleasure and will—to the praise of His glorious grace, which He has freely given us in the One He loves. In Him we have redemption through His blood, the forgiveness of sins, in accordance with the riches of God's grace that He lavished on us with all wisdom and understanding. Ephesians 1:3–8

You, Too, Are Adopted

L ois showed Jennifer pictures of her family at a party.

"Here's one of Dave," Lois said, pointing to her husband. "And those are his parents standing next to him."

Jennifer said, "Wow, Dave sure looks like his mom."

"But Dave was adopted," Lois replied.

Jennifer was surprised! She looked at the picture again but still thought Dave really looked like his mother.

When people spend a lot of time together, they often pick up certain traits from one another. They may say the same kinds of things or laugh the same way. Sometimes they even start to look alike. That's probably what happens to adopted children.

Do you know that every single Christian is adopted? The Bible tells us that when Jesus Christ died and rose again, all our sins were forgiven. God adopted us when we were baptized. He loves us so much that He has made us His children.

The more time we spend with God, the more He works in us so we start to "look" like Him. Other people will be able to tell that we are children of our heavenly Father. Think how great it would be to have someone say to you, "Of course, you're one of God's kids. You look just like Him!"

_____Let's do: What are some ways you resemble God? Write them on a piece of paper. (Examples: forgive others; am kind to my friends; help my parents without complaining.) Then pray that God would help you be more like Him in all areas.

_____Let's pray: Dear Lord, thank You for making me part of Your family. Please help me to (mention some things you wrote on your list) so I can be more like You. In Jesus' name. Amen.

J. L. A.

Calling Long-Distance

B ryan hung up the phone and turned around to see his mother standing next to him.

"Bryan, how long have you been on the phone?"

"I'm not sure. I called Grandma at two o'clock, though."

"It's already 3:15," his mom told him. "You were on the phone for more than an hour, and you know that's a long-distance call. That's going to be very expensive when the phone bill comes."

"I'm sorry, Mom," Bryan answered. "I was having such a good time that I forgot we have to pay for it later."

There's one person we can talk to for as long as we like, and it never costs us a thing—God. Every time we pray, we're having a conversation with our heavenly Father.

Do you have a best friend whom you can't wait to talk to every day? Well, that's the same way God feels about you. He wants you to talk to Him every day because He loves you. He loves you so much that He sent His Son, Jesus Christ, to pay the price for all your sins. So you see, you really can talk to God anytime you want to for free—the bill's already been paid.

Read from God's Word

"For I know the plans I have for you," declares the LORD, "plans to prosper you and not to harm you, plans to give you hope and a future. Then you will call upon Me and come and pray to Me, and I will listen to you. You will seek Me and find Me when you seek Me with all your heart." Jeremiah 29:11–13 ᑫ

_____Let's do: Write down three truths you know about prayer.

_____Let's pray: Dear heavenly Father, thank You for loving me so
             much that You have enabled me to call on You in
             prayer anytime, free of charge. Help me remember
             how important my conversations with You are.
             Through Jesus I ask this. Amen.

J. L. A.

Read from God's Word

But we see Jesus, who was made a little lower than the angels, now crowned with glory and honor because He suffered death, so that by the grace of God He might taste death for everyone. In bringing many sons to glory, it was fitting that God, for whom and through whom everything exists, should make the author of their salvation perfect through suffering. Hebrews 2:9–10 ✍

Living Conditions

Keisha stared as her father pointed to a little bathroom up a hill. How would she manage to survive a whole week of camping?

It didn't take long for Keisha to realize that without electricity, her hair dryer wouldn't work. There was no CD player or television. She couldn't get a bowl of ice cream from the freezer whenever she wanted.

Somehow Keisha made it through the week and even had some fun. But when she finally got back home, she had never been so thankful for modern conveniences.

When Jesus walked among us in Bible times, He may have noticed that many "heavenly conveniences" were missing here on earth. He left behind a home where no sickness or pain existed. He left behind a home where He could visit His friends anytime He wanted. On earth He found Himself crossing miles of dusty roads and deserts. He left behind a home where everyone knew Him personally and adored Him. On earth, people He loved turned against Him.

But Jesus didn't complain. He came to conquer death and to rise again. "He was delivered over to death for our sins and was raised to life for our justification" (Romans 4:25).

Jesus loved us so much that He didn't mind all those earthly inconveniences. To Him, we were worth it.

_____Let's talk: What inconveniences might Jesus have experienced on earth? Why do you think people are worth so much to the Lord?

_____Let's pray: Dear Jesus, thank You for Your love. I'm so glad You saved me for a future in Your heavenly home. In Your holy name, Lord. Amen.

K. M. M.

Heading Home

H old it still!" Matthew wriggled in the car's backseat as he moved the magnetic checker on the little board balanced on his brother's knee.

But our citizenship is in heaven. And we eagerly await a Savior from there, the Lord Jesus Christ, who, by the power that enables Him to bring everything under His control, will transform our lowly bodies so that they will be like His glorious body. Philippians 3:20–21

"Let's quit. I'm hot," complained Zachary.

"Mom!" whined Matthew. "Zach won't hold the board still!" At home the brothers enjoyed playing checkers. But on a car trip like this it wasn't much fun.

"Put the game away for now," said Mom. "When we get back home, you can play the real thing again."

Riding in a car doesn't provide ideal conditions for playing games. But even at home, ideal conditions rarely exist.

It isn't easy to live a Christian life in our sinful world. We try to praise and serve God in less than ideal conditions. Jesus knows how rough life can be for us. By His death, Jesus made it possible for less-than-ideal humans to look forward to a future in heaven.

Someday we will be in our real home in heaven for good. Paul reminds us in Ephesians 2:19, "You are no longer foreigners and aliens, but fellow citizens with God's people and members of God's household."

In heaven at last, none of us will feel hot, grumpy, cramped, hungry, itchy, or uncomfortable. We can "play" all day, praising our Lord for all eternity!

_____Let's talk: Why are we less-than-ideal people? Name some things you think you will like about heaven.

_____Let's pray: Lord, thank You for understanding when things are not perfect. Thank You for loving me enough to give me a wonderful home in heaven. In Jesus' name. Amen.

K. M. M.

The Living Spirit

Cody and his little sister Annie gazed from the backseat windows. Annie took a gulp of air and held her nose as they drove by some gravestones.

"What are you doing?" exclaimed Cody. "I don't smell anything funny around here."

"My friends do that when they pass a graveyard," she said. "It's to keep out the spirits. We don't want ghosts getting in us."

"That can't really happen when you pass a cemetery," explained Cody. "Besides, you already have a Spirit in you."

"I do?" asked Annie, her eyes wide.

Do you know what kind of spirit Cody meant? He didn't mean anything ghostly or evil, like what might be on TV or at the movies. He meant the Holy Spirit.

Paul told the Corinthians that God "put His Spirit in our hearts as a deposit, guaranteeing what is to come" (2 Corinthians 1:22). God's Spirit helps us know right from wrong and fight against temptations. He fills our hearts with faith, understanding, and love.

Have you been baptized? Do you trust in God and in His Son, Jesus, who brought you forgiveness for your sins? If you said yes to any of these, the Holy Spirit is living in you, making you stronger in love and faith.

_____Let's talk: Is there anything to fear from a graveyard? Why do you think God wants His Spirit to live in you? How do you know the Holy Spirit is in you?

_____Let's pray: Lord, thank You for Your Holy Spirit, who lives in me. Help me, Lord, to spread this love to others. In Jesus' name. Amen.

K. M. M.

The Jesus Touch

Michael kissed the dollar bill he'd just earned.

"Yuck!" said Nicole, his older sister. "Do you know how many people have touched that?"

"How many?" he said.

"Hundreds! And who knows how dirty their hands were—gross!"

Michael made a face. Holding the dollar by the edge, he gingerly put it in his savings envelope.

Jesus wasn't afraid to leave His perfect heavenly home for a dirty world. Jesus was touched by many hands and groping fingers. When Jesus walked down streets, people often followed Him, holding out their hands.

He didn't say, "Don't touch me!" or scold anyone by asking, "When was the last time you washed your hands?" Instead, He reached out His own human and sensitive hands to touch people back.

Jesus' hands touched dirt, germs, grime, grease, gross skin, dirty hair, crummy feet, crying eyes, bumpy bones, and bald heads. When He touched people, miracles happened. When He touched people, there was love. "And all who touched Him were healed" (Matthew 14:36).

Jesus knew there was something worse than outer dirt or ugliness: sin. Only Jesus can cure sin. His loving hands ended up with nail holes in them because of our sin. Through His loving forgiveness, we're washed clean.

Read from God's Word

And a woman was there who had been subject to bleeding for twelve years, but no one could heal her. She came up behind Him and touched the edge of His cloak, and immediately her bleeding stopped. "Who touched Me?" Jesus asked. When they all denied it, Peter said, "Master, the people are crowding and pressing against You." But Jesus said, "Someone touched Me; I know that power has gone out from Me." Then the woman, seeing that she could not go unnoticed, came trembling and fell at His feet. In the presence of all the people, she told why she had touched Him and how she had been instantly healed. Then He said to her, "Daughter, your faith has healed you. Go in peace." Luke 8:43–48 ✎

_____Let's talk: How do people get dirty on the inside? How did Jesus cure us of sin?

_____Let's pray: Dear Jesus, sometimes I feel dirty and ugly, even when I don't want to be. Thank You for washing away my sins in my Baptism to make me clean. Amen.

K. M. M.

The Master's Voice

"Sit, Ruffy!" J. J. said. "Sit!" Ruffy jumped up and licked J. J.'s face. "Not now, Ruffy," J. J. said, giggling. "Sit!"

"That dog needs obedience school," said J. J.'s dad. "But you'll have to take him yourself. He must learn to listen to his master's voice. That's you, J. J."

Ruffy finally did learn to sit, although he felt more like leaping and wagging his tail. But, of course, Ruffy didn't obey just anyone. He did what he was told only if J. J. said it. He learned to obey his master's voice.

Our Lord wants us to obey Him. We get advice from many sources: television and movies, magazines, textbooks, speakers, other adults, and friends. But Jesus said, "Blessed ... are those who hear the word of God and obey it" (Luke 11:28).

We can learn to obey God's will from our families, our churches, and Bible studies. We can learn to hear our true Master's voice. Obeying isn't always easy. But God doesn't expect us to follow Him all by ourselves. Remember that our Good Shepherd, Jesus, is leading us and helping us. He assures us: "My sheep listen to My voice; I know them, and they follow Me. I give them eternal life, and they shall never perish" (John 10:27–28).

_____Let's talk: Why do parents and teachers want us to obey them? Name some family rules you have. Why do you think God wants you to obey Him?

_____Let's pray: Dear Master and Lord, thank You for leading me to know Your voice as I study Your Word. Thank You for forgiving my failures. Help me obey You daily, with the help of Your Holy Spirit. In Jesus' name. Amen.

K. M. M.

A New Look on the Inside

Read from God's Word

Therefore we do not lose heart. Though outwardly we are wasting away, yet inwardly we are being renewed day by day. For our light and momentary troubles are achieving for us an eternal glory that far outweighs them all. So we fix our eyes not on what is seen, but on what is unseen. For what is seen is temporary, but what is unseen is eternal. 2 Corinthians 4:16–18

H ey," said Brian's dad, looking at the television, "I know that actress. She must be pretty old by now."

"She looks young, Dad. Are you sure it's the same person?" asked Brian.

"I remember her voice," said Brian's dad. "I guess she had a face-lift or two to keep herself looking young."

A face-lift, or plastic surgery, is done by a doctor to remove wrinkles or scars. The procedure usually makes people look younger.

People who get a "new look" often feel younger and more attractive. But a face-lift doesn't make a person younger. True change can come only from the inside. King David once sang that the Lord "satisfies your desires with good things so that your youth is renewed like the eagle's" (Psalm 103:5).

Realizing that Jesus, our Savior, forgives our sins every day, stays with us through good and bad times, and makes us feel young at heart. Earthly wrinkles and old age don't affect our eternal life. The Holy Spirit is alive in us, helping us grow in faith, giving us an exciting reason for living.

For a new look that really lasts, the prescription is simple: "If anyone is in Christ, he is a new creation; the old has gone, the new has come!" (2 Corinthians 5:17).

_____Let's talk: Think about a time you felt new on the outside. How does God renew us on the inside?

_____Let's pray: Lord, thank You for renewing me day by day with the Good News of Your forgiveness and salvation. In Jesus' name. Amen.

K. M. M.

The Greatest Mystery

Amy slowly walked to the dining room holding her latest mystery book, her eyes focused on the open page. "I'm coming," she added absentmindedly—just before she tripped on her brother's shoe and crashed into a chair.

"I was at a good part, Mom," said Amy as she rubbed her knee. "I can't wait to finish this mystery and start the next one."

The greatest mystery story of all is in the Bible.

It's a mystery how God could love us so much that He sent His Son to die for our sins—but He did. It's a mystery how Christ could redeem us and earn eternal life for us—but He did.

How can God know everything? How can He answer everyone's prayers?

Although we can't understand everything about God, we already know some of the most important things about Him. We know God made the world. We know He loves us. We know our Lord has a place in heaven for us because of Jesus.

And remember: This story isn't fiction!

The last chapter of this mystery for each of us will be reached in heaven. In the meantime, keep reading God's Word and learning about Him. Just don't stumble into a chair while you're doing it.

_____Let's talk: What's something great about the Lord that you already know?

_____Let's pray: Heavenly Father, I praise and thank You for the great mystery of Your love for me. In Jesus' name. Amen.

K. M. M.

Use Me, Lord

Read from God's Word

What, after all, is Apollos? And what is Paul? Only servants, through whom you came to believe—as the Lord has assigned to each his task. I planted the seed, Apollos watered it, but God made it grow. So neither he who plants nor he who waters is anything, but only God, who makes things grow. 1 Corinthians 3:5–7

"Hurry, Esther!" called Rebecca. "Where's your basket?"

"The big one? It's over there with lentils in it. Why do you—"

"Quickly, Esther, help me move the lentils out," Rebecca said. She began scooping lentils from the large basket into an earthenware pot. "Friends need the basket right away!"

Do you know which basket this might have been? Read Acts 9:19–25.

The Bible doesn't tell us whose basket Paul used or how he got it. But somebody had to have made it. Did the maker of the basket ever know how his or her talent saved Paul's life?

We may never know. But we do know that God uses ordinary, everyday things all the time in helping people.

Think of the pictures you draw, the projects you make, or the music you play. Maybe God will use something you do or make to help someone else. Think of your summer activities: playing ball, swimming, baby-sitting, biking, reading, traveling, and so on. You never know when the Lord may use things you say or do to bring someone closer to Him.

The message we share with others is simple but powerful: "Christ Jesus came into the world to save sinners—of whom I am the worst" (1 Timothy 1:15).

_____Let's talk: Think of something you enjoy doing during the summer. How might God use you in this activity to witness your faith in Him?

_____Let's pray: Dear Lord, thank You for using me to share Your wonderful love with others, in whatever way it happens. In Jesus' name. Amen.

K. M. M.

Read from God's Word

Blessed is he whose transgressions are forgiven, whose sins are covered. Blessed is the man whose sin the LORD does not count against him and in whose spirit is no deceit. Psalm 32:1–2 ᔌ

How Sin Is Like Sand

om, are you sweeping the cabin again?" asked Jenny.

"There seems to be sand from the beach everywhere!" said her mom, sweeping around the pile of clothes. "No matter where I sweep, there's always more."

Jenny felt the sand, all right. No matter how hard they tried to keep out the sand, more would come in.

We Christians often try to sweep our lives clean, to get rid of the sand of sin. But no matter how much we try, we aren't successful. Ezra prayed, "O my God, I am too ashamed and disgraced to lift up my face to You, my God, because our sins are higher than our heads and our guilt has reached to the heavens" (Ezra 9:6).

Only one person in the world has lived a completely clean life. That was God's Son, Jesus. Only Jesus, who had no sin, could pay for our uncleanness. When He did that on the cross, our sin was swept away by Jesus' righteousness so we could be saved for heaven.

In our lives, the sands of sin keep showing up—cross words and unkind actions. We can ask the Holy Spirit to help us contain these outbursts. But our real joy comes from knowing that our sins have been swept away—gone forever—because of Jesus.

_____Let's talk: Why was Jesus the only one who could pay for our sins?

_____Let's pray: Dear Jesus, only You could rescue me. Thank You for loving me and sweeping away all my sins. In Your name. Amen.

K. M. M.

A Smoldering Wick

Jesus said (quoting Isaiah), "'A bruised reed He will not break, and a smoldering wick He will not snuff out'" (Matthew 12:20). What is a smoldering wick? What might these words have meant to the Israelites?

In Bible times, houses were really dark at night. A little moonlight might come in through a tiny window in the wall, but that was it—no streetlights, no flashlights.

To provide light, Israelites used little oil lamps. A string-like wick burned on one end while the other end soaked up olive-oil fuel. They usually left these lamps burning all night. If the oil got too low, the wick would smolder or smoke up the entire house where everyone was sleeping.

The Israelites were comforted to think of the Lord watching over them during the dark night, keeping an eye on their needs. He was a protecting God. He was so protecting that He rescued them from an even greater darkness—their sins—by sending a Savior.

Jesus knows when we are like a smoldering wick—worn down from our sinning and discouraged by our lack of faith. After all, Jesus came to this world to rescue us from the darkness of sin. His Spirit guards our hearts and lives. His love is the oil that keeps us lit up with faith.

Read from God's Word

Aware of this, Jesus withdrew from that place. Many followed Him, and He healed all their sick, warning them not to tell who He was. This was to fulfill what was spoken through the prophet Isaiah: "Here is My servant whom I have chosen, the one I love, in whom I delight; I will put My Spirit on Him, and He will proclaim justice to the nations. He will not quarrel or cry out; no one will hear His voice in the streets. A bruised reed He will not break, and a smoldering wick He will not snuff out, till He leads justice to victory. In His name the nations will put their hope." Matthew 12:15–21

_____Let's talk: Why would a wick begin smoldering? What does the Lord do when we begin to "smolder"? How does the Lord help you when you are discouraged?

_____Let's pray: O Lord, it's comforting to know that You sent Jesus to rescue us from the darkness of sin. Thank You for the strength and comfort of Your Holy Spirit. In Jesus' name we praise You. Amen.

K. M. M.

Read from God's Word

For you were once darkness, but now you are light in the Lord. Live as children of light (for the fruit of the light consists in all goodness, righteousness and truth) and find out what pleases the Lord. Have nothing to do with the fruitless deeds of darkness, but rather expose them. For it is shameful even to mention what the disobedient do in secret. But everything exposed by the light becomes visible, for it is light that makes everything visible. This is why it is said: "Wake up, O sleeper, rise from the dead, and Christ will shine on you."
Ephesians 5:8–14 ✍

Wake Up and Smell the Coffee

Janey scrambled out of her tent. It was morning, and her parents were already by the campfire. The smells of bacon, eggs, and coffee made Janey feel glad to be awake. Mmm! Coffee especially smelled good. Her mom wouldn't let her drink it, but she loved that smell anyway.

There's an expression about coffee that goes, "Wake up and smell the coffee!" This means something like "Get with it," or "Find out what's going on."

We want people to "wake up and smell the coffee" about their need for God's forgiveness and love. The apostle Paul traveled all over the Mediterranean area telling people about God's saving grace. The Spirit used him to wake people up spiritually.

When Paul explained that Jesus died for people's sins, many believed in their Savior. They figured out that life was really about God's love and forgiveness. They were glad to be awakened to hear and learn the Good News of Christ Jesus.

It's the same for people in our day. Unless they hear the Good News of salvation, they won't believe in Christ. We can celebrate what Christ has done for us, then share the "wake up" news with others.

———Let's talk: How did Paul invite people to "wake up"?
List some ways we can do this too.

———Let's pray: Lord, thank You for waking me up to Your Good News of love and forgiveness. Help me tell others about You. In Jesus' name. Amen.

K. M. M.

Taking the Jesus Ride

M y shoe!" cried Amanda. The water ride swooshed her sandal away and down a waterfall. Amanda stared after it as she climbed into the ride's raft with only one shoe on. "Poor Harry," she moaned

"You named your shoe?" asked Meg.

"Sure," said Amanda, giggling. "Larry is still on my other foot. But Harry is gone."

Let's think of our life in Christ as a long ride. Worldly things (toys, games, clothes, money) often get in the way of our enjoying the ride. We may try so hard to save and collect things that we forget about life's real meaning—Jesus.

Collecting worldly things can't bring true happiness to anyone. Some people are so busy collecting possessions that they don't enjoy anything about the Jesus ride. Sometimes they get off before it's over by no longer trusting their Lord. They forget that at the end of the ride is eternal life in heaven.

There's only one way to stay on the Jesus ride of life. That is to trust that Jesus is our Savior. He holds onto us during the tough parts of life. He's with us to the end. He already paid our admission price to the ride by dying on the cross for our sins.

Then we won't need our shoes. We'll only need Jesus.

> **Read from God's Word**
>
> *Then He said to them, "Watch out! Be on your guard against all kinds of greed; a man's life does not consist in the abundance of his possessions." And He told them this parable: "The ground of a certain rich man produced a good crop. He thought to himself, 'What shall I do? I have no place to store my crops.' Then He said, 'This is what I'll do. I will tear down my barns and build bigger ones, and there I will store all my grain and my goods. And I'll say to myself, "You have plenty of good things laid up for many years. Take life easy; eat, drink and be merry."' But God said to Him, 'You fool! This very night your life will be demanded from you. Then who will get what you have prepared for yourself?' This is how it will be with anyone who stores up things for himself but is not rich toward God." Luke 12:15–21* ✑

_____Let's talk: Create a word tower listing names of worldly possessions. On the Jesus ride, what happens to those possessions when you die? to you?

_____Let's pray: Dear Savior, thank You for paying my way to eternal life. Help me trust in You rather than in my possessions. Amen.

K. M. M.

august

Contributors for this month:

Doris Schuchard

Mary Lou Krause

Glenda Schrock

Ruth Geisler

God's Team

Read from God's Word

Just as each of us has one body with many members, and these members do not all have the same function, so in Christ we who are many form one body, and each member belongs to all the others. We have different gifts, according to the grace given us. If a man's gift is prophesying, let him use it in proportion to his faith. If it is serving, let him serve; if it is teaching, let him teach; if it is encouraging, let him encourage; if it is contributing to the needs of others, let him give generously; if it is leadership, let him govern diligently; if it is showing mercy, let him do it cheerfully. Romans 12:4–8 ✍

S ome of the team chopped with their bare hands. Others kicked with their bare feet. Several picked up a friend and used his head as a battering ram.

This strange sport was a karate exhibition. Fifteen members of a karate team tried to demolish a 150-year-old house. They used their skills, working together.

Have your ever been part of a team? Maybe you're part of a school band or church choir. Or you help a group that cleans up and plants flowers in a park. It's fun to work toward a common goal.

You became a part of God's team, a child of God, in Baptism. In today's Bible reading, God's team is pictured as a body. Each part of your physical body—ear, hand, or stomach—has a different job to do. In the same way, God has given each person in His body special gifts and abilities too.

Just as God showed His love for us by sending Jesus to be our Savior from sin, we can show a kind of Christlike love. You might share your outgrown clothes with others. You can make a card for a neighbor who is ill. You can pray for your pastor and teachers. With Christ as our leader, we can use His gifts toward the goal—sharing His love.

_____Let's do: What are the special talents God has given you? Jot down some ways you can share His gifts with others.

_____Let's pray: Thank You, Jesus, for the gifts You have given me, especially (name them). Show me ways I can share Your love with others today. Amen.

D. S.

Read from God's Word

Show me Your ways, O LORD, teach me Your paths; guide me in Your truth and teach me, for You are God my Savior, and my hope is in You all day long. Remember, O LORD, Your great mercy and love, for they are from of old. Remember not the sins of my youth and my rebellious ways; according to Your love remember me, for You are good, O LORD. Good and upright is the LORD; therefore He instructs sinners in His ways. He guides the humble in what is right and teaches them His way. Psalm 25:4–9

Who Moved?

It was a perfect day for kite flying. Dad helped Andy reel out the string and watch the kite unfurl in the breeze. As it whipped across the sky, Andy ran back and forth across the grass, holding on tightly.

"Now, Andy," Dad called out, "don't go too far. Play where you can always see me."

"But Dad," Andy yelled back, "every time I look over, you've moved!"

Andy was so busy flying his kite he didn't realize he was the one moving. Dad was still there, watching him.

Have you ever heard the saying "If God seems far away, guess who moved?" Sometimes we don't feel close to God. We're upset when a friend doesn't invite us to a party. We don't clean our room because we watched TV instead. We're just too tired to have devotions and prayer time.

We step away from God when we make unwise choices, forget to show love, or miss our time with Him. When that happens, God wants us to know He is always there, loving and guiding us.

Sometimes our sins are like winds that blow the kite and we drift away from God. But God leads us to confess our sins. Jesus promises to forgive us. His death and resurrection mean He is always close to us. He hasn't moved at all!

_____Let's do: Is there something in your life that wants to blow you away from God? It may help to write it down. Pray about it. Jesus' forgiveness is sure.

_____Let's pray: Dear Jesus, thank You that I can always come to You, knowing You love and forgive me. Please forgive me for (confess your sin). Help me follow You always. Amen.

D. S.

Are You Thirsty?

Here's an easy recipe to try for National Watermelon Day today:

1. Chop 6 ice cubes in a blender or food processor.

2. Add 2 cups of seedless watermelon pieces and blend until slushy, about 1 minute.

3. Add 1 tablespoon of sugar or honey and blend 10 seconds. Pour the slush into glasses and enjoy!

Watermelons are a valuable source of drinking water in the deserts of Africa, where they originally came from.

Much of the nearby land of Israel is desert too. In Bible times, water was just as precious as gold. So when God's people became thirsty, God showed His care by supplying them with water. He provided a well full of water for Hagar and her son Ishmael in the desert. He gave the Israelites water from a rock. He sent a special messenger to Elijah with bread and water.

> **Read from God's Word**
>
> *O God, You are my God, earnestly I seek You; my soul thirsts for You, my body longs for You, in a dry and weary land where there is no water. I have seen You in the sanctuary and beheld Your power and Your glory. Because Your love is better than life, my lips will glorify You. I will praise You as long as I live, and in Your name I will lift up my hands. My soul will be satisfied as with the richest of foods; with singing lips my mouth will praise You. Psalm 63:1–5*

To satisfy our deep-down spiritual thirst, God sent Jesus. He invites us to come to Him and drink if we are thirsty (John 7:37). Jesus gives us life-giving water that gives us forgiveness of sins, daily needs, and eternal life.

If you're thirsty this summer, grab an ice-cold watermelon slush. But remember the refreshment that a "drink" of prayer, daily devotions, and worship with your Christian family brings. Jesus gives us the real water to live.

———Let's do: Think about how it feels to be thirsty. List things you can do when you're thirsty for Jesus.

———Let's pray: Dear Lord, thank You for sending Jesus to give us life-giving salvation. Amen.

D. S.

Your Will Be Done

Dwight L. Moody traveled around the world telling people about Jesus.

He was on a ship when part of a broken propeller smashed a hole in the ship. Water rushed in, and the ship began to sink. Pastor Moody had been in dangerous situations before, but this time he was really scared, thinking he had only hours to live.

He went to his cabin and got down on his knees. He asked God to take care of him and prayed, "Thy will be done." Then he went peacefully to sleep!

Pastor Moody was following Christ's example in prayer—whether he lived or died, he trusted God's will. In the Garden of Gethsemane, Jesus knew God could rescue Him from having to suffer and die on the cross. But Jesus wanted to do what pleased His Father. So He prayed, "Not what I will, but what You will." God's will was for Jesus to be the Savior of the whole world. We have life with Christ forever because of His victorious death and resurrection.

A few hours after Pastor Moody prayed, another boat saw the ship and towed them to safety. You can be sure that no matter how sinking your problems, God will be your rescue. Even if the answer isn't what you expected, you can trust God's will.

_____Let's talk: The gift of eternal life and opportunity to show His love to others are two things God wants for you. Can you list others?

_____Let's pray: I want Your will in my life, Lord. Show me what to do. Give me the courage to follow You. Amen.

D. S.

Looking for Answers?

"I-R-R-E-L-E-V-A-N-T," Ashu paused between each letter as she rolled the shiny penny around in her pocket for good luck. The judge smiled. Ashu had won the school spelling bee!

Many people believe a good luck charm can help them. Even in Bible times some of God's people were tempted to use charms called amulets, a carved stone or gem worn around the neck. People thought amulets would protect them from disease and harm.

God warned His people not to be led astray by charms. What does God want us to do instead? He tells us, "Trust in the LORD with all your heart and lean not on your own understanding" (Proverbs 3:5).

God is in control of our world. He knows the future and has a wonderful plan for your life—here and in eternity.

The next time you're faced with

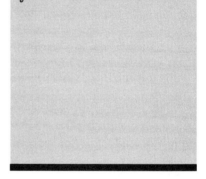

Read from God's Word

Consider it pure joy, my brothers, whenever you face trials of many kinds, because you know that the testing of your faith develops perseverance. Perseverance must finish its work so that you may be mature and complete, not lacking anything. If any of you lacks wisdom, he should ask God, who gives generously to all without finding fault, and it will be given to him. James 1:2–5

trouble or need help with a decision, remember today's Bible reading. It reminds us to pray and ask Jesus for wisdom. He gives us forgiveness for our sins, salvation, a heavenly home, and the power to love others. He will provide for our daily needs too and help us make wise decisions.

When it comes to shiny pennies, spend them or save them. But for real help, go to God—He has all the answers!

_____Let's do: Think of a time when God provided the answer to your need. Write a thank-You prayer for His goodness.

_____Let's pray: Let's pray: Dear Lord, give us Your wisdom on which to lean our hearts. Amen.

D. S.

Read from God's Word

For this reason, since the day we heard about you, we have not stopped praying for you and asking God to fill you with the knowledge of His will through all spiritual wisdom and understanding. And we pray this in order that you may live a life worthy of the Lord and may please Him in every way: bearing fruit in every good work, growing in the knowledge of God, being strengthened with all power according to His glorious might so that you may have great endurance and patience, and joyfully giving thanks to the Father, who has qualified you to share in the inheritance of the saints in the kingdom of light. For He has rescued us from the dominion of darkness and brought us into the kingdom of the Son He loves, in whom we have redemption, the forgiveness of sins.
Colossians 1:9–14 ✍

A Real Superhero

Roger keeps bugging Patty. Finally Patty has had enough and yells at Roger. They both end up in trouble.

"How can I help my friend Patty?" wonders Doug. "It's time to draw and unleash the powers of the Quail—patience, intelligence, and speed!"

When we see Doug turn himself into Quail Man in a cartoon, we might wish we were a superhero too. There are days when you feel on top of the world, like when you score the winning goal. Then there are bottom-of-the-world days when you play the wrong notes at your recital.

The disciples probably felt brave the night they climbed into a boat with Jesus. They could haul in loads of heavy fish. They were strong enough to row across a lake. But when the wind blew, the rain fell, and the waves threatened their boat, they didn't feel so heroic anymore. They called to Jesus, our real Superhero.

He is powerful enough to heal sickness, calm a storm, or save His people. He is the only one to overcome sin and death by rising from the dead. God wants to give us His strength to be patient, kind, and joy-filled. He wants to give us forgiveness and eternal life. He helps us every day to bear fruit and grow in Him (Colossians 1:10).

_____Let's talk: How is Jesus like a Superhero? How is He better?

_____Let's pray: Dear Lord, help me each day to find my strength in You. In Jesus' name. Amen.

D. S.

Celebrate Twice!

G uess the holiday by solving the puzzle below. Start with the letter *B* in the square. Move up, down, or diagonal from *B*—letter to letter until you've used all the letters and found the answer. (Hint: When this holiday first began, it was only for rich people. No cake and presents for common people.)

I	B	S
H	R	Y
T	D	A

When Christians began observing Jesus' birthday, people also began celebrating their own birthdays. In Germany there were the *Kinderfeste*, or "children's parties." The family woke the birthday child early with a cake. The candles on top equaled the child's age plus one for the "light of life" God gives.

You have two birthdays. On your first birthday you were born into your earthly family. On your second birthday, your Baptism, you were adopted into God's family. Because God loves you, He sent Jesus to win forgiveness, life, and salvation. In Baptism God washed you from sin, giving you His gifts. Now you are a new person, living for Jesus, trusting Him to be with you.

When is your Baptism birthday? Ask your family to share stories, photos, and the church bulletin from that day. Have a special devotion with today's Bible reading and a favorite hymn. Go ahead. Celebrate twice!

Read from God's Word

At one time we too were foolish, disobedient, deceived and enslaved by all kinds of passions and pleasures. We lived in malice and envy, being hated and hating one another. But when the kindness and love of God our Savior appeared, He saved us, not because of righteous things we had done, but because of His mercy. He saved us through the washing of rebirth and renewal by the Holy Spirit, whom He poured out on us generously through Jesus Christ our Savior, so that, having been justified by His grace, we might become heirs having the hope of eternal life. Titus 3:3–7 ✐

_____Let's do: What gifts did God give you on your Baptism? Write your two birthdays on the calendar. Celebrate both.

_____Let's pray: Thank You, Jesus, for the blessings You've given me in Baptism. Help me live as a new person in You. Amen.

D. S.

Safe!

Cherise thought the chickens were the most interesting things on her Grandpa's farm. "The hen hatches the baby chicks and takes care of them until they are big," Grandpa told her.

Mary Ann, a big hen, had 11 fuzzy babies. When she found a bug or a bit of feed, she clucked. Then all the chicks ran to see what treat she had for them.

One afternoon the shadow of a hawk passed low over the chicken yard. All the chickens froze. Cherise wondered if the hawk would try to carry off one of the chicks. But Mary Ann clucked a warning. All 11 babies were instantly under her strong wings. Mary Ann was protecting her children!

Baptism sets us apart as God's children. He faithfully takes care of us, much like Mary Ann. We live within the comforting sound of His loving voice. His power shelters us from the devil's attacks.

Nothing can harm our souls as we live in Christ. That is His sure, true, and faithful promise. We may be physically hurt in an accident or grow old and die, but our spiritual selves, our real selves, are beyond the devil's reach. Jesus suffered and died on the cross to pay for our sins. We are forever safe in Him.

_____Let's do: Write about a time when God protected you from harm.

_____Let's pray: Heavenly Father, thank You for taking care of me. I know I can always turn to You for help and protection. You love me with a father's love, and I also love You. In Jesus' name. Amen.

G. S.

A Team Mission

Out in the Kalahari Desert in Africa, things are tough. You travel hundreds of miles with a four-wheel-drive vehicle—sand up to the hubcaps—to find a few scattered Bushmen families. The environment is hot and hostile. No familiar food grows here. When you try to communicate with the people who live here, the only response you get is strange clicking sounds.

The Good News of Jesus and heaven is meant for the Bushmen also. To this end of the earth the Lord has called a very special missionary team. The missionary pastor is kind and friendly. The people love him. He also has the patience and talent to understand and write the language. His wife has courage; she isn't afraid to travel hundreds of miles through barren desert to get food and supplies. She can even fix the van if it breaks down.

God has made the missionary and his wife a team. They are delivering the most important message on earth: "God so loved the world that He gave His one and only Son, that whoever believes in Him shall not perish but have eternal life" (John 3:16).

You are always welcome to join the missionary team. Join with your prayers and offerings to reach the people of the world for the kingdom of heaven.

Read from God's Word

For this is what the Lord has commanded us: "I have made you a light for the Gentiles, that you may bring salvation to the ends of the earth.'" When the Gentiles heard this, they were glad and honored the word of the Lord; and all who were appointed for eternal life believed. The word of the Lord spread through the whole region. Acts 13:47–49

———Let's do: Check out the LCMS World Mission Web site at
                http://mission.lcms.org. Write about something
                new you learned about other missionaries.
                Join a missionary team as a prayer partner.

———Let's pray: Lord Jesus, I want to be on Your mission team.
                Help me pray for those who tell of Your salvation
                far from home. Amen.

M. L. K.

Read from God's Word

Though you have not seen Him, you love Him; and even though you do not see Him now, you believe in Him and are filled with an inexpressible and glorious joy, for you are receiving the goal of your faith, the salvation of your souls. 1 Peter 1:8–9

Joy Today

"The rule is, jam to-morrow and jam yesterday, but never jam to-day!" That's what the White Queen tells Alice in Lewis Carroll's *Through the Looking-Glass.* Maybe you know people who live like that.

We often hear people say they will be happy *when* or *if* something happens. They will be happy when they make the starting lineup. They will be happy if they get a new scooter. When they get to heaven, they will surely be happy!

Some people can't feel happy because they keep thinking about how things used to be. "I had fun when we lived in the other house." "I was really happy when Mom and Dad were still together."

Illness, divorce, or a lack of money can make life seem hard. We are all sad when we must give up a pet or someone we love. Jesus understands our sad times. He was sad sometimes too. But because of Him, we can feel joy even in times of sadness.

Jesus died on the cross to pay for our sins. He won for us the greatest reward of all—the salvation of our souls. We don't have to wait until we get to heaven to rejoice about that. As children of God, we are secure in that joy tomorrow, yesterday, and today.

_____Let's do: Rewrite the queen's statement to make it true for Christians. You might begin, "The Good News is . . ."

_____Let's pray: Dear Jesus, how glad I am that You are my Savior and friend! Help me to share my joy. Amen.

G. S.

God's Perfect 30

Zack and his dad were going through old papers from his great-grandparents' attic.

"Dad, look!" Zack said. "These are stories about World War I! They're all by Will Cole."

Dad nodded. "Will was my great-uncle. He was a war correspondent."

Zack read on. "What does '30' mean at the end of each story?"

His father thought for a minute. "I think that's the way reporters write 'The End.' One newsman always ended his column by writing, 'That's a 30.'"

The next day, as Zack sat in church, the pastor talked about God's plan for our salvation. Jesus was true man and true God. The plan was for Him to take all sins of all people upon Himself. Then, since death is the punishment for sin, Jesus would die in their place.

Jesus carried out the plan perfectly. From the cross Jesus cried out, "It is finished!" He was ready to die in victory. He had earned our salvation.

On the way home Zack and his father were talking about the pastor's message. Zack eyes twinkled as he made a connection from the day before to what the pastor said. "If Jesus had been a newsman, He could have said, 'That's a 30!'"

"Right you are, Zack. And that's news worth reporting."

_____Let's do: Research different ways to say, "It is finished."
For example, we sometimes say, "That's that."
The French say, "C'est fini." Draw the cross on
each of the statements.

_____Let's pray: Dear Lord Jesus, thank You for dying for my sake.
How glad I am that You are my Savior! Amen.

G. S.

Read from God's Word

Then Peter came to Jesus and asked, "Lord, how many times shall I forgive my brother when he sins against me? Up to seven times?" Jesus answered, "I tell you, not seven times, but seventy-seven times." Matthew 18:21–22

One More Time

What bothers you the most about your friend? Maybe she tells your secrets. Maybe she puts you down. Maybe he borrows your things and ruins them. Maybe he promises to do something but always forgets.

Most of us eventually reach a point where we've had enough. No matter what, we won't forgive our friend this time; we've already forgiven him so many times! But then our friend says, "I'm sorry." What are we supposed to do?

Simon Peter came to Jesus and asked how many times he should forgive his brother. Seven times? (Peter probably thought seven times was more than enough.) But Jesus replied that Peter should forgive his brother 77 times, or even 70 times 7. What Jesus meant was that Peter should forgive as many times as forgiveness was needed.

We all sin many times each day. Some of our sins are things we do that are wrong. Other sins are things we ought to do but don't. We often sin without even knowing it!

God knows when we sin. Every sin offends Him. Yet when we ask Him to forgive us, He does because Jesus already took the punishment for our sins. God places no limit on the number of times He forgives. As He forgives us, He expects us to forgive others.

_____Let's do: St. Paul wrote that love "keeps no record of wrongs" (1 Corinthians 13:5b). Write two sentences that explain the math of God's forgiveness.

_____Let's pray: Father, forgive me when I sin. Help me to forgive others. In the name of Jesus Christ. Amen.

G. S.

Another Way to Sing

When people at church praised Mika's singing, she felt really proud. She couldn't wait to sing a solo again.

But no one asked her to sing for the Praise Festival. Instead, she was asked to greet children. Mika got up the courage to talk to her Sunday school teacher. "I wanted to sing," she told her. "Everybody says I sing well."

Mrs. Pate smiled at her. "You have more talents than singing, Mika. Do you want to serve others with your talent? Or do you just want to show off?"

Mika thought. "I'm sorry," she finally whispered. "Please forgive me?"

Mrs. Pate hugged her. "Of course, I forgive you. Your singing brings joy to all of us. But this time we need your kindness and warm smile to greet others. We'll call this your humble service."

During the Last Supper Jesus washed His disciples' feet, usually a servant's job. Jesus showed that He was willing to serve others in the humblest way.

Read from God's Word

Young men, in the same way be submissive to those who are older. All of you, clothe yourselves with humility toward one another, because, "God opposes the proud but gives grace to the humble." Humble yourselves, therefore, under God's mighty hand, that He may lift you up in due time. 1 Peter 5:5–6

As His greatest service Jesus died on the cross to save all people from sin. There was no applause. It was a painful, ugly, humiliating task. But this was God's plan to save us. Jesus died willingly because of His great love for us. Such great love leads us to sing His praise and serve as He leads!

_____Let's do: Make two lists: What Jesus did for you.
              What you could humbly do for Him.

_____Let's pray: Dear Lord, forgive me when I become proud.
              Help me serve in any way You want. Amen.

G. S.

Take Your Stand!

Read from God's Word

Finally, be strong in the Lord and in His mighty power. Put on the full armor of God so that you can take your stand against the devil's schemes. Ephesians 6:10–11 ✐

Bigfoot Wallace was a legendary hero of the Texas frontier.

Once some men stole Bigfoot's horses, and he had to get them back. But he was 1 man against 40. The only thing handy for protection was a bunch of hickory nuts. So Bigfoot stuffed his clothing full of hickory nuts. He even filled his cap!

Bigfoot must have looked like a lumpy monster. All his enemies had were bows and arrows. He just stood there and let the arrows bounce off him. His enemies soon became confused and terrified. They threw down their weapons and ran away. Bigfoot calmly took his horses home.

Not all of us will have to face enemies who want to harm us physically. But we all have to face the attacks of the devil. The devil tries to draw us away from God. To stand up against the evil one, we need special protection.

In Ephesians 6, St. Paul urges us to put on the armor of God. God's armor consists of things like truth, righteousness, faith, and the Word of God. We also have the sure defense of Christ's sacrifice for us. Jesus paid for our sins with His death on the cross. Because He died for us, the devil has no power over us.

_____Let's talk: How would God's armor help you withstand criticism from your friends?

_____Let's pray: Heavenly Father, help me stand up for what is right and resist what is evil. In Jesus' name. Amen.

G. S.

Fun at the Beach

S arah always looked forward to the days when they could eat supper at the beach.

Sarah and her dad ran for the water. Dad dove under a wave and swam out beyond the breakers. Sarah walked into the water to her knees and then swam out to the calm water to be with her dad. It was fun to float on their backs and be lifted by the gentle swells. Sometimes seagulls swooped over them.

Later Sarah and Mom and Dad ate their sandwiches, enjoying the warm sun. By the time they cleaned up and built a sand castle, the air was getting cool.

Sarah almost fell asleep as she rode home in the backseat. Mom looked at her and smiled. "Did you have a good time?" she asked.

"I sure did," Sarah said.

What's the best time you have ever had? Do you know why you can have such good times? It's because Jesus loves you so much. He gives you a special kind of joy that only Christians have. It's the joy that comes from knowing Jesus died for you and rose again. Sometimes you have great times. Sometimes you have problems. But God loves you at all times.

Read from God's Word

I have seen the burden God has laid on men. He has made everything beautiful in its time. He has also set eternity in the hearts of men; yet they cannot fathom what God has done from beginning to end. I know that there is nothing better for men than to be happy and do good while they live. That everyone may eat and drink, and find satisfaction in all his toil—this is the gift of God. I know that everything God does will endure forever; nothing can be added to it and nothing taken from it. God does it so that men will revere Him. Ecclesiastes 3:10–14 ⤣

_____Let's do: Make a list of fun things you have done this summer. Thank God for those times.

_____Let's pray: Thanks, Lord, for fun times with my family. I owe all these good times to Your goodness and mercy. Keep us all in Your love, for Jesus' sake. Amen.

R. G.

Read from God's Word

Have we not all one Father? Did not one God create us? Why do we profane the covenant of our fathers by breaking faith with one another? Malachi 2:10

What Happened at the Park

Janeen saw Tamika walk into the park. "Tamika, hi!" she yelled.

Tamika smiled. But as she walked past the basketball court, some kids stared at her. "What's wrong with your hand?" one of them asked.

Tamika looked at the ground. Her left arm was much shorter than her right arm, and it didn't really end with a hand—just two fingers and a thumb.

Tamika's eyes filled with tears.

By the time Janeen got home, she was crying too. "Honey, what's the matter?" her grandmother asked.

Janeen told Grandmother what the kids had done. "They made Tamika cry," she sobbed. "They were mean!"

Grandmother hugged Janeen. "I don't think they meant to be mean. Do you think Tamika's hand looks funny?"

"No," Janeen answered. "I don't even notice it."

"Tamika's blessed to have a friend like you," Grandmother said. "Do you know, when Tamika was born, her little hand didn't even have a thumb? The doctor did an operation and turned one finger into a thumb so she could hold things. God has made her a very special person.

"God made each person different. He loves us and sent Jesus to make each of us His own. Why don't you call Tamika?"

"Okay," Janeen smiled. "I'm glad I have such a special friend."

_____Let's talk: What makes each of your friends special?

_____Let's pray: Thank God for some things that make you and your friends special.

R. G.

The Camping Trip

Kurt was waiting on the porch with his sleeping bag when Uncle Dan and Mark drove up. "Bye, Mom," he yelled.

After their arrival at the camp Kurt and Mark put on life jackets and jumped into a small river.

Later Kurt watched the campfire. "This was a great day," Kurt said.

"Maybe one more thing would make it just perfect," Uncle Dan said. He got out some marshmallows and helped Kurt and Mark toast them over the fire. Then they ate the golden brown marshmallows and chocolate bars between two graham crackers.

"They're called s'mores," Mark laughed, "because you always want s'more."

"We have had a good time today," Uncle Dan said. "It reminds me of the first miracle Jesus did when He lived on earth. He helped people have a good time."

"Oh, I know," Kurt said. "Jesus was at a wedding, and He changed water into wine."

Uncle Dan added, "Jesus cares about us in many ways. Not only did He die to take our sins away and give us a fantastic home in heaven, but He also cared enough to give us a lot of fun here on earth."

"That's right," Mark said. "At the wedding Jesus' friends thought His wine at the end was the best thing."

"Just like the s'mores," Kurt laughed.

———Let's do: Read John 2:1–11. List good things God has given you. Place the list where you can see it every day.

———Let's pray: Thank You, Lord, for all the good times and good things You give me. I praise You for Jesus, who makes it possible for me to be Your child. Amen.

R. G.

Read from God's Word

That day when evening came, He said to His disciples, "Let us go over to the other side." Leaving the crowd behind, they took Him along, just as He was, in the boat. There were also other boats with Him. A furious squall came up, and the waves broke over the boat, so that it was nearly swamped. Jesus was in the stern, sleeping on a cushion. The disciples woke Him and said to Him, "Teacher, don't You care if we drown?" He got up, rebuked the wind and said to the waves, "Quiet! Be still!" Then the wind died down and it was completely calm. He said to His disciples, "Why are you so afraid? Do you still have no faith?" They were terrified and asked each other, "Who is this? Even the wind and the waves obey Him!" Mark 4:35–41 ✍

The Calm after the Storm

Jesus had been talking to the people all day. The other disciples and I sat with Jesus in our boat so the people could crowd along the shore to hear Him.

Finally Jesus was so tired that He lay down at the back of the boat and fell asleep.

All at once a wind like a tornado crashed into us! Waves started to come in on top of us. I looked back at Jesus. He was sound asleep!

My friends and I shook Him and yelled, "Jesus, can't You tell there's a storm? Don't You care about us?"

Jesus woke up. He talked to the wind and the waves, just like He'd talked to the people all day. "Peace! Be still!" He said.

We couldn't believe it! The wind stopped blowing and the water was smooth as glass.

"Why were you afraid?" Jesus asked. "Don't you have faith?"

We looked at one another. We'd seen Jesus do so many things. What would He do next?

What makes you feel afraid? The dark? Having someone angry with you? Jesus is stronger than things that make you afraid. He is even stronger than sin or death. He has won a victory over them for you. You can trust this Jesus, for He loves you and is always beside you.

_____Let's do: Write about a time when knowing Jesus made you feel calm about a problem.

_____Let's pray: Dear Jesus, thank You for being with us through the storms of our life and granting us Your peace. Amen.

R. G.

Every Day

Tina saved her program and took the disk out of the drive. Tina was glad her teacher was showing her how to write her own programs.

James called his new song "Thunderstorm Blues." His mom had shown him how some songs have a pattern of running bass notes. The low notes sounded neat with the melody James heard in his head and found on the piano keys.

"A ... B ... C ..." Ki Jin said each letter of the alphabet as she pointed to it. "Excellent!" her teacher smiled. A few weeks ago Ki Jin could speak only Korean, but now she was learning English too.

What's the newest thing you have learned to do? We learn new things at school, home, church, even when we go on vacation. God's world is so big and exciting, and He teaches us new things every day. God gives us the talent to learn new things.

Read from God's Word

"His master replied, 'Well done, good and faithful servant! You have been faithful with a few things; I will put you in charge of many things. Come and share your master's happiness!' ... 'For everyone who has will be given more, and he will have an abundance. Whoever does not have, even what he has will be taken from him.'" Matthew 25:23, 29

God gives us other talents too—the talent to praise Him for sending Jesus, the talent to share His love, the talent to help and forgive people, the talent to tell our friends about Jesus. We want others to share in the Kingdom that Jesus gives us—God's reign of mercy, peace, and full forgiveness.

When you think about it, you're a very talented person!

_____Let's do: What new things are you learning this week? What is something you would really like to learn how to do? Ask God to help you.

_____Let's pray: Dear Father, it's great to be able to do so many things. Help me use my talents for the good of Your kingdom. In Jesus' name. Amen.

R. G

Read from God's Word

People were bringing little children to Jesus to have Him touch them, but the disciples rebuked them. When Jesus saw this, He was indignant. He said to them, "Let the little children come to Me, and do not hinder them, for the kingdom of God belongs to such as these. I tell you the truth, anyone who will not receive the kingdom of God like a little child will never enter it." And He took the children in His arms, put His hands on them and blessed them. Mark 10:13–16 ✍

In the Way

Nicole walked outside and heard the whir of the Weed Eater. "Stay away, honey," her dad called. "This might kick something into your eyes."

Nicole sighed and went into the kitchen. "Nicky, get out of here. Can't you see I'm on the phone?" her brother yelled.

Do you ever feel like you're in the way? You might be trying to help people, but instead you seem to bother them. Jesus' disciples once felt that some children were getting in their leader's way.

Some mothers were bringing their children to be blessed by Jesus. But the disciples thought the children would bother Jesus. "Take the children back home," the disciples said. "Jesus is too busy to see them."

But Jesus said, "Let the children come to Me. I love them. They belong to My Father and will go to heaven with Me."

Your parents and teachers may get so busy or troubled with a problem that they tell you not to bother them. That doesn't mean they don't love you. They are just lost in their own thoughts.

When this happens, talk to the One who always has time for you. Jesus gave His entire life and even died for you so that through faith you would belong to Him forever. He is eager to listen to you anytime.

_____Let's talk: When was the last time someone made you feel
like you were in the way? How did you feel?
If this happens again, how will you handle it?

_____Let's pray: Dear Lord Jesus, You know all things. You know that
I often need someone to listen to me and treat me as
important. Thank You for always being there for me.
I love You very much! Amen.

R. G.

Sometimes I Worry

Read from God's Word

"Are not two sparrows sold for a penny? Yet not one of them will fall to the ground apart from the will of your Father. And even the very hairs of your head are all numbered. So don't be afraid; you are worth more than many sparrows." Matthew 10:29–31

Travis hated it when his mom was in the hospital. Now, although she was home, her back still hurt.

Travis's dad sat down beside him. "What's wrong? Did it scare you to see Mom in pain?"

Travis sighed. "I hate to have Mom sick. And what about the bills?"

"Well, the hospital is expensive," said Dad. "But she's going to be fine—that's what's important."

"But don't you worry sometimes?"

"Sure," Dad said. "I worry about you and Mom and having enough money. But I also think about that nest the sparrows built under the roof last year."

"I remember that," Travis said.

"Do you know that if one of our baby sparrows had fallen out of the nest, God would have known about it? God cares even more about us. God even knows how many hairs you have on your head!"

Travis laughed. Dad laughed too. "God knows all our needs—especially our need for a Savior. And He loves us so much that He sent Jesus to suffer and die for our sins. If God will take care of that great big problem, He will also take care of all our little needs. When I remember that, I don't worry. Why don't you go see Mom?"

Travis hugged his dad and ran into the house.

_____Let's talk: How does it feel to know that God knows every little thing about you and cares what happens to you?

_____Let's pray: Do you feel worried about something? Tell God about it.

R. G.

Sometimes I Feel Special

Read from God's Word

It was He who gave some to be apostles, some to be prophets, some to be evangelists, and some to be pastors and teachers, to prepare God's people for works of service, so that the body of Christ may be built up until we all reach unity in the faith and in the knowledge of the Son of God and become mature, attaining to the whole measure of the fullness of Christ. Then we will no longer be infants, tossed back and forth by the waves, and blown here and there by every wind of teaching and by the cunning and craftiness of men in their deceitful scheming. Instead, speaking the truth in love, we will in all things grow up into Him who is the Head, that is, Christ. From Him the whole body, joined and held together by every supporting ligament, grows and builds itself up in love, as each part does its work. Ephesians 4:11–16 ✎

Todd saw an ad that said WIN A BIKE! SEND IN YOUR NAME TODAY! NO TRICKS!

Todd read the ad carefully. He didn't have to send money or write a story—just send in his name. It seemed too good to be true. Todd had been praying for a bike every night for weeks.

Todd showed the ad to his mom. "Look at this, Mom. Should I send my name in?"

Mom read the ad carefully. "You might as well try."

Six weeks later Todd opened a letter that said "Congratulations! A gift certificate for $150 is enclosed."

The next night as Mom drove them to the bike shop, Todd asked her to stop the car for a minute. "What's wrong?" she asked.

"God gave me this bike," he said. "Let's stop and thank Him."

Todd's bike is something like the special gifts God gives to you. God sent His Son, Jesus, to die on the cross and rise again so all your sins are forgiven. In your Baptism, God gave you the gift of faith so you can believe in Him and live in heaven one day. God helps you tell your friends and family about Jesus.

God's gifts are all free—no tricks, no strings attached.

_____Let's talk: What's the biggest surprise you ever had? What is the best gift God has given you?

_____Let's pray: Dear God, I want You to know how grateful I am. Thanks for everything, especially for Jesus. Amen.

R. G.

Nida from Pakistan

Nida learned to speak English in Pakistan. When she started school in America, she was very quiet. But she could do all her work, and she always said "thank you" when someone helped her.

One day Melody showed Nida her gel pens at recess. "Would you like to draw some pictures?" she asked.

"Yes," Nida smiled.

Melody and Nida sat on the grass together. Melody wrote her name using a different pen for each letter.

"That is pretty," Nida said. "I can write my name in Urdu."

"Wow, that's neat!" Melody commented. "You must be smart to know two alphabets."

"I learned them at my former school," Nida said. "It was easy."

God desires that we love other people just as much as we love ourselves. When you meet someone new, put yourself in her place. Would you like someone to talk to you? You might ask her to play or eat lunch with you. You might help her.

Jesus was friendly to new people, wasn't He? Jesus was even known as "a friend of sinners" because He came to suffer, die, and rise from death to save everyone—including you and me—from sin. You can ask Jesus to help you talk to new friends and share this same kind of love with them.

Read from God's Word

One of them, an expert in the law, tested Him with this question: "Teacher, which is the greatest commandment in the Law?" Jesus replied: "'Love the Lord your God with all your heart and with all your soul and with all your mind.' This is the first and greatest commandment. And the second is like it: 'Love your neighbor as yourself.' All the Law and the Prophets hang on these two commandments." Matthew 22:35–40

———Let's talk: How does having Jesus for a friend help you be a friend to other people?

———Let's pray: Ask God to show you how to help a new friend this week.

R. G.

Read from God's Word

"So he got up and went to his father. But while he was still a long way off, his father saw him and was filled with compassion for him; he ran to his son, threw his arms around him and kissed him. . . . We had to celebrate and be glad, because this brother of yours was dead and is alive again; he was lost and is found.'" Luke 15:20–32 ✍

Living High—Until . . .

I thought I was really smart. I was tired of doing the same old things at home. I asked my dad to give me the share of his money that would be mine when he died. Then I ran away.

I stayed up all night if I felt like it. If I saw something I wanted, I bought it. I had fun day and night.

But pretty soon I ran out of money. Each day I got hungrier and weaker. Finally a farmer said I could work feeding his pigs, but he couldn't afford to pay me.

I threw buckets of scraps to the pigs. Even the servants who worked for my dad had plenty of food to eat, and I was in a pigpen, starving to death. I wished I could take back everything I'd done wrong.

I pushed myself up from the ground. I knew what I had to do. I would go back home and say, "Dad, I've sinned. I'm not good enough to be your son. Please let me work for you."

I started the long walk home. I stared at the ground and wished I hadn't done so many stupid things. Before I knew what was happening, my dad ran toward me and hugged me and kissed me. He wasn't angry at all!

——Let's talk: Read Luke 15:20–32. How are you like the son who spent all his money? How is God like the father?

——Let's pray: Dear God, I am sorry for my sins. Please forgive me for Jesus' sake. Amen.

R. G.

Whom Do You Imitate?

L iesl flipped her legs over her head and landed standing up on the playground. Amy sighed. If she tried a cherry drop off the bars, she'd break her head.

Amy wanted to let her hair grow long like Liesl's thick, blonde hair that fell below her waist. Amy's hair was thin and brown and stopped at her shoulders.

Amy loved to stay overnight at Liesl's house. It was much bigger than her house.

Liesl was kind to everybody at school. Every once in a while Amy wondered if she was jealous of Liesl. But she decided she wasn't. She loved her family and home. She would just like to be more like Liesl.

Do you ever wish you could imitate someone else? We all admire some people and try to do things like they do.

The best person to imitate is Jesus. Think of playing follow the leader, with Jesus as your leader. He will help you imitate the good things that your friends do and stay away from the bad things. He also thought enough of you to die for you so your sins would be forgiven. When you think of imitating Jesus, think of the love He gave to the whole world.

Read from God's Word

So whether you eat or drink or whatever you do, do it all for the glory of God. Do not cause anyone to stumble, whether Jews, Greeks or the church of God—even as I try to please everybody in every way. For I am not seeking my own good but the good of many, so that they may be saved. Follow my example, as I follow the example of Christ. I praise you for remembering me in everything and for holding to the teachings, just as I passed them on to you.
1 Corinthians 10:31–11:1

_____Let's talk: What good qualities do you have that someone else might want to imitate? How do you get the power to imitate Jesus?

_____Let's pray: Lord Jesus, please be my leader every day. Amen.

R. G.

Read from God's Word

When I came to you, brothers, I did not come with eloquence or superior wisdom as I proclaimed to you the testimony about God. For I resolved to know nothing while I was with you except Jesus Christ and Him crucified. I came to you in weakness and fear, and with much trembling. My message and my preaching were not with wise and persuasive words, but with a demonstration of the Spirit's power, so that your faith might not rest on men's wisdom, but on God's power. 1 Corinthians 2:1–5

The Most Important Thing

Thea thought of doing her science project on bones when the doctor said she could keep the X-ray of her broken finger.

People couldn't believe the chicken bone tied in a knot. That had been easy—Thea's dad had helped her soak a bone from a chicken leg in acid overnight. Then they rinsed it with water and baking soda. The bone bent like rubber.

Thea had found that people are taller in the morning than they are at night. That's because at night liquid fills in the spaces around the little bones called vertebrae in your backbone and then it runs out during the day. Thea measured herself and her mom and dad every morning and night for a week. Then she made a chart. Now everybody wanted to run right home and measure themselves.

Have you ever worked on a project or a lesson that helped you learn a lot of new things?

There is one thing you already know that is more important than any other fact in the world. Jesus was put to death on a cross and came alive again so you can go to heaven. Knowing we have such a wonderful Savior makes us excited to learn more about Him and the world He has given us.

_____Let's do: On a piece of paper, write three of the newest facts you have learned. Write three facts about Jesus.

_____Let's pray: Dear Father, thank You for the wisdom You give me as I learn new things. And thank You for the best wisdom— knowing and trusting Jesus as my Savior. Amen.

R. G.

A Faith Full of Fizz

op the top. Whishh! That's the fresh fizz sound of soda. The fizz tickles your face and sparkles on your tongue.

Now it's hours later. You rush into the house after a hot, dusty game. Your soda is still standing on the table. One thirsty gulp finds it F–L–A–T.

Sometimes our faith is like that. It seems to fizzle out. It's easy to forget how great God really is—so great that He sent His own dear Son to save us. Sometimes our pep for serving the Lord gets used up doing other things, selfish things. We may feel too tired to be helpful or kind. The faith fizz that sparkles with loving deeds has gone flat.

Before God's people settled down in the Promised Land, Joshua called them together for a pep talk. He reminded them of all that God had done for them. God had rescued them and cared for them. "Be very careful to ... love the LORD ... and to serve Him with all your heart and all your soul," Joshua told them.

The Holy Spirit can put this kind of fizz into your faith. Let your helpful deeds and kind words continually bubble over to others. Thank the Lord enthusiastically in all you do!

Read from God's Word

Then Joshua summoned the Reubenites, the Gadites and the half-tribe of Manasseh and said to them, "You have done all that Moses the servant of the LORD commanded, and you have obeyed me in everything I commanded. For a long time now—to this very day— you have not deserted your brothers but have carried out the mission the LORD your God gave you. Now that the LORD your God has given your brothers rest as He promised, return to your homes in the land that Moses the servant of the LORD gave you on the other side of the Jordan. But be very careful to keep the commandment and the law that Moses the servant of the LORD gave you: to love the LORD your God, to walk in all His ways, to obey His commands, to hold fast to Him and to serve Him with all your heart and all your soul." Then Joshua blessed them and sent them away, and they went to their homes. Joshua 22:1–6 ✑

———Let's talk: From what has God rescued or saved you? What are some things that take the "fizz" out of your faith? Who or what can help you thank the Lord more enthusiastically?

———Let's pray: Heavenly Father, thank You for sending Jesus to rescue us from the devil. Send Your Spirit to pep up our faith so we can serve You enthusiastically. Amen.

M. L. K.

Read from God's Word

Who can discern his errors? Forgive my hidden faults. Keep Your servant also from willful sins; may they not rule over me. Then will I be blameless, innocent of great transgression. May the words of my mouth and the meditation of my heart be pleasing in Your sight, O LORD, my Rock and my Redeemer. Psalm 19:12–14

Close Up

How perfect the world looks, I thought, as we cruised along in our jet. Trees were tucked beside gently curving streams. Houses and buildings were lined up in tidy rows. But when our plane landed, the world didn't look so perfect close up. Streets were littered. The rivers were dirty. Some buildings were crumbling.

In a way, my grandma views me from a distance. I visit her every summer. She notices the good things I do. She thanks me for my courteous manners. But I know the real me. Crabby, sometimes sassy. Jealous of others. Wanting my own way. Lazy. Complaining. Not a pretty picture.

Even if others don't see our faults, we know they pollute our lives. In Psalm 90:8 God tells us that our secret sins are exposed in the light of His presence. God knew about the pollution of sin in our lives before we were born. That's why He sent Jesus to suffer and die—so our sins could be covered with His righteousness.

Jesus' saving work changed God's view of us. Because of Jesus' life and death, all our sins, even secret sins, are covered with His perfect and beautiful garment of salvation. Clothed in Christ's righteousness, we can enter heaven and celebrate with joy in the presence of God.

_____Let's talk: Which sins pollute your life? How does the Holy Spirit strengthen us to fight against sins?

_____Let's pray: Jesus, Your blood and righteousness are beautiful clothes. Thank You. Amen.

M. L. K.

The Sunny Side of the Clouds

Read from God's Word

Who shall separate us from the love of Christ? Shall trouble or hardship or persecution or famine or nakedness or danger or sword? As it is written: "For your sake we face death all day long; we are considered as sheep to be slaughtered." No, in all these things we are more than conquerors through Him who loved us. For I am convinced that neither death nor life, neither angels nor demons, neither the present nor the future, nor any powers, neither height nor depth, nor anything else in all creation, will be able to separate us from the love of God that is in Christ Jesus our Lord. Romans 8:35–39 ✍

The nice thing about flying is that you can rise above the dark, gloomy sky and view the world of uninterrupted sunshine.

A lot of people live on the gloomy side. Troubles, poverty, or lack of love cloud their vision. Life seems dark and hard, with no ray of cheer to ease their burdens.

Su-Lin's family was poor. Her father died when she was three years old, and her mother was frequently sick. Su-Lin had to work hard. She had to get up early to help with cooking and laundry.

It would have been easy for Su-Lin to see only the gloomy side of her life. But Su-Lin's mother had taught her to treasure God's Word. One of her favorite verses said, "In all things God works for the good of those who love Him" (Romans 8:28). Su-Lin thought about God's love. Since He loved her so much that He sent His own Son, Jesus, to save her, surely He would care in other ways as well.

Su-Lin felt happy about God's forgiving love. She saw His sunshine coming through in the loving care of those around her. Her hard work trained her for success in school. She felt rich with good friends. Despite her troubles, Su-Lin lived each day in the glorious sunshine of God's love.

_____Let's do: Draw and identify some "clouds" in your life. What are some ways God's love has shined on you? Draw in the rays of sun. Add a cross to remind you of Jesus.

_____Let's pray: Lord, I rejoice in the sunshine of Your love and forgiveness. Use me to spread Your light to others. In Jesus' name. Amen.

M. L. K.

Sewer Rescue

Read from God's Word

I waited patiently for the LORD; He turned to me and heard my cry. He lifted me out of the slimy pit, out of the mud and mire; He set my feet on a rock and gave me a firm place to stand. He put a new song in my mouth, a hymn of praise to our God. Many will see and fear and put their trust in the LORD. Blessed is the man who makes the LORD his trust, who does not look to the proud, to those who turn aside to false gods. Many, O LORD my God, are the wonders You have done. The things You planned for us no one can recount to You; were I to speak and tell of them, they would be too many to declare. Psalm 40:1–5

Juanita and a few of her friends were playing in a ditch near their home. As the girls prepared to head home, a thunderous downpour tumbled out of the sky.

Almost instantly, flash flood waters swirled down the ditch. Juanita's friends glanced back to see her struggling against the swift current, hands outstretched. Then she was gone, swept into the sewer with the sudden rush of swirling water.

After searching all night, rescue crews gave up hope of finding Juanita. Early the next morning, some distance away, workmen were checking the sewer line for damage. As they opened a manhole, they noticed the girl far below.

"I held onto a crack," explained the bruised but safe Juanita as she was rescued.

Without warning we are frequently swept away by the devil's stormy temptations. Unless we are rescued, eternal death in hell threatens us. God, our heavenly Father, loved His children and sent Jesus to rescue all people from sin, eternal death, and the power of the devil.

King David said that sin had dragged him down into a slimy, hopeless pit. He felt sorry for his sins and begged God to forgive him. God's forgiveness was complete. Many of David's psalms are songs of praise to God for rescuing him from the devil and the awful hole of sin.

_____Let's talk: What are some ways that the devil may tempt you to sin? What would you say to someone who feels sorry that he or she has sinned?

_____Let's pray: Lord, make us strong against the stormy attacks of the devil. Forgive our sins for Jesus' sake, and lift us from the pit of sin to Your heavenly home. Amen.

M. L. K.

I Am Sending You!

Ben could have been a computer programmer or an engineer. He was smart. He was a go-getter. Instead, today Ben molds lives. He influences young children, and he comforts the elderly. Each day is an opportunity, an adventure.

Ben is a DCE. That stands for Director of Christian Education. He was called to help lead people to know Jesus as their Savior. People of all ages hear Ben share his faith.

One day at chapel Ben called LaShonda to come and put on a white T-shirt. It covered her spotted dress. He put a shiny gold crown on her head. "This is a reminder of your Baptism," Ben said. "Jesus' righteousness covers all the spots of our sin. We are children of the King. We'll live with Him in heaven."

The children remembered the Good News about Jesus that had been told in a special way.

Read from God's Word

After this the Lord appointed seventy-two others and sent them two by two ahead of Him to every town and place where He was about to go. He told them, "The harvest is plentiful, but the workers are few. Ask the Lord of the harvest, therefore, to send out workers into His harvest field. Go! I am sending you out like lambs among wolves. Do not take a purse or bag or sandals; and do not greet anyone on the road. When you enter a house, first say, 'Peace to this house.' If a man of peace is there, your peace will rest on him; if not, it will return to you." Luke 10:1–6

God is using Ben to tell many people about Jesus' love every day. The Bible says: "The harvest is plentiful, but the workers are few." Each day many people die in their sins because they haven't heard about Jesus, their Savior. To people rejoicing in Jesus' love, God says, "Go. I am sending you to tell others!"

_____Let's talk: What special talents has God given you for sharing the Good News about Jesus? What could you tell someone who doesn't know Jesus' love? Ask your pastor or teacher about different kinds of church work.

_____Let's pray: Lord, show me what I can do for You so others may share Your glory too. Amen.

M. L. K.

september

Needed Rest

"Want to work on your pitching tomorrow?" Andrew asked.

"No," replied Chris. "I'm going to church, and besides, my arm needs a rest."

"A rest?" Andrew didn't know that pitchers perform much better after their muscles have had time to rest and get stronger.

Even God rested. He didn't rest to get more strength or fix mistakes. He worked for six days creating the world and rested on the seventh because He wanted to. He rested to celebrate.

Years later, when God gave the Ten Commandments on Mount Sinai, He required His children to rest on the Sabbath. The people of Israel would rest and see how perfectly God had provided for them. They would rest and celebrate God's goodness.

Sometimes we skip a special kind of celebration rest—Sunday worship. Our sinful desires tempt us into thinking that other things, like pitching practice or just sleeping in, would benefit us more.

Read from God's Word

God saw all that He had made, and it was very good. And there was evening, and there was morning—the sixth day. Thus the heavens and the earth were completed in all their vast array. By the seventh day God had finished the work He had been doing; so on the seventh day He rested from all His work. And God blessed the seventh day and made it holy, because on it He rested from all the work of creating that He had done. Genesis 1:31–2:3

If we skip worship, we miss its blessings. In church we gather with our family in Christ to sing and celebrate God's glory. We pray for one another. We listen to the pastor tell of Jesus' death and resurrection, the forgiveness of sins, and the gift of heaven. We receive strength in God's Word and Sacraments. We are gifted with the rest we need to celebrate and go on.

_____Let's talk: What are your favorite parts of Sunday worship?

_____Let's pray: Dear heavenly Father, thank You for giving us
Sunday as a special day to celebrate You. In Jesus'
name we pray. Amen.

R. B.

Read from God's Word

Trust in the LORD and do good; dwell in the land and enjoy safe pasture. Delight yourself in the LORD and He will give you the desires of your heart. Commit your way to the LORD; trust in Him and He will do this: He will make your righteousness shine like the dawn, the justice of your cause like the noonday sun. Psalm 37:3–6

Center Lines

"Why are there lines on the highway?" asked Dominique.

"Those lines help to keep people safe as they travel," Dad explained. "We share the road with others. Lines on the road divide it into lanes. It's one way to keep us safe and get us where we want to go."

We have guidelines for our life journey too. God gives us His guidelines in the Bible. His Word shows us the way to live—like the centerline on the highway. Hard as we try, we can't stay in our place near the centerline. We do things like fight over who gets the best seat (swerve toward the curb) or cheat on a quiz (off in the ditch). We can't live the way God wants us to, so we wander off the road.

What hope do we have? We have Jesus. He lived perfectly in place on the road! Jesus did what we could never do, and He did it in love for us. When His work on earth was done, He died on a cross and rose from death for each of us. Through faith in Jesus, God offers us forgiveness of sins and life everlasting. God gives us His grace through His Word and Sacraments so we might be with Him each day until we journey to heaven.

_____Let's do: Sketch your life as a road or highway. Draw a sign that asks God to be the center of all you do.

_____Let's pray: Dear heavenly Father, thank You for loving and caring for us. Help us share Your love with others. Amen.

R. B.

Free to Sing

I t had been a disappointing day for Rachel—a squabble with her best friend and the discovery of overdue library books under her bed. So she put in a new CD and started to sing.

Rachel sometimes hits sour notes and has been known to sing off-key, sending the dog right out of the room. Sometimes singing helps her feel better; other times it doesn't.

What happens when we *act* off-key? What if we mess up our thoughts or actions? What if we complain or talk back? What if we lie and then lie about lying? What a sour song, a sin medley!

Our conscience, informed by God's Word, can't stand to have us involved in that sin medley. It reminds us we are not acting or reacting in God's way. We know our awful actions are not okay; we are led by God to confess our sins.

God puts His arms around us and covers our sin-sour notes with His grace. God forgives our sins because Jesus set us free from sin through His perfect life and death and resurrection. Through Jesus' sacrifice, God gives us freedom to talk and walk a "new song." Even when we mess up our freedom in Christ, God loves us and forgives us again and again for Jesus' sake.

Read from God's Word

"Then you will know the truth, and the truth will set you free." They answered Him, "We are Abraham's descendants and have never been slaves of anyone. How can you say that we shall be set free?" Jesus replied, "I tell you the truth, everyone who sins is a slave to sin. Now a slave has no permanent place in the family, but a son belongs to it forever. So if the Son sets you free, you will be free indeed." John 8:32–36

_____Let's do: Describe God's work in your life in a musical way.
            Sing your favorite hymn about Jesus.

_____Let's pray: Dear heavenly Father, help us sing out the freedom
            Jesus won for us. In Jesus' name we pray. Amen.

R. B.

Securely Rooted

Read from God's Word

I pray that out of His glorious riches He may strengthen you with power through His Spirit in your inner being, so that Christ may dwell in your hearts through faith. And I pray that you, being rooted and established in love, may have power, together with all the saints, to grasp how wide and long and high and deep is the love of Christ, and to know this love that surpasses knowledge—that you may be filled to the measure of all the fullness of God. Now to Him who is able to do immeasurably more than all we ask or imagine, according to His power that is at work within us, to Him be glory in the church and in Christ Jesus throughout all generations, for ever and ever! Amen. Ephesians 3:15–21 ✍

Justin pulled, using all his weight. He finally pulled the stubborn cabbage plant out of the ground.

"What are these funny hair-like strings?" he asked his dad.

"They're roots. They hold the plant firmly in the ground," explained Dad. "The fine root hairs soak up water from the soil to feed the plant. Without them, the plant would blow over in the breeze."

We need to be strongly rooted so when the winds of sin blow in our direction, we can stand firm. When we are tempted, we need a source of strength bigger than ourselves to keep us strong and well rooted.

Our roots will sink deep and secure in God's "soil." When Jesus died on the cross and rose again, He saved us from sin and all the evil winds the devil can blow at us. In His Word, we learn how God promises to guard and protect us from harm and to comfort us when we are afraid or sad.

God's redeeming water in Baptism has power over the devil, our own sinful ways, and death itself. The Holy Spirit continues to feed us through God's Word, which is taught to us by Christian parents, Sunday school teachers, and pastors. Whenever we hear God's Word, the Holy Spirit strengthens our root system—our relationship with God.

_____Let's do: Draw the root system of a plant. Record the events of your Baptism or spiritual growth around the roots.

_____Let's pray: Dear heavenly Father, help us stay rooted in Your Word so we can grow strong and healthy as Your children. In Jesus' name we pray. Amen.

R. B.

Labor Day Off

Why did they name the holiday "Labor Day"? For many people, it's a holiday. They might sleep late, play with friends, or go swimming and have a picnic. It's more of a rest day than a labor day.

Actually, it is called Labor Day to celebrate how hard people work on *other* days. A hundred years ago people got very few holidays. They worked six or seven days a week, 12 or more hours a day. They needed a day off. In 1894, President Grover Cleveland made Labor Day a national holiday in the United States. Soon it became a holiday in Canada too.

Does life ever seem like hard labor to you? You work hard in school. You work hard to get along with your friends. Maybe sometimes school and friends don't work out so well. Do you ever feel tired of that—or sad or discouraged about it?

Jesus promises us a day off. He says, "Come to Me, all you who are weary and burdened, and I will give you rest." Somehow, He'll help us learn whatever we need to learn. He'll be our best friend, right there with us, even when we're "on the outs" with the other kids.

Jesus is giving us His "rest" every day—now and forever in heaven.

> ## Read from God's Word
> *Jesus said, "I praise You, Father, Lord of heaven and earth, because You have hidden these things from the wise and learned, and revealed them to little children. Yes, Father, for this was Your good pleasure. All things have been committed to Me by My Father. No one knows the Son except the Father, and no one knows the Father except the Son and those to whom the Son chooses to reveal Him. Come to Me, all you who are weary and burdened, and I will give you rest. Take My yoke upon you and learn from Me, for I am gentle and humble in heart, and you will find rest for your souls. For My yoke is easy and My burden is light." Matthew 11:25–30* ✍

—————Let's talk: Jesus labored very hard to give us an eternal "holiday." How? What did He do?

—————Let's pray: Dear Jesus, thank You for working so hard for us— even dying on a cross! Thanks for giving us a day off and for being with us every day! Amen.

C. F.

It's in the Heart

Read from God's Word

For we brought nothing into the world, and we can take nothing out of it. But if we have food and clothing, we will be content with that. People who want to get rich fall into temptation and a trap and into many foolish and harmful desires that plunge men into ruin and destruction. For the love of money is a root of all kinds of evil. Some people, eager for money, have wandered from the faith and pierced themselves with many griefs. But you, man of God, flee from all this, and pursue righteousness, godliness, faith, love, endurance and gentleness. Fight the good fight of the faith. Take hold of the eternal life to which you were called when you made your good confession in the presence of many witnesses. 1 Timothy 6:7–12 ✐

Dario's brother, Habil, was going to college. He was getting all the new stuff—phone, computer, clothes, and now, a party. It wasn't fair.

Dario was jealous of his brother. It was just a tiny thought and then it turned ugly—into a giant attitude problem. Now this big, major, rumbling giant of an attitude problem was controlling Dario's heart.

I'll show them, he thought as he stayed in his room all day, avoiding the happy crowd. Just when he began to have regrets, he heard a knock at his door.

"There you are. May I come in?" asked Habil.

"I guess," mumbled Dario, half-surprised and half-glad.

"Where have you been? I missed you at the party. Won't you come and celebrate with me?" asked Habil.

Habil's kind words had an effect on Dario's attitude. Dario found himself apologizing, "I'm sorry that I've been so grumpy."

Habil found Dario—but God found him too. He led Dario to confess and apologize. He finds us in the same way when we are sinful and weak. He reminds us that He loves us and that He sent Jesus to take the punishment for our self-centeredness and our jealousy. Jesus' death and resurrection brought forgiveness and eternal life to all God's children. And that's something to celebrate.

_____Let's talk: Have you ever been robbed of joy by jealousy? What might you pray for the next time you feel jealous?

_____Let's pray: Dear heavenly Father, help us see our blessings and praise You for them. Thank You for sending Jesus to be our Savior. In His name we pray. Amen.

R. B.

Take My Hand

ever cross the street unless you hold someone's hand. That was the rule for three-year-old Sarah, who needed someone to guide and protect her.

"My sheep listen to My voice; I know them, and they follow Me. I give them eternal life, and they shall never perish; no one can snatch them out of My hand. My Father, who has given them to Me, is greater than all; no one can snatch them out of My Father's hand. I and the Father are one." John 10:27–30

As we cross through life, we might grab hands that encourage us to want more—certain clothes, shoes, or toys. If those hands could talk, they would say, "Come with me. I'll take you across to Happy Land." We might grab our friends' hands and be led into dangerous intersections of thinking. Those hands might say, "Come with me to the crossroads of excitement and popularity." Sometimes we discover in time that we were being tempted to grasp the hand of a false friend—but other times we sin. Ever since we were born, sin has grabbed us, leading us away from God and filling us with false hope.

God's hands will never lead us the wrong way or fill us with false hope. God's hands provide us with all we really need to live on earth. God's hands reached out beyond our earthly needs and provided a cure for sin in Jesus. And this perfect Jesus let death grasp Him on the cross. Jesus hung and died there, paying a price for sin we could not pay. His victorious, nail-pierced hands support us each day and will welcome us to heaven.

_____Let's talk: Share a time when you were in danger and you received a helping hand.

_____Let's pray: Dear God, we are thankful for Your protecting hands. We especially thank You for sending Jesus to be our friend and Savior. In His name we pray. Amen.

R. B.

Read from God's Word

Let the word of Christ dwell in you richly as you teach and admonish one another with all wisdom, and as you sing psalms, hymns and spiritual songs with gratitude in your hearts to God.
Colossians 3:16

Good Nutrition

The fifth graders kept a journal of every meal they skipped or ate at a fast-food restaurant and why. Alyssa's list looked like this:

Monday—Supper at Burger World after soccer practice

Tuesday—Skipped breakfast because I overslept

Friday—Pizza at church with youth group

Sunday—Breakfast at The Big Egg after church

Cullen's list was much shorter and looked like this:

Wednesday—Pizza at Pizza Pizzazz after hockey game

Sunday—Breakfast at The Big Egg after hockey practice

If Cullen is eating most of his meals at home, then it's likely he is getting the vitamins and minerals his body needs. If Alyssa eats mostly pizza and burgers, then her body is probably missing nutrients.

What food does our spirit need? It needs God's Word, which satisfies our hunger to know God and to understand His love.

Some children are starving. They skip listening to God's Word in church and Sunday school. They miss God's spiritual food.

God still loves them and wants them to live with Him forever in heaven. That's why He sent His only Son, Jesus, to die on a cross for everyone. God promises that whoever believes in Jesus will have eternal life. You're not starving when you know Christ and have the "good food" of God's Word!

_____Let's do: For one week, keep track of the times you read, study, or listen to God's Word.

_____Let's pray: Dear Jesus, we're sorry we put other things in life ahead of You. Forgive us and help us. Amen.

S. C.

Acts of Courage

Read from God's Word

Be on your guard; stand firm in the faith; be men of courage; be strong. Do everything in love.
1 Corinthians 16:13–14 ✐

Pulling somebody from a burning house. Diving into a swimming pool to save a drowning child. These are examples of courageous and heroic acts. In our lives as Christians, courage is not always shown in heroic acts.

It's natural to pray in church or before we go to sleep. It's comfortable to talk about Jesus with our friends in Sunday school. But how do we act when we're not at home or with other Christians?

Do we always pray before eating in school or when we're at a restaurant? Do we talk to our friends about Jesus?

The Bible passage encourages us to "stand firm in the faith; be men [and women, girls and boys] of courage," but we do not always have the courage to share our faith. We are afraid people might make fun of us or think we are weak or stupid. Even Peter, one of Jesus' disciples, pretended he did not know Jesus because he was afraid of what people would think.

We can pray, asking God to give us the courage to live and share our faith. And when we fail to have that courage, God will forgive us because Jesus died on the cross for all of our sins. His courage is ours in life and death.

_____Let's do: Write about opportunities you have to be a courageous Christian, living and sharing your faith.

_____Let's pray: Dear Jesus, thank You for loving us even when we do not have the courage to show our love toward You. Help us to show our love for You. Amen.

S. C.

God Takes Care of Us

Read from God's Word

"Therefore I tell you, do not worry about your life, what you will eat or drink; or about your body, what you will wear. Is not life more important than food, and the body more important than clothes? Look at the birds of the air; they do not sow or reap or store away in barns, and yet your heavenly Father feeds them. Are you not much more valuable than they? Who of you by worrying can add a single hour to his life?" Matthew 6:25–27

Danilee's mom had cancer and was very sick. Danilee did her best to clean and fix their meals.

Danilee was worried. What would happen to her if her mom died? She hadn't seen her dad since she was five, and her grandparents had died a few years ago.

Danilee felt guilty for worrying about herself. But she thought, *If Mom dies, she gets to go to heaven—but who will take care of me?*

Every night before they said their bedtime prayers, her mother would say, "Danilee, will you read to me about how God takes care of the birds and the flowers?" Then Danilee would get her mom's Bible and read Matthew 6:25–34. When she was finished, her mother would say, "Remember, Danilee, God loves you more than birds and flowers. He sent Jesus here to die for you and me."

One day Danilee came home and saw a woman sitting by her mother on the couch. "Come here, Danilee," her mother said. "I want you to meet Moriah, your godmother. You haven't seen her since you were a baby. She's going to stay with us until I get well."

Danilee was happy. God answered her prayers by providing for her care and for her mom's—just as He provided a Savior for her sins.

_____Let's do: Write about the biggest thing you've ever worried and prayed about. How did God answer your prayers?

_____Let's pray: Dear Father, thank You for taking care of us and always giving us everything we need. In Jesus' name. Amen.

S. C.

Looks Aren't Everything

Mercedes and Junior were at the humane society, choosing a kitten. "I want the cute one with the black paw," squealed Mercedes.

"How about the little gray one?" suggested their grandmother.

"No way!" Mercedes and Junior said in unison. "That one's too small and ugly."

The Lord sent Samuel to anoint a new king for His people. Samuel went to the house of Jesse. When he saw Jesse's oldest son—big, strong, handsome Eliab—Samuel immediately thought he was the one God wanted.

But God told Samuel not to choose Eliab. God said, "The LORD does not look at the things man looks at. Man looks at the outward appearance, but the LORD looks at the heart." The Lord had chosen Jesse's youngest and smallest son, David, who grew up to be a great king.

Read from God's Word

When they arrived, Samuel saw Eliab and thought, "Surely the LORD's anointed stands here before the LORD." But the LORD said to Samuel, "Do not consider his appearance or his height, for I have rejected him. The LORD does not look at the things man looks at. Man looks at the outward appearance, but the LORD looks at the heart." 1 Samuel 16:6–7

God does not choose us based on how we look or act. It's a good thing, because we are not able to keep our hearts and minds pure and holy. We are sinful. Yet the Bible assures us that we are nothing less than "sons [and daughters] of God through faith in Christ Jesus" (Galatians 3:26). As His children we wear the "good looks" that Jesus gave us—His robe of righteousness. We are free to live as God's beautiful children.

_____Let's do: Write about a time when you were misjudged or when you misjudged another person. How can God help you in those kinds of struggles?

_____Let's pray: Father, create in me a clean heart, and renew a steadfast spirit within me. In Jesus' name. Amen.

S. C.

Read from God's Word

Finally, brothers, whatever is true, whatever is noble, whatever is right, whatever is pure, whatever is lovely, whatever is admirable— if anything is excellent or praise-worthy—think about such things. Whatever you have learned or received or heard from me, or seen in me—put it into practice. And the God of peace will be with you. Philippians 4:8–9

A Little Bit

"I'm sorry about getting mad earlier, Mom." Cordell said. "But I don't understand why you won't let me go see that movie. It only has a few bad parts."

"Add a teaspoon of this to the cookie dough," Mom said, handing Cordell a small plastic bag.

Cordell opened the bag. "Ugh, it smells awful! What is it?"

"It's from the compost pile. Just add one little teaspoon."

"But, Mom, compost is garbage!" Cordell protested.

"But it's only a *little* bit," replied his mother. "If watching a movie with a few bad parts is okay, then surely a little bit of ..."

"Okay, I get it," interrupted Cordell. "But, Mom, the world is full of bad stuff. I can't spend the rest of my life in my room."

"You're right, but there's no need to purposely watch and listen to the bad stuff. Our hearts and minds are naturally filled with enough sinful thoughts."

"Hey," said Cordell, "my Sunday school teacher said that whatever is in our hearts and minds will show up in what we say and do."

"That's right," said Mom. "Jesus gave His life so we would be free from sin. He will fill our hearts and minds with good stuff."

"Yep," said Cordell. "And let's keep the garbage where it belongs."

_____Let's do: Write about the last time you weren't allowed to do something you wanted to. Why weren't you allowed to do it? What do you think about it now?

_____Let's pray: Dear Jesus, please fill our hearts and minds with Your love and help us turn away from the bad things in the world. Amen.

S. C.

A Member of the Club

"There's no catch, Dad!" Jacques said confidently. "It's free. When I join the club, I get to pick out six free CDs. The CD club will automatically send me a new CD every month, and all I have to do is buy four more CDs this year. Please, Dad!"

Father agreed to let Jacques join the club. Four weeks later the CDs arrived with a shipping and handling bill for $10.50. Jacques hadn't expected to pay shipping charges but he sent in the payment, determined to keep his promise.

The next month, Jacques received another CD in the mail. It wasn't exactly what he wanted. And it cost more money than the local department store charged. He sent in the payment and began to worry. How would he buy the CDs his membership required?

For the next several months, Jacques felt very poor. All the money he earned went to the CD club. Finally, he completed his obligation and canceled his membership.

Read from God's Word

He saved us, not because of righteous things we had done, but because of His mercy. He saved us through the washing of rebirth and renewal by the Holy Spirit, whom He poured out on us generously through Jesus Christ our Savior, so that, having been justified by His grace, we might become heirs having the hope of eternal life. This is a trustworthy saying. And I want you to stress these things, so that those who have trusted in God may be careful to devote themselves to doing what is good. These things are excellent and profitable for everyone. Titus 3:5–8 ✍

As baptized children of God, we have been given a free membership into God's family. Unlike Jacques's CD club, there is no catch. As sinners we could never "meet the commitments" to earn God's favor on our own. But through Jesus' perfect life and death, we have a fully paid membership into the family of God.

———Let's talk: Have you or your friends ever started a club? How is it like being part of God's family? How is it different?

———Let's pray: Dear Father, thank You for sending Jesus to be our Savior and for giving us the gift of eternal life. Amen.

S. C.

The Holy Cross

For Christians, the cross is a symbol of our salvation. It reminds us that Jesus died on the cross as payment for our sins so we could live with Him forever in heaven.

The Mormon religion teaches that the cross is a sign of pain and suffering. They do not display crosses. People of the Jewish faith don't have crosses in their temples or synagogues. They don't believe that their salvation comes from Jesus. Jehovah's Witnesses think that Jesus died on the cross for the sins of Adam, not the whole world. Muslims know that Jesus lived, but they think He somehow escaped being crucified and just made it look as if He was.

How sad for these and other non-Christians who don't know or believe that Jesus died on the cross to pay for the sins of the entire world!

Whenever we see a cross, we are reminded of John 3:16: "For God so loved the world that He gave His one and only Son, that whoever believes in Him shall not perish but have eternal life." Let us pray that God would send His Holy Spirit into the hearts of all nonbelievers so they might know the love and victory gift Jesus gave in His life and death on the cross.

_____Let's do: Do you know somebody who does not know Jesus? Write his or her name in your journal and draw a cross above the name daily until you get a chance to tell that person about our Savior.

_____Let's pray: Dear Father, please send the Holy Spirit to spark faith in nonbelievers so they might know of Your love and plan of salvation through Jesus Christ. Amen.

S. C.

Wild Cards!

What is baseball coming to? The first-place teams in the divisions are pretty strong. But some of the wild-card teams have no business being in contention! They've lost more games than they've won and still could make it to the World Series!

In the old days, you had to be good to keep playing in October. How can they let average teams into the series?

In today's Bible reading, certain Pharisees complained to Jesus' disciples about something like this. They thought they were the good people. And they couldn't understand why Jesus let bad sinners into His company.

Jesus explained that His whole mission was to save sinners. His death on the cross was for the very purpose of taking away sin. He didn't come to earth because people are good. He came because no one is good. Everybody needs a Savior.

Read from God's Word

As Jesus went on from there, He saw a man named Matthew sitting at the tax collector's booth. "Follow Me," He told him, and Matthew got up and followed Him. While Jesus was having dinner at Matthew's house, many tax collectors and "sinners" came and ate with Him and His disciples. When the Pharisees saw this, they asked His disciples, "Why does your teacher eat with tax collectors and 'sinners'?" On hearing this, Jesus said, "It is not the healthy who need a doctor, but the sick. But go and learn what this means: 'I desire mercy, not sacrifice.' For I have not come to call the righteous, but sinners." Matthew 9:9–13 ✍

When you think about it, we're not like dynamite, first-place teams, are we? We're really not even as good as the wild-card contenders. We're losers in sin through and through. Isn't it wonderful? Jesus came for sinners like us! And in Jesus' league, sinners like us—losing records and all—are always welcome to play.

_____Let's talk: How does your sin make you like a losing baseball team? Does God see you as a loser? Why not?

_____Let's pray: Father, thank You for putting me on Your team forever despite my sin, for the sake of Jesus. Amen.

C. F.

More Than Plenty

H ave you ever gone blueberry picking? You drive out into the country until you see a sign: U PICK EM. The owner of the field gives you a bucket, and you start picking. Then you go home and eat them!

Sound good? In most parts of the country the picking season is nearly over, so you might want to go soon. Don't worry, though. There are always plenty of berries left. That's the best part! No matter how many people have been out picking before you, you'll still fill your bucket.

As the Israelites entered the Promised Land, God gave special instructions about picking their fields. They were not to harvest every last olive or grape or sheaf of grain. They were to leave some so poor people could come later and pick the rest.

God would always make sure there was more than enough for everyone. God blessed Israel with such rich harvests that an owner could have all he needed and still leave plenty for others.

God always blesses us too! He gives us family, food, clothes, and a home. More than that, He gives us love and forgiveness and eternal life through Jesus. Everything we need—and enough to share!

_____Let's talk: Why is God so generous? With whom can you share His abundant love?

_____Let's pray: Dear God, thank You for everything, especially faith in Your Son. Help me to share. Amen.

C. F.

Do You Believe Me?

I've got something really exciting in this box! Let me just check and see ... Yep, it's still in there. Know what it is? It's a $100 bill! That's right. This little box sitting next to my computer has a $100 bill inside. See?

Oh, that's right. You can't see. But it's there. It's green, about, oh, six inches long and maybe two or three inches wide. And it's got a picture of Ben Franklin on it. See, I told you I had a $100 bill in the box.

Long before Jesus was born, God told people such as Noah and Abraham and Moses that a Savior would come someday. They never saw Jesus, but they believed God's promises. That's called faith.

We haven't seen Jesus either, but the Bible says Jesus came to earth and lived as a real human being. It tells us Jesus died on the cross for our sins and then rose again to give us eternal life. Do you believe that? Even though you haven't seen Jesus? Even though you haven't seen heaven? That's faith, God's gift to us through the Holy Spirit.

Okay, shall I show you the $100 bill? Sorry, I can't. Faith doesn't work that way. But it is in there. Believe me.

Read from God's Word

Now faith is being sure of what we hope for and certain of what we do not see. This is what the ancients were commended for. These were all commended for their faith, yet none of them received what had been promised. God had planned something better for us so that only together with us would they be made perfect. Hebrews 11:1–2, 39–40

_____Let's talk: Faith believes things we can't see. But will we ever see the One we've believed in—Jesus? When? What do you think that will be like?

_____Let's pray: Dear Jesus, though I don't see You now, I believe in You. Please keep my faith strong until I see You in heaven. Amen.

C. F.

How to Find Fish

Grandpa told us there were plenty of fish in the pond, but all we could see was the thick layer of bright green scum.

"How will we find the fish?" six-year-old Rachel wondered.

"Don't worry. The fish will find us," my wife assured her.

That's the way fishing works, isn't it? Your bait is in the water and the fish come to you.

Peter, Andrew, James, and John were fishermen, but they weren't fishing when they met Jesus. They weren't looking for Jesus. Jesus came looking for them. Jesus called, "Come, follow Me."

A lot of people spend a lot of time and effort trying to find God. They try out different religions. They work hard to do what they think God would like. But all our looking will never find God.

Fortunately, Christ Jesus finds us! In His Word, right now, He's reaching out to us. He comes looking to give us the forgiveness He earned for everybody on the cross. And to those He finds, He gives a place in His heavenly kingdom.

After Jesus found them, Peter and the others "caught" people for Jesus by telling them He was their Savior. We can go fishing for people too. And even if we can't see how we'll ever catch a thing, don't worry. Jesus will find them.

_____Let's talk: Why did Jesus come looking for you? For whom could you fish for Jesus?

_____Let's pray: Dear Jesus, I have a friend I'd like to "catch" for You. Please move _____ to believe in You when I tell about Your love. Amen.

C. F.

Strike the Pose!

The wide receiver catches the pass ... He breaks into the clear ... To the 10, to the 5 ... Touchdown! The crowd goes wild! TV cameras zoom in to catch the antics of Mr. Touchdown.

Maybe it's a dance. Maybe a football spike or a Heisman Trophy pose. But it's broadcast for fans nationwide to enjoy.

In backyards and on school playgrounds, those antics are imitated by hundreds of would-be football pros. In their eagerness, they imitate the people they wish to become.

Even before we were born, God planned what we should become. Today's Bible reading says that God has been planning to make us like Jesus, and now it's happening!

When we were baptized, we became God's children, just as Jesus is God's Son. Every time we hear His Word, God is shaping us to live like Christ. Someday, in heaven, our bodies will even be glorified like Jesus' body.

Read from God's Word

For those God foreknew He also predestined to be conformed to the likeness of His Son, that He might be the firstborn among many brothers. And those He predestined, He also called; those He called, He also justified; those He justified, he also glorified. Romans 8:29–30

We can love people like Jesus did. We can serve others as Jesus served when He gave His life on the cross to pay for our sins. We can let others know what Jesus is like by the way we play and talk and work. We can imitate Jesus for everyone to see!

_____Let's talk: What to you is the best part of being like Jesus? Can you let others see it?

_____Let's pray: Heavenly Father, thank You for making me Your child and giving me a home in heaven with Your Son. Help me to be like Him every day. Amen.

C. F.

Read from God's Word

He was despised and rejected by men, a man of sorrows, and familiar with suffering. Like one from whom men hide their faces He was despised, and we esteemed Him not. Surely He took up our infirmities and carried our sorrows, yet we considered Him stricken by God, smitten by Him, and afflicted. But He was pierced for our transgressions, He was crushed for our iniquities; the punishment that brought us peace was upon Him, and by His wounds we are healed. Isaiah 53:3–5

Who Am I?

What is it?
    Can you guess?
A crowd gathers round it. They laugh.
    They shout.
They tug it. They beat it.
    They give it a clout.
They strike it. They bruise it.
    It hangs from a tree.
They pierce it. They crush it.
    Its insides spill out.
They mob it. They grab it.
    For what do they see?
The one that they broke gives
        them prizes—for free!
    Can you guess what it is?

    It's a piñata! A piñata is a party tradition in Mexico, parts of the United States, and other countries. It is brightly colored pottery or papier-mâché shaped like an animal or some other figure. It's filled with candy and hung overhead by a rope. Blindfolded children try to break the piñata with a stick. And when they do, there's a mad scramble for the goodies! Everybody has a great time!

Who am I? Can you guess?
    A crowd gathers round Me. They laugh. They jeer.
    They tug at Me, beat Me. They nail Me up here.
    They strike Me. They bruise Me. They hang Me up high.
    They crush Me. They pierce Me, not shedding a tear.
    They spill out My blood, and I let them. But why?
    That these and all sinners may live when I die.
    Can you guess who I am?

_____Let's do: Draw or imagine a piñata exploding. What are the prizes Jesus gives us?

_____Let's pray: Lord Jesus, I don't always remember how terrible Your suffering and death was. Thank You for going through it for me! Amen.

C. F.

Refrigerator's Open

G abriel was barely one year old, but there she stood at the refrigerator reaching for the grape jelly. As we watched her, we knew she would make a mess, but we were thrilled for her to help herself.

We always hear about the younger son who left home, blew it all, and came back. The beauty of the story is that the father eagerly welcomed him home. Jesus was teaching us that God always forgives us and welcomes us back when we sin because Jesus died for those sins.

There was another son in Jesus' parable. The older son was angry when his brother returned. "All these years I've been slaving for you," he complained to his father. "Yet you never gave me even a young goat so I could celebrate with my friends."

You know what? That older brother had been missing something all along. "My son," the father said, "you are always with me, and everything I have is yours." Not only a young goat, but also the whole refrigerator was always open to him.

That's the way our heavenly Father is with us. Everything He has (and that's everything!) He gladly gives us. His love. His forgiveness. Eternal life. Milk and bread and jelly. As far as God is concerned, His refrigerator is our refrigerator.

Read from God's Word

Jesus continued: "There was a man who had two sons. The younger one said to his father, 'Father, give me my share of the estate.' So he divided his property between them. Not long after that, the younger son got together all he had, set off for a distant country and there squandered his wealth in wild living. . . . and he began to be in need. . . . So he got up and went to his father. . . . 'Father, I have sinned against heaven and against you. I am no longer worthy to be called your son.' But the father said to his servants, 'Quick! Bring the best robe and put it on him. Put a ring on his finger and sandals on his feet. Bring the fattened calf and kill it. Let's have a feast and celebrate. For this son of mine was dead and is alive again; he was lost and is found.' So they began to celebrate. . . . The older brother became angry . . . 'My son,' the father said, 'you are always with me, and everything I have is yours. But we had to celebrate and be glad, because this brother of yours was dead and is alive again; he was lost and is found.'" Luke 15:11–32 ✍

———Let's talk: What do you like best about God saying that everything He has is yours?

———Let's pray: Dear Father, thank You for being such a dear Father. Amen.

T. R.

Real Reality

The jet fighter rumbles down the runway, gaining speed. The wheels bump, the cockpit bounces, and you are airborne.

You climb through the clouds, soaring overhead. Then suddenly you plunge toward earth, diving toward a canyon. Finally you pull up and burst through the sound barrier.

What a trip! And you never left "The Mach 1 Adventure." You were strapped into a seat that bounced and rolled. Your eyes were glued to a screen five stories tall—all inside a theater.

It looked, sounded, and felt real. It was not reality, but *virtual* reality!

It's easy to think that what we see and feel is real. Usually it is. It's much harder to understand that invisible things can be real too. But there is a whole reality out there we can't see.

We can't see our heavenly Father. We've never seen Jesus in the flesh. We can't see His angels. We forget how real they are when we need them the most. When you're worried, your Father in heaven is making the right stuff happen. Even when you're lonely, Jesus is in your room with you. And when you're afraid, God's angels are there, holding a shield in front of you. You can't see them, hear them, or feel them. But that's the *real* reality.

_____Let's talk: How do you feel knowing Jesus is right here in the room with you now?

_____Let's pray: Dear Lord, although I can't see You with my eyes, open my heart to know You're always with me. Thanks! Amen.

C. F.

Valuable Treasures

S omewhere beneath the rolling waves lay a Spanish ship that sank long ago. When the ship went down in a storm, a Spanish king's fortune was instantly lost.

Nearly 300 years later Mel Fisher decided to devote his life to finding that Spanish ship. The search was very demanding and often discouraging. But finally Mr. Fisher and his crew found the treasure. The sunken gold and silver, worth $400 million, was their dream come true.

Finding a treasure worth millions of dollars would surely be exciting. Having so much money might give a person some happiness in this life. But in today's Bible reading we are told about a different kind of treasure, the treasure that lasts forever.

In the Gospel of Matthew, a man was willing to sell all he had in order to buy a field so its treasure would belong to him. Each time we read and study the Bible, we learn more about our greatest treasure, God's mercy and the forgiveness of sins.

Read from God's Word

"The kingdom of heaven is like treasure hidden in a field. When a man found it, he hid it again, and then in his joy went and sold all he had and bought that field. Again, the kingdom of heaven is like a merchant looking for fine pearls. When he found one of great value, he went away and sold everything he had and bought it." Matthew 13:44–46

When Jesus died on the cross, He purchased this priceless treasure for us. For Jesus' sake, God in His grace gives us the treasure of His kingdom— eternal life with Him. This heavenly treasure is far greater than any treasure found on earth, even one as valuable as Mr. Fisher's.

_____ Let's talk: What do you think Mr. Fisher did with his treasure? What does our heavenly treasure do for us? How can we share?

_____ Let's pray: Father in heaven, You have given us all we need. Thank You for also giving us the greatest treasure, eternal life with You. Help us to share it with others. Amen.

K. A. S.

Read from God's Word

"Therefore everyone who hears these words of Mine and puts them into practice is like a wise man who built his house on the rock. The rain came down, the streams rose, and the winds blew and beat against that house; yet it did not fall, because it had its foundation on the rock. But everyone who hears these words of Mine and does not put them into practice is like a foolish man who built his house on sand. The rain came down, the streams rose, and the winds blew and beat against that house, and it fell with a great crash." Matthew 7:24–27

Build on the Rock

Jesus told a parable about what happened to two houses during a storm. One man had built his house on the sand. His house looked fine—until the storms came. Then the wind and the rain destroyed it.

Another man built his house on a rock base. This solid foundation made the house able to withstand the raging storm.

Jesus is the solid ground on which we can build our lives. Our faith in Jesus enables us to survive danger and trouble. When the devil tempts us to feel worthless and guilty, Jesus, our solid foundation, assures us of His love and forgiveness.

The lives of people who do not know Jesus may at first seem okay. But then the storms of life and the temptations of the devil begin to blow and rage around them. Without faith in Jesus as their foundation, they're in danger of being totally lost.

God strengthens the faith foundation of our lives in many ways. One way is through devotions we read each day, like those in this book. Memorizing passages from the Bible and worshiping in church are other good ways to let the Holy Spirit build our faith on the solid rock of Jesus, the Word.

———Let's talk: Can you think of other ways your faith is strengthened? Why is it good to know that Jesus will never fail to support you?

———Let's pray: My hope is built on nothing less Than Jesus' blood and righteousness; ... On Christ, the solid rock, I stand; All other ground is sinking sand. (*LW* 368:1)

K. A. S.

Sharing Troubles

Read from God's Word

I have learned to be content whatever the circumstances. I know what it is to be in need, and I know what it is to have plenty. I have learned the secret of being content in any and every situation, whether well fed or hungry, whether living in plenty or in want. I can do everything through Him who gives me strength. ... And my God will meet all your needs according to His glorious riches in Christ Jesus. To our God and Father be glory for ever and ever. Amen. Philippians 4:11–20

"Hey, Jennifer, why the long face?" asked Marianne.

"Oh, no reason," replied Jennifer.

"Come on, Jen. I'm your best friend. Tell me what's wrong."

Jennifer told Marianne about the problems her parents were having. She confessed that it was hard to concentrate on schoolwork with so many problems at home.

Marianne listened. Her parents had gone through some of the same things. She understood how upset Jennifer felt.

When Jennifer saw that Marianne understood what she was going through, it made her feel better. Her problems seemed easier to face. She knew that by talking with her friend, she could get through this difficult time.

That night, before going to bed, Jennifer read her Bible. She found that Paul also had troubles—and friends who shared those troubles with him. He thanked the friends for sharing his trouble.

Jennifer wrote a note to Marianne, thanking her for listening. Then she thanked Jesus for giving her a friend like Marianne. She also thanked God, who gives us everything we need, including friends to share our troubles with.

Jesus is that kind of friend. He will help us through any problem. His cross is the proof of His eternal love for us. He died that we might have forgiveness.

_____Let's talk: Do you have a friend who depends on you in hard times? Who is always your best friend? Why?

_____Let's pray: Thank You, Jesus, for being our friend. Help us always remember that we can bring our problems to You in prayer. Thank You for the friends You give us. Help us be a friend to others. Amen.

K. A. S.

Read from God's Word

We must pay more careful attention, therefore, to what we have heard, so that we do not drift away. For if the message spoken by angels was binding, and every violation and disobedience received its just punishment, how shall we escape if we ignore such a great salvation? This salvation, which was first announced by the Lord, was confirmed to us by those who heard Him. God also testified to it by signs, wonders and various miracles, and gifts of the Holy Spirit distributed according to His will.
Hebrews 2:1–4

Drifting Away

Aaron and Jamal had been paired to lead on the family canoe trip. Since they were far ahead of the others, they devised their own fun as they waited for their pokey relatives.

They were unaware that their canoe was drifting in a swift current toward tricky white water. Suddenly, their canoe tipped and toppled them over. Both boys gasped for air as they struggled to keep their heads above the churning water. By the time the other canoes arrived, the boys had recovered from the horror of their drifting.

In today's Bible reading, we see that there is another kind of drifting—a spiritual drifting. Cares and worries of this world can cause our attention to drift away from Jesus. We may focus our lives on having the right clothes or certain friends. Faith in Christ, the forgiveness He offers for our sins, and the new life He brings may become less important to us.

The Bible can be our compass. It points out where we have drifted, reveals the correct course, and gives us new strength to follow it. Traveling through life with our Savior is great because He guarantees us peace, love, and forgiveness. When we sail with Jesus, we can look forward to being in heaven with Him.

_____Let's talk: What are some things in life that can cause you to drift away from faith in Jesus? What helps keep you on course?

_____Let's pray: Lord Jesus, You have promised to guide us and keep us safe in life. Please help us each day to look to You as our compass and guide. Help us always stay on the course You have set for us. Amen.

K. A. S.

Not to Worry

What if I don't get an A on this test? What if I don't get to pitch at that next ballgame?

Are you a worrier? A newspaper recently reported that people can now hire a company called a "worry service" to worry for them. Students can hire the service to worry about their tests in school.

The Bible tells about people who were worriers. Martha worried that her sister Mary wasn't helping. The disciples of Jesus worried about the children bothering the Lord when their mothers brought them to Him. They also worried about a terrible storm and having enough to feed 5,000 people who came to hear Jesus teach.

Jesus always knew what to do. He assured Martha that listening to His life-giving Word was more important than housework. The Savior let the disciples know that He loved having the children with Him. When His disciples feared for their lives on the sea, Jesus calmed the storm. He also miraculously fed thousands with a small amount of food.

Each morning you can wake up knowing that Jesus is watching over you. He will provide you with all you need each day. He loves you and forgives you all the time. That's why you can throw all your worry on the Lord—because He cares for you.

Read from God's Word

Therefore humble yourselves under the mighty hand of God, that He may exalt you in due time, casting all your care upon Him, for He cares for you.
1 Peter 5:6–7

_____Let's talk: What things do you sometimes worry about? How can you let Jesus take your worries for you?

_____Let's pray: When the worries of each day get in the way, help me, Jesus, to pray and ask You to take my worries away. Amen.

K. A. S.

Read from God's Word

"You are the light of the world. A city that is set on a hill cannot be hidden. Nor do they light a lamp and put it under a basket, but on a lampstand, and it gives light to all who are in the house. Let your light so shine before men, that they may see your good works and glorify your Father in heaven." Matthew 5:14–16 ✍

Why Be S.A.D.?

Mallory has a sickness the doctors call S.A.D., seasonal affective disorder.

This sickness occurs in the winter, when there is less sunlight. When it's dark, your brain makes a substance called melatonin to help you sleep. Mallory's brain needs plenty of sunshine to keep it from making too much melatonin.

Mallory's doctor has suggested that she spend more time outside early in the morning. Mallory has found that taking the time to be in the sunshine can help keep her from getting depressed.

The Bible tells us that you and I can become spiritually discouraged. In order to be strengthened we need to spend time in our spiritual sunshine, Jesus Christ. He said, "I am the Light of the world. Whoever follows Me will never walk in darkness, but will have the light of life" (John 8:12).

Jesus enlightens our minds with His Word. He brings us the Good News of forgiveness. Sin can drag us down and make us feel bad. When we know we're forgiven, the burden of our sins is removed from our hearts. We feel more alive and full of joy.

Although winter days offer less sunshine, our hearts will never be without the light of life, Jesus. His forgiveness and love will keep our days filled with "Son-shine."

_____Let's talk: What causes Mallory to feel depressed? What helps make her feel better? What can make our days seem dark? How does God's forgiveness brighten our days?

_____Let's pray: Lord, You are my light in dark times. You are always there to brighten my day. Thank You. Help me share Your sunshine with others. Amen.

K. A. S.

It's No Fake!

Years ago some Russian children claimed that they saw space creatures 12 feet tall with small heads. This story was later shown to be a fake.

There are people who believe that the Bible is full of stories made up in someone's imagination, like the story about space creatures.

In 1975 archaeologists in Syria made an amazing discovery. They found an ancient library containing more than 17,000 inscribed clay tablets.

On these tablets one can read about biblical people such as Abraham, David, and Saul. Recorded there are some events similar to those in the Bible.

We don't need proof from archaeology to help us believe what the Bible says. But these findings remind us that the stories of the Bible are not made up. They are true.

The apostle Peter wrote to his fellow believers that they could be sure

Read from God's Word

For we did not follow cunningly devised fables when we made known to you the power and coming of our Lord Jesus Christ, but were eyewitnesses of His majesty. For He received from God the Father honor and glory when such a voice came to Him from the Excellent Glory: "This is My beloved Son, in whom I am well pleased." And we heard this voice which came from heaven when we were with Him on the holy mountain. And so we have the prophetic word confirmed, which you do well to heed as a light that shines in a dark place, until the day dawns and the morning star rises in your hearts.
2 Peter 1:16–19

of the Bible's message. Peter saw the miracles Jesus performed. Jesus even healed Peter's mother-in-law. Peter assured his friends that Jesus was really God's Son. They could be certain that He paid for their sins on the cross. They could look forward to being in heaven with Jesus.

You can believe the message of the Bible; it came from God Himself. Jesus' love has paid for your sins. That's no fake!

_____Let's talk: What is your favorite "hard to believe—yet really true" part of God's Word?

_____Let's pray: Thank You, heavenly Father, for showing us that all You have told us in the Bible is true. Help us share Your forgiveness and love with those around us. Amen.

K. A. S.

Read from God's Word

Therefore, if anyone is in Christ, he is a new creation; old things have passed away; behold, all things have become new. Now all things are of God, who has reconciled us to Himself through Jesus Christ, and has given us the ministry of reconciliation, that is, that God was in Christ reconciling the world to Himself, not imputing their trespasses to them, and has committed to us the word of reconciliation. Now then, we are ambassadors for Christ, as though God were pleading through us; we implore you on Christ's behalf, be reconciled to God. For He made Him who knew no sin to be sin for us, that we might become the righteousness of God in Him.
2 Corinthians 5:17–21 ✍

Who Paid for Sin?

A 14-year-old boy in Florida broke into his school and caused a lot of damage. The police and the boy's father arrived on the scene. The father said, "I take total responsibility. His sin is my sin."

The father took out a bank loan to pay for the damages. And during the next few weeks he brought his entire family to the school to clean and paint.

When you hear this story, do you feel angry about what the boy did? Do you think the family should not have helped the boy out of his mess? Perhaps you think he alone should have paid for the damage he caused.

Think for a moment about the things you have done wrong. Some sins you have had to pay for. Some you got away with.

God has compassion and mercy on us because of Jesus' death on the cross. Instead of making us pay for our sins, God sent Jesus to pay for them on the cross. Now, when God looks at the hearts of those who believe in Jesus, He doesn't see our sin. Instead, He sees the perfection of Christ.

There is no need for you or me to take out a bank loan to pay for our many sins. Jesus has paid the price for us in full!

——Let's talk: Why do you think the father paid for his son's sins? Why did God pay for our sins? How might we respond to God's gift of forgiveness?

——Let's pray: Bold shall I stand in that great day, Cleansed and redeemed, no debt to pay; For by Your cross absolved I am From sin and guilt, from fear and shame. (*LW* 362:2)

K. A. S.

october

LaVerne Almstedt

Phil Lang

Craig Otto

Becky Peters

Suzanne Ramsey

Using the Right Words

Read from God's Word

"No good tree bears bad fruit, nor does a bad tree bear good fruit. Each tree is recognized by its own fruit. People do not pick figs from thornbushes, or grapes from briers. The good man brings good things out of the good stored up in his heart, and the evil man brings evil things out of the evil stored up in his heart. For out of the overflow of his heart his mouth speaks." Luke 6:43–45

Steven pinched his finger in his toy and yelled, "Ow!" followed by a bad word.

Nathan said, "Sh-h-h! My mom's home!" Steven thought it was funny to curse and not get caught. He began saying, "Ow!" and the bad word every time he snapped a piece onto the toy. The boys giggled uncontrollably.

Nathan's mother didn't hear Steven curse—but God did. Nathan felt guilty because he laughed about a word that didn't follow God's Word.

The Bible teaches that we curse because of sinful desires inside us. "For out of the overflow of his heart his mouth speaks." Steven's heart was not set on pleasing God so his words were not pleasing either. Nathan's heart was not set on pleasing God either. He was just going along with his friend.

God wants us to speak pure, kind words and help others do the same thing. When we fail, He calls us to repent. God leads us to say, "I'm sorry. Please help me get rid of sinful desires in my heart. I want my words to reflect Your love."

A prayer like that shows a heart that overflows with faith, confident that Jesus died for your sins—even the sin of cursing. Led by the Spirit, we can choose our words more carefully.

_____Let's talk: Who can tell you if a word is okay to use? If someone curses, what could you say to him or her? Memorize a short, caring response.

_____Let's pray: Dear Lord, I need Your forgiveness. I haven't always used words You would be proud of. Thank You for showing me the way to live. In Jesus' name. Amen.

C. O.

Did You Say Something?

K enny had the amazing ability to stop listening.

His father was telling the family he would build a new workshop in the garage. He followed the explanation by asking Kenny, "Can you help me clean the garage on Saturday?"

Kenny didn't look up. Kenny didn't answer.

"Kenny, are you there?"

"What?" Kenny was startled.

The whole family laughed—even Kenny! He was glad to help his father clean the garage, but he hadn't heard him.

God's people haven't always listened to their heavenly Father either. During the time of Joel, people stopped listening to God. To get their attention, He said, "Return to Me with all your heart." God wanted everyone to know He would give the Holy Spirit.

Sometimes we're so busy we forget to listen for God's promises. We sometimes "tune out" God because we think we already know everything we need to.

But God says in His Word, "Return to Me with all your heart." He wants to bless us with power to do good things for others. And we can through the power of the Holy Spirit, whom we received at Baptism.

Listen! Today God calls each of us to hear His Word. He reminds us that we are forgiven because of Jesus and empowered to do good works in His name!

> **Read from God's Word**
>
> *"Even now," declares the LORD, "return to Me with all your heart, with fasting and weeping and mourning." Rend your heart and not your garments. Return to the LORD your God, for He is gracious and compassionate, slow to anger and abounding in love, and He relents from sending calamity. Who knows? He may turn and have pity and leave behind a blessing—grain offerings and drink offerings for the LORD your God. Joel 2:12–14*

_____Let's do: Have your parents asked you to do something, and you haven't done it yet? Ask their forgiveness, and then get the job done.

_____Let's pray: Lord, help me remember You are speaking to me each day. I want to hear Your Word and do good things to honor You. In Jesus' name. Amen.

C. O.

Read from God's Word

But now, this is what the LORD says—He who created you, O Jacob, He who formed you, O Israel: "Fear not, for I have redeemed you; I have summoned you by name; you are Mine. When you pass through the waters, I will be with you; and when you pass through the rivers, they will not sweep over you. When you walk through the fire, you will not be burned; the flames will not set you ablaze."
Isaiah 43:1–2 ✍

When Someone Doesn't Go

"Uncle Jeff is going to church with us!" cried Jamie.

As Jamie and Susan talked, their mother said a silent prayer for Jeff. He had married her sister years before and had gone to church with her only five times.

"Mom," asked Susan, "is Uncle Jeff a Christian?"

Mother opened the Bible and read, "Fear not, for I have redeemed you; I have summoned you by name; you are Mine."

She explained, "God loves Uncle Jeff and knows his name too. He is baptized like you, but he has forgotten how important it is to love, obey, and worship God."

"What can we do for him?" asked Jamie.

"Pray," her mother answered. "We love Uncle Jeff so much we want him to share the blessings we have from being close to Jesus."

Maybe someone in your family doesn't go to church often. God is disappointed and you might worry that He will stop loving that person. But even when a Christian fails, God's love doesn't fail the one who turns back to Him and asks forgiveness.

God sent His only Son, Jesus, to redeem sinners. "Fear not, for I have redeemed you." He redeemed us through the blood of Jesus, who died on the cross. Each day we turn to our Savior, trusting in the forgiveness He won for us.

_____Let's do: Write about someone you would like to go to church more often. Say a prayer for that person now, and invite him or her to church this week.

_____Let's pray: Dear Lord, thank You for redeeming me. I am Your child, and I pray that others see Jesus' love in me. In His name I pray. Amen.

C. O.

A Sign of Jesus' Coming

Read from God's Word

"Now learn this lesson from the fig tree: As soon as its twigs get tender and its leaves come out, you know that summer is near. Even so, when you see all these things, you know that it is near, right at the door. I tell you the truth, this generation will certainly not pass away until all these things have happened. Heaven and earth will pass away, but my words will never pass away." Matthew 24:32–35

Lee spent every Saturday at Grandma and Grandpa's farm raking the leaves.

Lee asked his grandfather, "Why do the leaves change color and drop?"

Grandpa said, "When trees lose their leaves, it's a sign that winter's coming."

Each season is different for a tree: in spring the leaves bud, in summer they're green, in fall they lose their green color, and in winter there are few or no leaves.

When Jesus spoke about judgment at the end of the world and the gathering of God's people into heaven, His disciples asked, "When will this happen, and what will be the sign of Your coming?" (Matthew 24:3).

Jesus said the changing leaves on a tree were a sign: "When you see all these things, you know that it is near."

Leaves are always changing, so does that mean Jesus is coming soon? Yes. It could be in three years, three hundred years, or longer. But He could come back today or tomorrow to take us to heaven.

We prepare ourselves by remembering what God did for us in our Baptism. He washed away our sins and filled us with His Holy Spirit. The Spirit leads us to repent of sinful behavior, to trust that Jesus loves and forgives us, and to look forward to His return with joy.

———Let's do: Draw a picture of Jesus coming on the clouds in the sky. Put these words from Revelation 22:7 on it: "Behold, I am coming soon!"

———Let's pray: Jesus, have mercy on me, a sinner, and prepare me for Your coming. Amen.

C. O.

Shouting and Singing

At sporting events, fans cheer and scream encouragement to the participants.

Have you ever acted like a sports fan in church? It would be an unusual church where people cheer, "Go, God!" or scream encouragement to the pastor.

In church we are honoring God, not praising one another or applauding a performance. We come to church to praise the God who made us, to give thanks for His Son's sacrifice on the cross, and to pray in the power of the Spirit.

The writer of Psalm 66 says, "Shout with joy to God," but quickly adds, "All the earth bows down to You; they sing praise to You." The Holy Spirit, working through these words of Scripture, leads us to church so we can confess, bow, and sing to the One who is truly worthy: Jesus.

Long ago an excited crowd shouted "Hosanna!" to celebrate Jesus' arrival in Jerusalem. They didn't know He was going to be crucified. Maybe they would have bowed silently as He passed by if they had known He'd soon die for them.

It seems you have a good reason to sing praise to God and say, "How awesome are Your deeds!" God's love in Christ is a special gift for crowds in every generation ... and for you. Rejoice!

_____Let's do: Ask your parents what their favorite hymns are and why they are special.

_____Let's pray: Lord, You are awesome. Help me to pray joyfully in church and at home. In Jesus' name. Amen.

C. O.

Different from Us

A boy talked about a girl and used a word that was not very nice. It was a word to describe all people of her nationality in a negative way.

One student knew it was wrong and reported the incident. The teacher, the principal, and the girl's parents all became involved in teaching the class about racism.

Even Peter had to learn about racism (not accepting people who are different). He had spoken poorly about Gentiles, even wondering if they could believe the same faith as those who were born Jewish. Peter learned that people of all races may worship Jesus.

"I now realize how true it is that God does not show favoritism," said Peter, "but accepts men from every nation who fear Him and do what is right."

We're called to love people of different color, those with different body size, sense of humor, or interests. When we tell others we don't like a classmate, we sin against that person and against God.

Jesus died for that person, just as He died for you. He offers His forgiveness for our quick judgments about others and our prejudiced attitudes toward those who are different. So let's pray that as new creations in Christ, we would act and speak in a God-pleasing way toward those whom God loves.

Read from God's Word

Then Peter began to speak: "I now realize how true it is that God does not show favoritism but accepts men from every nation who fear Him and do what is right. You know the message God sent to the people of Israel, telling the good news of peace through Jesus Christ, who is Lord of all. You know what has happened throughout Judea, beginning in Galilee after the baptism that John preached—how God anointed Jesus of Nazareth with the Holy Spirit and power, and how He went around doing good and healing all who were under the power of the devil, because God was with Him." Acts 10:34–38

_____Let's do: Write the words to the song "Jesus Loves the Little Children." Illustrate all or part of the text.

_____Let's pray: Dear Lord, You are a good and gracious God, giving salvation for all through Jesus Christ, Your Son. Use me as a witness to His love. In Jesus' name. Amen.

C. O.

Read from God's Word

When the LORD was about to take Elijah up to heaven in a whirlwind, Elijah and Elisha were on their way from Gilgal. Elijah said to Elisha, "Stay here; the LORD has sent me to Bethel." But Elisha said, "As surely as the LORD lives and as you live, I will not leave you." So they went down to Bethel. 2 Kings 2:1-2

Friends Stay Friends

Caleb's mother asked, "Would you like a big birthday party?"

"I'd rather just have Alex," Caleb responded.

Alex joined Caleb's class early in grade school and from then on the two had been best friends. Over the years they changed a lot, but their friendship remained strong.

Caleb's mother said, "You're really blessed to have such a good friend."

Do you remember examples from the Bible of people who remained loyal friends? Ruth chose to stay with Naomi, Jonathan pledged to protect David, and Elisha said he'd stay beside Elijah through a difficult time.

Friendships are tested. You may wonder if your friend understands your fears. What will happen to our friendship if my family moves to a new neighborhood?

The song "Stay with Us" (*AGPS* 221) is a prayer asking the Lord to be our friend in times of trouble: "Walk with us, the road will bend: make all our weeping, wailing end. Wipe our tears, forgive our fears: Jesus, lift the heavy cross."

Jesus walks with you when you face changes in your family or at school. He carried "the heavy cross"—all our burdens and sinfulness—when He died. Then He rose to life, showing that our burdens aren't too great for Him to bear.

Good friends are important, and Jesus is our best Friend!

_____Let's do: Write an invitation to a friend, inviting him or her to dinner. After the meal, share a devotion.

_____Let's pray: Lord Jesus, make me a loyal friend whom others can trust. Amen.

C. O.

God's Balloons

Jeremy Cookie launched a helium-filled balloon in Elmira, New York. He hoped it would go as far as Canada and win $500 for his school. Months later he learned that the balloon had traveled 8,000 miles to East Africa.

A boy in Kenya found the balloon and wrote to Jeremy. Jeremy had forgotten about the balloon and the prize money for the school. Now he had a new friend.

Our Sunday school sent up balloons with Bible passages in them. We wanted God's love in Jesus to be carried far and near. It was great to hear from people who found the brightly colored balloons and read the Bible words.

We are God's balloons as we reach out to others in love. We may never go as far as Kenya—but we can be a colorful balloon for God right where we are! We can spread the word about Jesus, who died for all.

Read from God's Word

For, "Everyone who calls on the name of the Lord will be saved." How, then, can they call on the one they have not believed in? And how can they believe in the one of whom they have not heard? And how can they hear without someone preaching to them? And how can they preach unless they are sent? As it is written, "How beautiful are the feet of those who bring good news!" Romans 10:13–15

How about your neighbors across the street? They invite you over for picnics. They may be looking for something more in their lives. Ask your parents to invite them to church with you.

Our Bible reading tells us the way to spread the joy of Jesus: hear, preach, send. What are other ways we can spread the message that "Jesus is Lord and Savior of all"?

_____Let's talk: Where would you like to send God's love? To whom would you give it? What would you say to them?

_____Let's pray: Pray for someone you know who doesn't know Jesus. Ask God to use you to reach this person with His love.

L. A.

Read from God's Word

This is the message we have heard from Him and declare to you: God is light; in Him there is no darkness at all. If we claim to have fellowship with Him yet walk in the darkness, we lie and do not live by the truth. But if we walk in the light, as He is in the light, we have fellowship with one another, and the blood of Jesus, His Son, purifies us from all sin.
1 John 1:5-7

Sin Buildup

Last December we tried to light the candles on our Advent wreath, which had been used for many years. Wax had built up around the wicks and the candles wouldn't light. We scraped away the wax and cleaned the candles. Then they burned brightly again.

Sin, the bad things we do and the good things we don't do, can build up in our lives too. Sin separates us from the light of God's love. When it does, others cannot see the light of Christ reflected in us.

It's easy to say, "All people sin." To look at our sins is harder.

Mom tells you to clean your room, but you want to go play. Under the bed goes the junk. Mom asks, "Is your room clean?" You answer, "It sure is!" Sin build-up.

Math has never been an easy subject for you. When Mrs. Squibb assigns a zillion problems, you moan. When Lisa offers you her homework to copy, you have a way out of the situation. More sin build-up.

God provides a clean-up plan. Through His Word, the Holy Spirit moves us to take a look at our life, confess our sins, and turn to Jesus. His death on the cross for us cleans us from all sin. Now we can live our lives for Him. Now His light can burn brightly in us.

_____Let's do: Think of some ways that sin builds up in your life. How can Jesus' love and forgiveness make a difference in your life?

_____Let's pray: Faithful Savior, You know all our sin. Thank You for forgiving us. Help us shine brightly for You. Amen.

L. A.

A Record Name

$\mathcal{S}$ee how fast you can read this name: Adolph Blaine Charles David Earl Frederick Gerald Hubert Irvin John Kenneth Lloyd Martin Nero Oliver Paul Quincy Randolph Sherman Thomas Uncas Victor William Xernes Yancy Zeus Wolf + 585. How would you like to write *that* at the top of each assignment? His name was shortened to Mr. Wolf + 585.

No matter how long or short your name is, Jesus knows you. He calls you to follow Him. Our Bible reading tells of Jesus as the Good Shepherd.

You are that lost sheep whom Jesus calls and cares for as His own. Each one of us is very important to God.

You have other names people call you: You are son or daughter, friend, brother or sister, and student; you may be ballplayer, singer, reader. ... The list goes on and on.

Most important, you are Christian. Jesus died for your sins. He has given you His name. And He has given you other names, such as forgiven, loved, humble, faithful, kind, obedient, unselfish, and joyful. This list could go on and on.

Wear your names proudly. You are God's child. He knows you and loves you. Your name is in His book. Rejoice and praise Him!

Read from God's Word

"I tell you the truth, the man who does not enter the sheep pen by the gate, but climbs in by some other way, is a thief and a robber. The man who enters by the gate is the shepherd of his sheep. The watchman opens the gate for him, and the sheep listen to his voice. He calls his own sheep by name and leads them out. When he has brought out all his own, he goes on ahead of them, and his sheep follow him because they know his voice." John 10:1–4

———Let's talk: How can people know you are God's child? When you don't act like a Christian, how does Jesus help you?

———Let's pray: Jesus, thank You for Your love. Help us wear the name Christian so others see You. Amen.

L. A.

Bought and Renewed

Read from God's Word

"I will sprinkle clean water on you, and you will be clean; I will cleanse you from all your impurities and from all your idols. I will give you a new heart and put a new spirit in you; I will remove from you your heart of stone and give you a heart of flesh. And I will put My Spirit in you and move you to follow My decrees and be careful to keep My laws." Ezekiel 36:25–27

Becky's family laughed at her desk. The front of one drawer was falling off, deep scratches covered the top, and the entire desk wobbled. She said only two words, "Just wait."

Becky reattached the front of the drawer. She tightened every joint in the desk to make it sturdy. Then she stripped the dirty, scratched paint and sanded the entire desk. Finally Becky applied a wood stain and protective seal.

Her family was amazed. The desk looked great. Her two children even argued about who got to use it.

God does the same with us. When we were weak and covered with sin, He bought us and paid for us with the blood of Jesus. Then He changed our attitudes and behaviors so other people can see His love in us.

Becky's desk couldn't renew itself. Neither can we change ourselves by our own power. God gives us His Spirit to help us do His will.

With daily use, her refinished desk will weaken and become dirty again. Living in a sinful world and our own sin make us weak and dirty with sin. That's why we depend on God to wash away our sins. We rejoice in the strength He gives us to do His will, living as His people.

_____Let's talk: What do you do when you find yourself weak and sinful? How can you thank God for renewing you?

_____Let's pray: Dear Father, thank You for making me Your child and a new person through Jesus. Help me to share Your love with others. In Jesus' name. Amen.

B. P.

Persistence Pays

Today is the anniversary of the day Christopher Columbus landed in the New World.

We know that Columbus was persistent. Columbus was sure he could reach the Indies by sailing west. He asked King John to support his trip. The king tricked Columbus and gave his maps and charts to his own sea captain.

Columbus didn't give up. He asked King Ferdinand and Queen Isabella of Spain to finance his trip. Six years later, the queen finally agreed.

When his crew was afraid of sea monsters and wanted to turn back, Columbus refused. His men even threatened to throw Columbus overboard. But Columbus persisted, determined to reach his goal.

Jesus persisted in His goal too. Determined to do His Father's will, Jesus saved all people from their sin. The job took great love, courage, and strength. But by His death on the cross, Jesus showed us how to truly persevere.

God tells us to be persistent in doing His will. Because of our sin, we are not able to persevere in a sinful world. Because of Jesus, God forgives us when we fail and gives us new power to persevere.

Unlike Columbus, we don't seek an earthly reward. We look forward to the reward of heaven, which God promises to all who persevere.

Read from God's Word

So do not throw away your confidence; it will be richly rewarded. You need to persevere so that when you have done the will of God, you will receive what He has promised. Hebrews 10:35–36

———Let's talk: In what areas do you have trouble persevering? What are the blessings of doing God's will?

———Let's pray: Dear Jesus, thank You for persevering for my sake. Please give me power to persevere and to do Your will. Amen.

B. P.

The Big Battle

Robert loves football. On Friday nights he goes to the local high school game. On Saturdays he watches the college games on television. On Sunday afternoons he watches the pros. Robert seldom misses a Monday night football game.

Why does Robert like football? It's the competition—two teams fighting for possession of the ball. The players give all they've got. Uniforms get dirty. Helmets crash.

But Robert is involved in a much more important game that lasts his entire life. His team captain is stronger and wiser than anyone. What is it?

It's the game of life—Robert against the devil. The devil fights hard to take away Robert's faith in Jesus, to knock him off God's team, and to steal his place in heaven.

Jesus is our team captain. He's always by our side, coaching us, forgiving our failures, and giving us strength to fight the devil. When our faith becomes weak, He reminds us that His power is greater than the devil's. He proved that with His death and resurrection.

Jesus pulls us to our feet, gives us a pep talk, and sends us back into the game—a game He has already won for all of us.

_____Let's do: What does the Bible reading say is your uniform for battle against the devil? Make up a cheer for Jesus.

_____Let's pray: Dear Jesus, thank You for being my team captain and Savior. Please give me all I need to fight the devil. Amen.

B. P.

Foolish or Wise?

Would you trade a pound of gold for a pound of salt? That's what people in the country of Ghana did around the year A.D. 1000. The West Africans had plenty of gold, but salt was scarce. They needed salt in their diets to replace what they lost through perspiration and to preserve their food.

Merchants in the Sahara Desert north of Ghana traded their salt for gold, then they sold the gold to the Europeans.

Salt could be as valuable as gold! Most people throw away the salt they spill. Would you throw away gold?

Some people think believing in Jesus is more foolish than trading a pound of gold for a pound of salt. To save us from sin and eternal death, Jesus had to die. Jesus said if you want to be first, you have to put yourself last. How can Good Friday be "good"? Can you see why Christianity doesn't make sense to some people?

Read from God's Word

For the message of the cross is foolishness to those who are perishing, but to us who are being saved it is the power of God. For it is written: "I will destroy the wisdom of the wise; the intelligence of the intelligent I will frustrate." Where is the wise man? Where is the scholar? Where is the philosopher of this age? Has not God made foolish the wisdom of the world? For since in the wisdom of God the world through its wisdom did not know Him, God was pleased through the foolishness of what was preached to save those who believe. ... For the foolishness of God is wiser than man's wisdom, and the weakness of God is stronger than man's strength. 1 Corinthians 1:18–25 ✎

The Bible says that God is stronger and wiser than people. We don't have to be strong. We don't have to understand everything about God. Our all-knowing, all-powerful, loving God gives us everything we need for salvation—forgiveness through Jesus and faith in His promises. Rejoice! God's gifts are more valuable than all the riches in the world.

———Let's talk: What do you think these Bible words mean: "The weakness of God is stronger than man's strength"? How can we be truly wise?

———Let's pray: Dear heavenly Father, You alone have all wisdom and power. Please give me wisdom and faith to follow You. Amen.

B. P.

Read from God's Word

Give thanks to the LORD, call on His name; make known among the nations what He has done. Sing to Him, sing praise to Him; tell of all His wonderful acts. Glory in His holy name; let the hearts of those who seek the LORD rejoice. Look to the LORD and His strength; seek His face always. Remember the wonders He has done, His miracles, and the judgments He pronounced. Psalm 105:1–5 ✑

Praise Him with Poetry

Poems are written in different styles, shapes, and sizes. Some poems are long; some are short. Some rhyme; some don't. Some poems are serious; some are silly. Some poems like this one have only two lines.

Upon the cross He paid the cost
So I would be no longer lost.

A syllable poem is fun to write. The first line has one syllable. The second line has two syllables. For every line you write, you add one more syllable. This poem has six lines:

God
Loving
Sinful us
Sending Jesus
Forgiving our sins
Sharing heaven with us!

King David used poetry to respond to God's blessings in his life. He wrote psalms—poems that can be sung—about all sorts of experiences and feelings. Whether David was happy or down in the dumps, he wrote poetry to express his thoughts and feelings. When David had problems, he turned to God for help. When things were going well in David's life, he praised God. Can you talk to God about your joys and sorrows through poetry?

_____Let's do: Read some of the psalms. Write a poem that tells your feelings about God right now. (Your poem can be any style, shape, or size, with or without rhyme.)

_____Let's pray: Heavenly Father, hear me pray. Thank You for taking my sins away. Send Your Spirit to me each day. Show Your love in all I do and say. Amen.

B. P.

First Things First

D o you have a baby book? If so, it probably records your first tooth, your first steps, your first words, and your first day of school.

The word *first* means "before any others" or "most important." What comes first for you? Setting goals and working to achieve them is wise, as long as you do something else first.

In the Old Testament, King Jehoshaphat of Judah and King Ahab planned to attack an Israelite city that had been taken over by another country. But Jehoshaphat told Ahab, "First seek the counsel of the LORD."

God warned the two kings that disaster would come from their planned attack. But they didn't listen, and King Ahab was killed.

King Jehoshaphat's advice is still important today. God invites us to study His Word and to seek His will. Through His Spirit, God enables us to put Him first. Through His Son, God forgives us for those times when we sin and put other things before Him.

Read from God's Word

For three years there was no war between Aram and Israel. But in the third year Jehoshaphat king of Judah went down to see the king of Israel. The king of Israel had said to his officials, "Don't you know that Ramoth Gilead belongs to us and yet we are doing nothing to retake it from the king of Aram?" So he asked Jehoshaphat, "Will you go with me to fight against Ramoth Gilead?" Jehoshaphat replied to the king of Israel, "I am as you are, my people as your people, my horses as your horses." But Jehoshaphat also said to the king of Israel, "First seek the counsel of the LORD." 1 Kings 22:1–5 ✍

God is first to listen, forgive, guide, and empower us to do His will. He richly blesses us in our work to reach our goals.

_____Let's talk: What goals have you set for yourself? How will you put God first in what you do with your life?

_____Let's pray: Dear Father, thank You for always listening to me. Help me always to first seek You and Your will and then follow it. Amen.

B. P.

God's Plans

"We planned a camping trip, but our car broke down."

"I started my homework, but then unexpected guests came over."

"Mom planned to have a party, but Grandma got sick."

Have you ever noticed how plans don't always work out? We make plans for all sorts of things—work, play, people to see, and places to go. But other things get in the way. Unexpected things happen or forgotten commitments arise. Sometimes we become frustrated. Other times we simply say, "That's life!"

Psalm 33:11 says, "The plans of the LORD stand firm forever." That means what God plans, He will do. When sin first came into the world, God promised to send His Son, Jesus, to save us from sin and eternal death. Many years later, Jesus came to the world, died on the cross, and rose again—just as God's prophets had foretold, just as God had planned. Now we can be sure of God's forgiveness and a joyful life in heaven.

This doesn't mean that everything that happens to us will be good. But God can use anything that happens and make good come out of it.

Think about all the plans you make. Some work out, some don't. Isn't it great to know that God's plans for us always work out?

_____Let's talk: What do you think people mean when they say, "I'm planning to . . . God willing"? What are some of your plans? How can you entrust them to God?

_____Let's pray: Dear Lord, thank You for all the good things You've planned for me. Please help me to remember that You are in charge of my life. Amen.

B. P.

The Crown

enni Simpson shivered with excitement. The stadium was packed with people and fancy cars carried girls wearing beautiful dresses onto the field. Jenni cheered loudly when her sister's name was announced. Then the crowd quieted to hear who would be the queen.

"And now, the 2004 homecoming queen—Miss Rachel Simpson!" Everyone cheered as a crown was placed on Rachel's head.

As the girls left the football field, Jenni told her grandpa, "When I'm in high school, I'm going to be the queen so I can wear a beautiful crown and have everyone cheer for me."

"Jenni," Grandpa said later, "do you know that you will get to wear a crown forever? And everyone in heaven will cheer for you."

Jenni looked amazed. "Why would I get a crown in heaven?"

"When Jesus died on the cross, He made you righteous, or holy, forgiving all your sins. Every day He gives you the faith and power to live as His child. People who remain faithful to Jesus will wear His righteousness and His crown of glory! Best of all, you will live with Jesus in heaven forever.

"I'm very happy for Rachel tonight," Grandpa continued, "but I'm even happier to see Jesus' love living inside of Rachel and you." Then he gave Jenni a hug.

Read from God's Word

I have fought the good fight, I have finished the race, I have kept the faith. Now there is in store for me the crown of righteousness, which the Lord, the righteous Judge, will award to me on that day—and not only to me, but also to all who have longed for His appearing. 2 Timothy 4:7–8

——Let's talk: Contrast Rachel's two crowns. How are they different?

——Let's pray: Dear Jesus, keep me faithful to You so I will wear Your crown of glory in heaven. Amen.

B. P.

Read from God's Word

Do you not know? Have you not heard? The LORD is the everlasting God, the Creator of the ends of the earth. He will not grow tired or weary, and His understanding no one can fathom. He gives strength to the weary and increases the power of the weak. Even youths grow tired and weary, and young men stumble and fall; but those who hope in the LORD will renew their strength. They will soar on wings like eagles; they will run and not grow weary, they will walk and not be faint. Isaiah 40:28–31

Energy to Spare

Fifteen-year-old Sachi runs a three-mile race that takes her down dirt paths and over hills.

Sachi spent the entire week preparing for the race, running more than 20 miles! On Saturday Sachi raced the three-mile course in 30 minutes and 36 seconds.

It's no wonder Sachi went right home, collapsed on her bed, and slept. Two hours later she woke up and moaned, "I'm still tired! I can't move."

Think of all God does for you every day. He watches over you, protecting you from danger. He listens to your prayers, answers them, and provides for all your needs. He forgives your sins and through the Holy Spirit works faith in your heart. He guides your thoughts and actions. He does all of this for you and every one of His people throughout the world!

Read the Good News in Isaiah 40:28. God never gets tired. He works 24 hours a day, every day. He never sleeps or goes on vacation. But the good news doesn't end there. Continue reading verses 29–31.

God shares His strength and energy with us. We never have to be too tired to do what God wants us to do. We can trust in God and use His strength to live as His own energetic, faithful children.

_____Let's talk: What are some specific ways God helped you today? How did He help others you know?

_____Let's pray: Thank You, Lord, for being so awesome. Thank You for lifting me up when I'm weary. Please give me strength always to please You. Amen.

B. P.

Absolute Understanding

Read from God's Word

Great is our Lord and mighty in power; His understanding has no limit. Psalm 147:5 ✍

"What's your favorite Bible verse?" Ms. Reilly asked her class.

Becca raised her hand. "I like Psalm 23: 'The LORD is my shepherd, I shall not be in want.'"

Then George spoke. "Here's one: 'I am with you always.'"

"Ask and it will be given to you; seek and you will find; knock and the door will be opened to you," offered Amie.

Jake spoke up. "How about John 11:35? 'Jesus wept.' I like it because I can memorize it."

Ms. Reilly remarked, "That verse tells me that Jesus had feelings just like I do. He felt happy, sad, angry, shy, and lonely. I know He understands my feelings too.

"I don't always want others to know my true feelings," she continued. "Sometimes I don't understand them. But Jesus completely understands me and loves me just the same.

"Another verse I really like says, 'Great is our Lord and mighty in power; His understanding has no limit.' When I think of that verse, I know I don't have to understand my own feelings or why things happen in the world. And I can trust God to understand and to do what's best. He loved each of us so much He gave His Son to die for us so our sins are paid for. That's power and understanding."

_____Let's talk: What is your favorite Bible verse? What does it tell you about God and you?

_____Let's pray: Almighty God, thank You for understanding me, even when I don't understand myself. Help me to live for You. Amen.

B. P.

Read from God's Word

I call on You, O God, for You will answer me; give ear to me and hear my prayer. Show the wonder of Your great love, You who save by Your right hand those who take refuge in You from their foes. Keep me as the apple of Your eye; hide me in the shadow of Your wings. Psalm 17:6–8 ✐

The Apple of His Eye

"Look at your apple closely," Mrs. Meyer said to her students. "Notice its color, spots, blemishes, and bumps. How is the stem pointing? Now close your eyes and picture your particular apple."

Then Mrs. Meyer asked her students to put their apples together in a basket. She mixed up all the apples and laid them out on a table. Next she said, "Come find your own apple."

Could you find one red apple in a pile of 30? In Mrs. Meyer's class, every student found his or her own apple!

Maybe you thought that all apples look alike. However, each apple is unique. It has bumps and spots. Its color varies here and there. Its stem may be straight or crooked, long or short, and so on.

Each apple is unique and so are you. There is nobody just like you. Even in a crowd of millions of people, God can pick you out. He looks at you and says, "You are special! My Son, Jesus, was punished for your sins and died for you." God the Father takes great pleasure in you, the "apple of [His] eye" (Psalm 17:8). He wants you to live with Him forever.

When you eat your next apple, remember that you are the "apple" of God's eye!

_____Let's do: Pick an apple out of a bag of apples, study it, and put it back. Can you find it again? What is special about you?

_____Let's pray: Dear Father, help me remember that You made me special and redeemed me through Jesus, Your Son. Amen.

P. L.

Horse Race

Did you know that horses do not like to race ahead of each other? To run in the front feels dangerous. They would rather run in the middle of the herd for protection.

The key to success is the jockey. A winning horse will only run ahead of another horse for the jockey.

Sometimes we are like those horses—afraid. What will happen when we leave our old neighborhood? What will our friends say about our looks after we get braces? When our parents get divorced, how will we trust them? How will we explain to our parents the conflict we caused at school?

We have little power in ourselves to solve some problems and no power whatsoever to solve others. The good news is that God helps us trust in Jesus to help. He helps us with our day-to-day struggles like friendships and braces. He has even taken the punishment for our sins—the condition we could never solve—upon Himself. His death on the cross for our sins means that we can race through every day as winners.

Each night we can thank the Lord for forgiveness of our sins and His guidance throughout the day. And each day He will give us the power to race forward as winning Christians.

Read from God's Word

If we have been united with Him like this in His death, we will certainly also be united with Him in His resurrection. For we know that our old self was crucified with Him so that the body of sin might be done away with, that we should no longer be slaves to sin. Romans 6:5–6 ✍

———Let's do: Say, sing, or illustrate a stanza of "Christ Be My Leader" (*LW* 365). Try to write a new stanza.

———Let's pray: Dear God, thank You for loving me enough to lead me. In Jesus' name. Amen.

S. R.

I'm Confused!

Read from God's Word

Then Philip ran up to the chariot and heard the man reading Isaiah the prophet. "Do you understand what you are reading?" Philip asked. "How can I," he said, "unless someone explains it to me?" So he invited Philip to come up and sit with him. Acts 8:30–31

Are you ever confused by words you hear? For example, when students first learn the Pledge of Allegiance, they may not hear "one nation, under God, indivisible" correctly. Since the word *indivisible* has no meaning to them, they may say "invisible."

Once, as a Sunday school class was practicing for the Christmas service, a little boy whispered to his teacher, "What's 'the tired onion world'?"

His teacher was puzzled. She asked where he had heard that in the Christmas story.

"In that one part," he answered, "where the king said 'the tired onion world' should be counted."

The teacher slowly repeated "the entire Roman world" for the little boy, explaining each new word for him.

Some of the stories and ideas in the Bible are easy to understand; others are harder. In the Bible reading for today, the Ethiopian asked for help to understand God's Word. God sent Philip to help him. Philip met him on the road "and told him the good news about Jesus" (Acts 8:35).

Do you understand everything you hear spoken in God's Word? Of course not. But we never need to be confused about God's words of love and forgiveness that tell us Jesus came to this world to save us from our sins.

_____Let's do: Think about Bible stories that were hard for you to understand. Write about them. Who helped you grow in your understanding?

_____Let's pray: Dear God, thank You for Your Holy Word. For Jesus' sake. Amen.

S. R.

Without a Leader

small flock of sheep was running around behind one another in a circle. They weren't going anywhere or following anyone. How silly. Maybe they were just being simpleminded creatures. Maybe they were just being sheep without a shepherd.

The Bible tells us that we are like sheep. Do we chase after the tails of sinful people and sinful ways? Yes. Do we follow our own sinful nature round and round and round and end up lost and troubled? Yes. We could say we were just being ourselves—our sinful selves, and we'd be right. In our helplessness we cry out for a shepherd to save us and lead us.

Jesus is that Shepherd. He can save and lead. As our Savior, He overcame the power of sin, death, and the devil. He lived each breath without sin and died carrying the sins of all. As our Leader He invites and empowers us through His Spirit to believe in Him.

Read from God's Word

Some wandered in desert wastelands, finding no way to a city where they could settle. They were hungry and thirsty, and their lives ebbed away. Then they cried out to the LORD in their trouble, and He delivered them from their distress. He led them by a straight way to a city where they could settle. Psalm 107:4–7

He gives us salvation and life forever in heaven. He sends us His Spirit to rescue us from silly circles of sinful thoughts and selfish plans. That Spirit helps us learn the true path to God in His Word and Sacraments.

Each day is a new day to be led by the Good Shepherd. Where will we go today?

———Let's do: Reread Psalm 107:4–7. What problems did the people have? How did God provide for them?

———Let's pray: Dear Father, I am sorry for those times when I have not followed You. Thank You for sending Jesus to be my Shepherd. Hear me for Jesus' sake. Amen.

S. R.

Read from God's Word

They devoted themselves to the apostles' teaching and to the fellowship, to the breaking of bread and to prayer. Everyone was filled with awe, and many wonders and miraculous signs were done by the apostles. All the believers were together and had everything in common. Selling their possessions and goods, they gave to anyone as he had need. Every day they continued to meet together in the temple courts. They broke bread in their homes and ate together with glad and sincere hearts, praising God and enjoying the favor of all the people. And the Lord added to their number daily those who were being saved. Acts 2:42–47 ✎

Pull Together

It was the last day of the pulling contest. Matthew hitched up his first team of two horses and pulled five tons of cement blocks—good enough for third place. An hour later he tried again, but they pulled only four tons of blocks.

The last event was the four-horse pull. Would they be able to pull their scores from the first round even though they were tired? A nine-ton pull might win a ribbon. Imagine his surprise when his four horses pulled an amazing 12 tons to win first place!

God does amazing things through His people. Today's Bible reading tells about the work and worship of believers in the early church. They worshiped God and told others about Jesus. This was the beginning of the congregation of believers pulling together in Jerusalem. In a world where people selfishly took care of only themselves, God strengthened the believers through Word and Sacrament so they could then show the love of Jesus wherever they went.

Christian churches today are like that. Young and old gather to hear and study God's Word, receive forgiveness of sins, and enjoy the fellowship of other believers. We praise God and receive His strength to help others. He tells us to pull together and gives us the power to do amazing things!

_____Let's talk: How is God working in your congregation?

_____Let's pray: Dear heavenly Father, thank You for keeping all believers close to You through Jesus and helping them reach out to others with Your strength. Amen.

S. R.

Call Who for What?

A woman came home one day to find her water pipes leaking. She quickly called a piano player. Another woman discovered a serious engine problem, so she phoned the dentist.

Did the right people get called? The dentist who was called to fix the car was also a great mechanic. The piano player who fixed the leaky pipes was also a plumber. Looks like the right people were called after all.

In our Bible reading, a carpenter helps a fisherman fish. Simon had spent all night casting his net for nothing. Then Jesus told Simon to throw his nets out again, and he did it! Why?

Because Simon had just seen and heard Jesus teaching about God. The message of God's love had entered Simon's heart. The Holy Spirit was working.

Jesus wanted Simon to know Him as Savior and follow Him as disciple. So Jesus came to show Simon in an unlikely way, with an abundant catch, that He was the Lord.

Jesus comes to help us in our sinful boats. Through the Word, God's Spirit is working, telling us of Jesus' abundant love, which paid the full price to free us from sin. Like Simon we are amazed and follow Jesus.

Read from God's Word

One day as Jesus was standing by the Lake of Gennesaret, with the people crowding around Him and listening to the word of God, He saw at the water's edge two boats. ... He got into one of the boats, the one belonging to Simon, and asked him to put out a little from shore. Then He sat down and taught the people from the boat. When He had finished speaking, He said to Simon, "Put out into deep water, and let down the nets for a catch." Simon answered, "Master, we've worked hard all night and haven't caught anything. But because You say so, I will let down the nets." When they had done so, they caught such a large number of fish that their nets began to break. ... When Simon Peter saw this, he fell at Jesus' knees and said, "Go away from me, Lord; I am a sinful man!" For he and all his companions were astonished at the catch of fish they had taken. Luke 5:1–9 ✑

————Let's do: Look for two ways God shows His abundant love for you.

————Let's pray: Dear loving Father, forgive me when I don't hear and follow You in my everyday life. Thank You for sending Jesus. In His name I pray. Amen.

S. R.

The Strong Foundation

Read from God's Word

For in Scripture it says: "See, I lay a stone in Zion, a chosen and precious cornerstone, and the one who trusts in Him will never be put to shame." 1 Peter 2:6

When the Morgan family moved to Indiana, they were hoping to buy a house with a big basement. But they found a house with a big kitchen, three bedrooms, a nice yard—but a tiny basement!

When the builders tried to dig for the basement, they found a huge rock, much bigger than the house. They couldn't move it, break it, or go around it.

Did the Morgan family buy that house without the big basement they wanted? They sure did!

"We will be safe," said Mr. Morgan. "Our house is resting on the strongest foundation in town!"

Unless they are built on Christ, our lives are like houses with no foundation. What we say, think, or do appears to be building up something powerful, something that will last forever. But when troubles blow or temptations rain down, lives without Christ crumble into heaps of angry words, unkind thoughts, and sinful actions. Where can we find help?

Children of God are grounded in Christ and strengthened through God's Word and Sacraments. We are grounded because Jesus took the weight of our sins to the cross. He gave us His salvation so that day in and day out, through life and death, our life is built by God's power on the sure foundation, Jesus Christ.

_____Let's do: Write about the Christian foundation of your faith.

_____Let's pray: Almighty Father, forgive me when I don't honor You as the cornerstone in my life. Thank You for being strong for me. In Jesus' name. Amen.

S. R.

Can You Balance?

Susan longed to ride the blue bike. It looked so easy.

Her parents said, "Just keep trying. It's really easy once you learn how to balance."

It was hard to keep trying, but she did. All at once she was doing it—she was riding her bike! Now she could feel the balance everyone had been talking about.

The first people, Adam and Eve, lived in perfect harmony (or balance) with God. They obeyed His rules and experienced His total love.

But what happened when Adam and Eve disobeyed God's command? Sin upset the balance, the perfect order of things.

People have been trying to fix the balance ever since. Some make the mistake of trying to live a perfect life so God will be happy with them. Others try to ignore God altogether.

Can people regain balance this way? No. Sin and our sinful nature will always pull us down. We do not want to obey God or accept His love.

Only God can fix the balance. He loved us so much that He sent Jesus for us. Our sins were carried on Jesus' shoulders to Calvary. His perfect life took away the sins of the topsy-turvy world. And His perfect love gives us faith to be His child.

Read from God's Word

But because of His great love for us, God, who is rich in mercy, made us alive with Christ even when we were dead in transgressions—it is by grace you have been saved. And God raised us up with Christ and seated us with Him in the heavenly realms in Christ Jesus, in order that in the coming ages He might show the incomparable riches of His grace, expressed in His kindness to us in Christ Jesus. Ephesians 2:4–7

_____Let's do: Write down three words you think of when you think of balance. Draw a cross above each one.

_____Let's pray: Dear Jesus, I am sorry when I forget to follow Your ways. Thank You for forgiving my sins. Amen.

S. R.

Time to Relax!

When Sierra was a little girl, she collected bottle caps. They weren't valuable or useful, but they were fun to have.

Do you know someone who has a collection? Maybe they have fossils, baseball cards, teddy bears, or comic books. Collecting is fun. When we do fun things, it helps us enjoy life.

Do you have a hobby? Maybe you like to read, draw, or take care of your pet. It is important that people have the chance to do something they enjoy. Why?

People who have a hobby or take part in a relaxing activity are usually healthier. They are sharper mentally and live longer than people who work hard all the time and never relax.

When God created the world, He worked for six days. Then on the seventh day He rested. God gave us a wonderful example in this: do what needs to be done and then relax!

The Lord also set up something special for us to do when we take that time to rest. We can praise Him for sending Jesus to save us from our sins! We can do that anytime, but we do it in a special way when we spend time in church and Sunday school.

May God be a part of, and bless, your relaxing times.

_____Let's do: Ask someone about his or her hobby (surprise your pastor and ask him). Think about a new idea for a hobby.

_____Let's pray: Dear Father, thank You for time to relax and worship You. Forgive me when I have not taken enough time to enjoy Your blessings. In Jesus' name. Amen.

S. R.

HELP!

As Eric was about to clean up around a large bush, he heard some buzzing, but he didn't worry about it.

Dad looked just as Eric was reaching forward. "Stop!" he yelled. "There's a hornet's nest!"

Eric was wise enough to trust his dad. Dad had seen something dangerous—a hidden hornet's nest.

God called out to His people when they were in danger. In Jeremiah 46:27 God promises His people that He will save them. He tells them not to fear their enemies for He is more powerful.

God has saved us from afar. Long ago, at a place called Calvary, the devil attacked Jesus. Sinful men hurt and killed Him. But God was there. He let Jesus be killed—and counted it as the punishment for our sins. God the Father raised Jesus from the dead and He forgives us, for Jesus' sake.

We have enemies such as anger, fear, and sickness that threaten to hurt us. Who will protect us? God will! He gives us parents to teach us rules. He sends healing through doctors and medicines, and He calms our fears with a gentle word from a friend. Why? Because He loves us. God will always be with us, taking care of our earthly and heavenly needs.

Read from God's Word

"Do not fear, O Jacob My servant; do not be dismayed, O Israel. I will surely save you out of a distant place, your descendants from the land of their exile. Jacob will again have peace and security, and no one will make him afraid." Jeremiah 46:27

_____Let's talk: What are some ways God protects you?

_____Let's pray: Dear Lord, I believe that You watch over me with Your perfect and powerful love. Protect me from harm and keep me close to You. In Jesus' name. Amen.

S. R.

Read from God's Word

"Salvation is found in no one else, for there is no other name under heaven given to men by which we must be saved." Acts 4:12

Remember This Name

"I wish I had a different name," Jonathan told his mom one afternoon. "It doesn't seem very ..."

"Special?" finished Mom. "Your name was chosen for a reason that *does* make you special. A doctor told your dad and me that we'd never be able to have children. Then we found out you were on the way. We were so thankful! Your name means 'gift of the Lord.'"

Have you ever thought you'd like to change your name?

The first two people God created had special names. Adam means "from the earth" and Eve means "life."

Other people in the Old Testament had names with meanings. Some have taken the name Job to mean "he who turns to God." Isaiah's name means "the Lord saves."

Joseph was told by God to name his child "Jesus" because He was born to save His people from their sins. Jesus was punished for all the sins of all people for all time.

We pray to God in the name of Jesus. We encourage and bless each other in the name of Jesus. Honor and respect that name. Tell someone what that name means. Then they can share the wonder and blessing of His name!

_____Let's talk: What one good thing would you choose to have your name mean?

_____Let's pray: Dear Lord of all, thank You for loving me and calling me by name through Baptism. In Jesus' name. Amen.

S. R.

november

James Hahn

Tom Raabe

Dean Rothchild

Bonnie Schneider

Annette Schmacher

How to Scurry

Read from God's Word

Humble yourselves, therefore, under God's mighty hand, that He may lift you up in due time. Cast all your anxiety on Him because He cares for you. Be self-controlled and alert. Your enemy the devil prowls around like a roaring lion looking for someone to devour. Resist him, standing firm in the faith, because you know that your brothers throughout the world are undergoing the same kind of sufferings. And the God of all grace, who called you to His eternal glory in Christ, after you have suffered a little while, will Himself restore you and make you strong, firm and steadfast. To Him be the power for ever and ever. Amen. 1 Peter 5:6–11

Squirrels scurry here and there with their double-jointed hind legs, going up one tree and down the next. They glide around the trees and grass with their tails waving and bouncing as they go. They gather nuts and seeds for the coming winter. They don't look worried about anything attacking them—maybe that's because they have such keen eyesight!

Children scurry here and there, playing and learning all kinds of new things. They glide around waving hellos to their friends. They bounce back after an illness or a playground fall. They gather friends to play a game or materials to make a project. They don't look ...

Wait a minute. They *can* look worried! They can be worried about their grades and friends and pets and parents and their sins. Thoughts grow into worries, and worries can create anxiety.

God's children, young and old, don't have to be worried. In God's Word, Peter said, "Cast all your anxiety on Him [God] because He cares for you." God is inviting us to pray and bring our concerns to Him. As God's children, forgiven by Jesus' death and resurrection, we are washed clean in our Baptism. In Jesus we are living freely. Now we can scurry—not worry—around each day, secure in God's love.

———Let's do: List specific needs you or someone else may have, pray for them, and see how God answers those prayers.

———Let's pray: Gracious heavenly Father, as we scurry about this day, watch over us. In Jesus' name. Amen.

D. R.

Beware of the …!

Montel had a great view of the ball game. He wondered how he had been so fortunate to get that perfect view all to himself.

Soon he began to feel something crawling on his ankles. Ants! Montel's feet were on top a small anthill. Then he understood why no one had been sitting there.

People can be annoying like ants. We may become annoyed with ourselves when little things turn into worries. Wrong things we say and do can crawl into our conscience. We are bugged by sin.

We can move away from ants but only God can get rid of sin. God helps us feel bad and confess, or tell Him we are sorry for what we did wrong. John said, "If we confess our sins, He [God] is faithful and just and will forgive us our sins and purify us from all unrighteousness."

Read from God's Word

If we confess our sins, He is faithful and just and will forgive us our sins and purify us from all unrighteousness. 1 John 1:9 ✍

Jesus carried our sins to the cross. He laid down His life to earn forgiveness of sins for all people. His resurrection shows the Father's acceptance of His payment. How marvelous to hear God speaking to us when we hear our pastor say, "I forgive you all your sins" in the church service. Our lives have been delivered from the sin that crawls in us and through us. We are free.

———Let's do: Write a list of sins in two columns like two rows of ants on a march. Put a cross on the page in a way that reminds you of God's forgiveness of all sin through Jesus.

———Let's pray: Gracious heavenly Father, send Your Spirit to help us to confess our sins and know that Your forgiveness is for us. Help us to live as Your children. In Jesus' name and for His sake. Amen.

D. R.

Screech and Holler

Read from God's Word

At the sixth hour darkness came over the whole land until the ninth hour. And at the ninth hour Jesus cried out in a loud voice, "Eloi, Eloi, lama sabachthani?"—which means, "My God, My God, why have You forsaken Me?" When some of those standing near heard this, they said, "Listen, He's calling Elijah." One man ran, filled a sponge with wine vinegar, put it on a stick, and offered it to Jesus to drink. "Now leave Him alone. Let's see if Elijah comes to take Him down," he said. With a loud cry, Jesus breathed His last. The curtain of the temple was torn in two from top to bottom. Mark 15:33–38

While on vacation, Mr. and Mrs. Ramirez were startled at five in the morning. They were sleeping on the pullout couch in their friends' family room. The family's two pet birds began to chirp and chatter loudly as the room grew light in the dawn. There was no more sleeping. Mr. Ramirez named those two annoying birds "Screech" and "Holler."

We run into other kinds of screeches and hollers that startle us. A traffic accident on the way to school scares our family and disables our car. Screech! The ball comes straight to us in a soccer game and our own player runs in front of us and steals the play. Holler! We are surprised by the ugly screeches and hollers that can start in our sinful hearts.

When unexpected things happen, it is a reminder that we are sinful and live in a sinful world. We holler about injustice, but really deserve the punishment of sin. God, in love, sent His Son to take the punishment. The real injustice of all times was done for us on the cross. There, Jesus cried out in a loud voice the screech of real pain and punishment. The perfect Son of God did nothing wrong. He did everything right for us so we could be with Him forever.

_____Let's do: Use the Ten Commandments to prepare for confessing your sins before God in church. Jesus says this truth: "I forgive you all your sins."

_____Let's pray: Gracious Father, bring us the comfort and peace that come from knowing our sins are forgiven. In Jesus' name. Amen.

D. R.

No Guarantees

D olly needed kindergarten puppy classes to learn good behavior. She learned leash manners and good behavior.

It took almost two years for Dolly to become obedient. During those years she often forgot what her owners taught her and she continued to make mistakes. Sometimes she even did wrong things on purpose. But her owners tried to be patient and consistent. Eventually Dolly got a certificate that says she passed kindergarten. But there were no guarantees that she would be a perfect dog.

God wants us to be obedient too. He gives us His Word as a guide. In His Law He tells us to obey those in authority over us. Christian parents, teachers, pastors, and other leaders try to direct us according to God's Word. They aren't always successful, and neither are we. We are sinful—in our words, deeds, thoughts, and our very nature.

Read from God's Word

Your attitude should be the same as that of Christ Jesus: Who, being in very nature God, did not consider equality with God something to be grasped, but made Himself nothing, taking the very nature of a servant, being made in human likeness. And being found in appearance as a man, He humbled Himself and became obedient to death—even death on a cross! Therefore God exalted Him to the highest place and gave Him the name that is above every name, that at the name of Jesus every knee should bow, in heaven and on earth and under the earth, and every tongue confess that Jesus Christ is Lord, to the glory of God the Father. Philippians 2:5–11 ✍

But God is patient with us. He sent Jesus, who "humbled Himself and became obedient to death—even death on a cross!" Jesus kept the Law of God perfectly. He died and rose victorious. He offers us more guarantees than a certificate for passing kindergarten. And He gives us all good things—death and resurrection with Him, His righteousness, His keeping the Law perfectly, forgiveness, eternal life—in Baptism. What a blessing!

_____Let's do: List the tasks your parents expect you to carry out. How does the new life you have been given in Baptism enable you to joyfully carry out those tasks? Read Galatians 2:20.

_____Let's pray: Heavenly Father, thank You that I am forgiven— joined to Christ by Baptism into His death and resurrection. Help me live this day to Your glory. In Jesus' name. Amen.

D. R.

A Gift of Love

L aura washed the few dishes left in the sink, swept the kitchen floor, and emptied the trash can.

"Hi, Laura," said Mom. "Wow! Everything looks great!"

"Is there anything else I can do for you, Mom?" asked Laura.

"I'm happy you want to help me, but why are you doing all this housework?" asked Mom.

Laura relied shyly, "My birthday is next week. I thought if I did some extra work I might get a special gift."

Laura is doing what seems natural—working to earn something. For many of us, a gift is hard to receive without thinking that something should be given in return.

The most precious gift of all comes from Jesus, and there is absolutely nothing we can do to earn it. He freed us from sin by dying on the cross and then coming alive again. Even now He is at work preparing a heavenly place for us by His baptizing, preaching, and absolving us from sin. It is in these "earthy" things right in front of us that Jesus Himself is giving us His gift of love: His forgiveness, eternal life, and salvation.

Mom gave Laura a big hug. "Laura, you don't have to earn your gift! I want to give you one because you are my daughter and I love you."

_____Let's talk: What's the best gift in the world? Whom can you tell about Jesus' gift of eternal life?

_____Let's pray: Dear Jesus, thank You for loving us. Thank You for earning for us the gift of eternal life. Amen.

B. S.

Opposites

Winter is *five* months long in North Dakota! Eventually spring arrives. Then summer. Then fall. Then winter returns.

Like the seasons, everything has its time. We welcome a new baby and may say a tearful good-bye to a great-grandparent. We cry with our friends when they are hurting and laugh with them over a funny story. We cut up pieces of construction paper and put them together again to make an art project. We find our homework and lose our socks. We learn how to multiply fractions one day and how to divide them the next.

What is the meaning of all this change? Under God's control the seasons roll around—even long seasons like winter in North Dakota. Under His control friends are bonded and families formed. Under His guidance we go to school and learn new things.

Although life brings many changes, God's love and mercy remain constant. Under His grace we endure the changes life brings. God shows us our errors and sinful nature by His Word of Law, His commandments, which we have not kept. He also brings us the gift of forgiveness and eternal life through Jesus. He sends us into each new day with the promise of His forgiveness in Jesus—and a love that will never change.

> **Read from God's Word**
>
> *There is a time for everything, and a season for every activity under heaven: a time to be born and a time to die, a time to plant and a time to uproot, a time to kill and a time to heal, a time to tear down and a time to build, a time to weep and a time to laugh, a time to mourn and a time to dance, a time to scatter stones and a time to gather them, a time to embrace and a time to refrain, a time to search and a time to give up, a time to keep and a time to throw away, a time to tear and a time to mend, a time to be silent and a time to speak, a time to love and a time to hate, a time for war and a time for peace. Ecclesiastes 3:1–8* ✍

_____Let's do: Write seven sets of opposites. Thank God for them.

_____Let's pray: Heavenly Father, we see change all around.
We are thankful that Your love and forgiveness
for us never change. Amen.

D. R.

Read from God's Word

"Salvation is found in no one else, for there is no other name under heaven given to men by which we must be saved." Acts 4:12 ∽

Special Names

L ook at this sample list. What category do you think your name fits into?

Biblical—Abraham, Hannah, Sarah, Daniel

Historical—Conrad, Agnes, Leopold, Victoria

Presidential—Thomas, Madison, Taylor

Virtuous—Blythe, Justine, Faith, Hope

World figures—Frederick, Nicholas, Catherine, Isabella

Movie stars—Ashton, Gwyneth, Brittany

Sports figures—Tiger, Martina, Venus

No matter what category your name is in, or even if you didn't find a category for your name, one unlisted category fits us all. We are all sinners. Abraham, Brad, Mickey, and Steffi are all sinners. And as sinners, nothing about us or in us can save us from sin. We need God, who comes from outside of us, to claim us and to save us.

God did that in Jesus. It was Jesus who paid for the sins of all people. Because of Jesus' work, God claims us as His. In the name of Jesus we have salvation. "For there is no other name under heaven given to men by which we must be saved."

When we were baptized in the name of the Father and of the Son and of the Holy Spirit, we received God's name. In our Baptism, God came to us and said, "You are Mine!" Now His perfect name belongs to us. We are named Christian.

_____Let's do: Ask your parents why they chose your name for you. Does it have special significance in your family?

_____Let's pray: Heavenly Father, thank You for calling me to be Your own in Holy Baptism. Help me to live to Your glory and forgive me when I don't. In Jesus' name. Amen.

D. R.

I Need My Daddy!

Read from God's Word
"And call upon Me in the day of trouble: I will deliver you, and you will honor Me." Psalm 50:15

It had been six months since Tyler and his grandfather had been together. It didn't take long, however, for them to become the best of buddies.

One day during their visit, Tyler was riding his bicycle. Suddenly he hit a bump in the sidewalk, and the bike tipped. Grandpa tried to catch him, but didn't reach him in time. His knee and arm hit the sidewalk, and he immediately began to cry. Grandpa helped him up and tried to comfort him. "I need my daddy!" he sobbed as the tears trickled down his cheeks. He finally stopped crying when his daddy held him.

We have a heavenly Daddy who cares for us even more than our dads, moms, or grandparents. When someone calls us a name or makes fun of us, when we do poorly on a test, His arms are open. When we don't make the team or get the part in the play, He is always there. Our heavenly Daddy invites us to call on Him. He provides, protects, and cares for us in all our troubles.

When our skinned-up hearts are aching or our consciences suffer because of our sins, our heavenly Daddy is ready to scoop us up in His arms and forgive us.

_____Let's do: Jot down some times you have been hurt. Who helped you? Thank God for those persons.

_____Let's pray: Dear Father, thank You for comforting us when we are hurt and for forgiving us when we do things that hurt You and others. Amen.

J. H.

Read from God's Word

But when the kindness and love of God our Savior appeared, He saved us, not because of righteous things we had done, but because of His mercy. He saved us through the washing of rebirth and renewal by the Holy Spirit, whom He poured out on us generously through Jesus Christ our Savior, so that, having been justified by His grace, we might become heirs having the hope of eternal life. This is a trustworthy saying. And I want you to stress these things, so that those who have trusted in God may be careful to devote themselves to doing what is good. These things are excellent and profitable for everyone. Titus 3:4–8 ✐

One Red Ornament

It wasn't even close to Christmas, but the ornament hung from the center of the classroom ceiling. Can you guess why Mr. Hahn might have one red Christmas ornament suspended in that room? Was it because ...

It was still there from last year?

It represented Mars in the solar system model?

It served as a reminder?

Yes. The ornament was a daily reminder that Jesus was God's mercy plan for the sinful world.

Mr. Hahn knew this year's students would need mercy just as much as last year's students. So he left the ornament hanging.

Whenever the friendships got rough in that classroom or someone lost their patience, they had *one* red ornament to remind them God was the only *One* who could help.

Whenever mistakes in long division led students to cheat, the one *red* ornament hung as a reminder that God sent Jesus to shed His *blood* for all people.

Whenever children had a chance to read God's Word or discuss the Sacraments, they could see the beautiful love God has for His church. They could look at the one red *ornament*.

One red ornament. One more reminder of the love God provides for His church and *in* His church when He "saved us through the washing" of Baptism.

_____Let's do: Jot down the gifts God gives you today!

_____Let's pray: Dear God, thank You for the gifts You give me every day, especially the gift of Jesus. Amen.

J. H.

Watch Out for the Hook!

Grandpa, can I hold one of your lures?" asked Chris.

"Sure," Grandpa said, "watch out for the hook! It could hurt."

Chris examined a rainbow-colored one. "Why do you have so many different kinds?"

Grandpa explained, "Because each kind of fish is interested in a different size, shape, and color of an object. But all those lures do the same job. That's to trick the fish into thinking it is something good to eat."

The devil also uses lures to tempt us into sin. He tries to trick us into believing that it is okay to cheat once in a while or to steal something. The devil wants us to think it is okay not to help someone or to disrespect our parents. Sometimes he wants us to think that no one will know. And sometimes we listen to him and get hooked.

We've all been hooked by our sinful acts and our sinful nature. We can't escape. Only Jesus can set us free. The fisherman can remove the hook and release the fish, but our release cost Jesus His life. He died and rose again so we would be free from the penalties of sin. Because of Jesus, we have forgiveness and new life here on earth and forever in heaven. The devil's hooks cannot hold us.

Read from God's Word

When tempted, no one should say, "God is tempting me." For God cannot be tempted by evil, nor does He tempt anyone; but each one is tempted when, by his own evil desire, he is dragged away and enticed. Then, after desire has conceived, it gives birth to sin; and sin, when it is full-grown, gives birth to death. Don't be deceived, my dear brothers. James 1:13–16

_____Let's do: Think of times when you have been forgiven. Write down times when you forgave someone else. What does it mean to say, "Because of Jesus we are forgiven, and now forgive"?

_____Let's pray: Dear Father, thank You for rescuing us from sin and setting us free. Help us to resist the devil and his lures. Amen.

J. H.

God Never Sleeps

Read from God's Word

I lift up my eyes to the hills—where does my help come from? My help comes from the LORD, the Maker of heaven and earth. He will not let your foot slip—He who watches over you will not slumber; indeed, He who watches over Israel will neither slumber nor sleep. The LORD watches over you—the LORD is your shade at your right hand; the sun will not harm you by day, nor the moon by night. The LORD will keep you from all harm—He will watch over your life; the LORD will watch over your coming and going both now and forevermore.
Psalm 121 ✍

Grant and his friends were amusing themselves by jumping from a swing. Each one tried to jump farther than the last.

When it was Grant's turn, he pumped as high as he could and launched himself out over the farthest mark. That was the good news. The bad news was that he landed on his arm. And his arm was clearly broken.

The doctor decided that Grant would need surgery. Grant was afraid—he'd never had surgery. The doctor tried to help by carefully explaining what would happen while Grant was asleep.

Grant's dad helped too. He said, "Although you may be sleeping during surgery, Grant, God never sleeps. He will watch over you every minute." Grant began to feel better after his dad reminded him about God's love and care.

What a comfort to know that the God who never sleeps is always watching, protecting, and caring for us. He knows all our needs—especially our need for a Savior. His loving and protecting care sent Jesus to earth to be our Savior from sin.

He continues to share His forgiveness and salvation through the work of the pastor at church in preaching, absolving, and distributing Christ's body and blood in the Sacrament.

_____Let's do: Write down names of people who watch over you and protect you. Thank God for those people and for His care.

_____Let's pray: Father, thank You for watching, protecting, and caring for us. Help us to trust You. Fill us with peace. In Jesus' name we pray. Amen.

J. H.

In the Box

One day as he was working in the garage, Jim's neighbor Amanda stopped in to see what he was doing. He explained that he was cutting some pieces of oak to make Christmas presents for his friends.

Amanda noticed a box next to the saw that had pieces of wood in it. "Why did you throw those pieces in the box?" Amanda questioned. Jim told her they were mistakes. He explained that there was no way to correct a cutting mistake. He could only throw it away because he couldn't use it.

Our sin is like these miscuts and we deserve to be thrown away. God didn't throw us away—although He could have. He didn't say, "I don't have room in this project for a sassy third grader or a back-talking daughter." In fact, He came into the world to save sinners. He reached into the scrap box of our sinful lives and gave us His perfection. He works faith in our hearts so we can believe in Jesus as our Savior. He gives us Baptism to create faith, and feeds and sustains that faith by His absolution, preaching, and the Sacrament of the Altar. All these fulfill His plan for our lives—we are forgiven.

Read from God's Word

Here is a trustworthy saying that deserves full acceptance: Christ Jesus came into the world to save sinners—of whom I am the worst. But for that very reason I was shown mercy so that in me, the worst of sinners, Christ Jesus might display His unlimited patience as an example for those who would believe on Him and receive eternal life. Now to the King eternal, immortal, invisible, the only God, be honor and glory for ever and ever. Amen. 1 Timothy 1:15–17

_____Let's do: Write down some things that are valuable to you. Remember to thank God that you are valuable to Him.

_____Let's pray: Dear God, thank You for forgiving my sins. Thank You for loving and rescuing me. Amen.

J. H.

Read from God's Word

You see, at just the right time, when we were still powerless, Christ died for the ungodly. Very rarely will anyone die for a righteous man, though for a good man someone might possibly dare to die. But God demonstrates His own love for us in this: While we were still sinners, Christ died for us. Romans 5:6–8

GPS

James and his friends had traveled to the Gulf of Mexico for a salt-water fishing adventure. The weather was ideal—sunny, with only a slight breeze.

Once the boat was in the water, they moved out into the gulf. The shoreline seemed to shrink and finally disappeared. When they were about 20 miles from shore, they headed even farther to a place where the fish were biting. James didn't catch any fish, but it was a nice day just the same.

As they began to head home, James wondered how they would ever find their way back. He saw no land.

The owner of the boat said James shouldn't worry because the boat had GPS—Global Positioning System. He explained that two satellites circling the earth provided the boat's exact location and the direction they needed to return to shore. Without the GPS, they would have been lost.

Sin causes us to be separated and lost from God. On our own, we are helpless to make our way back to Him. But God's Plan of Salvation—His GPS—provided the way back to Him. He sent Jesus to die and rise in payment for our sins. Jesus is the only way we can get to heaven. Because of Him we no longer need to fear being lost forever.

_____Let's do: Write out God's GPS. How and where does He carry it out?

_____Let's pray: Dear Jesus, thank You for rescuing us from sin, death, and the devil. Thank You for Your gift of eternal life. Amen.

J. H.

Pieces of Gold

Whitney spotted a pile of leaves and ran. She jumped into the gold leaves, lay on her back, and looked up at the trees. Every time the breeze moved the branches, more leaves showered to the ground. They looked like pieces of gold dropping softly through the air.

Whitney pretended she was very rich as she imagined all the leaves as gold. Her dad laughed and explained that people are rich in more things than gold or money. "Happiness," he said, "does not come from what you have. Think of all those gold leaves as God's blessings."

Whitney began to think about the "gold" that had been showered on her—Christian parents, good friends, lots of clothes, plenty of food, a nice home, and ... Her thoughts went on and on. The more she thought, the more she realized her dad was right. God had made her rich with blessings. She had become God's child in Baptism. God showered her with blessings—especially faith in Jesus as her Savior.

Whitney had many things to be thankful for this Thanksgiving. She was God's child and, best of all, He had given her His golden treasures—forgiveness of sins and life everlasting.

Read from God's Word

How great is the love the Father has lavished on us, that we should be called children of God! And that is what we are! The reason the world does not know us is that it did not know Him. 1 John 3:1

_____Let's do: Draw a plant. Write one thing for which you are thankful on each leaf. Start with Jesus.

_____Let's pray: Dear God, help us to give You thanks each day for all Your gifts to us. We thank You for sending Jesus to give us forgiveness of sins and eternal life. In His name we pray. Amen.

J. H.

Read from God's Word

"I will put My Spirit in you and you will live, and I will settle you in your own land. Then you will know that I the LORD have spoken, and I have done it, declares the LORD." Ezekiel 37:14

Our Bones Will Live

No one has ever seen a live dinosaur, but we know a lot about them—how they lived, what they looked like, what they ate. From just a few bones, entire dinosaur skeletons have been recreated. Their bones tell us about these mighty animals that once roamed the earth.

The prophet Ezekiel was granted a strange vision of dry bones, lifeless and bleached by the sun.

"Can these bones live?" the Lord asked him. Ezekiel knew the Lord could make them live if He wanted to. The Lord told Ezekiel to speak His Word to the bones. He did, and the bones became covered with muscle and flesh and came to life.

Our skeleton is made up of bones. After death, it's only a matter of time until bones are all that's left of our bodies.

We know God brought us eternal life in Jesus by removing our sins by the cross and speaking His forgiveness to us. We also know the human body will one day wear out and will die physically. But God will bring our bodies back to life again. When Jesus returns visibly, our bones will come back together and support our resurrected, perfect bodies to live for all eternity. The guarantee is Christ's triumph over death and the grave through His resurrection.

_____Let's talk: Read Ezekiel 37:1–14. What has God done and given in Baptism so our bones can live now and into eternity in heaven? How does the promise of life after death affect the way you think and live?

_____Let's pray: Your love for us is so great, Lord. Thank You for showing it to us in Your Son, Jesus. May we live in Him now and always. Amen.

T. R.

Eyes on the Cross

Leoni had trained hard and long for the track meet. She ran and ran, trying to build up her endurance.

"There will be times when you want to quit," her father had told her. "But you can't stop. I'll be at the finish line to cheer you on."

As Leoni rounded the final turn her lungs burned, her legs felt numb, and the inside of her mouth was as dry as a desert. Every cell in her body cried, "Quit! Save yourself all this pain."

But Leoni could see the finish line. She saw her dad cheering her on. She found strength to endure to the end.

Christians need endurance too. Worldly success, money, and popularity all seem more appealing than the discipline of following Jesus.

With every step along the way in our Christian lives, we have Jesus to inspire us. He didn't quit His difficult race. He was beaten and scourged, mocked and spat upon, and finally nailed to the cross—all for our sins. At the end He won a victory for all people. More than an inspiration, He is our Savior with us throughout our difficult race.

With our eyes on His cross, supported by Jesus living in us through faith, we can finish the race and receive His prize of eternal life.

Read from God's Word

Therefore, since we are surrounded by such a great cloud of witnesses, let us throw off everything that hinders and the sin that so easily entangles, and let us run with perseverance the race marked out for us. Let us fix our eyes on Jesus, the author and perfecter of our faith, who for the joy set before Him endured the cross, scorning its shame, and sat down at the right hand of the throne of God. Hebrews 12:1–2

———Let's talk: What does the cross of Jesus 2,000 years ago mean for your life today? (Read Romans 6:3–4.)

———Let's pray: Lord, help us to live with our eyes on Your cross. May the power of Your forgiveness keep us faithful to the end. In Jesus' name. Amen.

T. R.

Read from God's Word

Seek the LORD while He may be found; call on Him while He is near. Let the wicked forsake His way and the evil man his thoughts. Let him turn to the LORD, and He will have mercy on him, and to our God, for He will freely pardon. "For my thoughts are not Your thoughts, neither are your ways My ways," declares the LORD. "As the heavens are higher than the earth, so are My ways higher than your ways and My thoughts than your thoughts." Isaiah 55:6–9

Doing It His Way

arty's father had told him to rake the leaves in the direction the wind was blowing and to wear work gloves. But Marty didn't want anyone else to do his thinking for him. He decided to rake the leaves without gloves *against* the wind.

Marty had built a large pile of leaves, but many more had escaped in the steady wind. He noticed the large blisters that were forming on his hands. One had already broken and stung quite a lot. Marty began to regret doing things his own way.

"I want to do it my way." How often have we heard or said those words? In the Garden of Eden, Adam and Eve wanted to do things their way. God had made them in His image, sinless and holy. But at the tree of the knowledge of good and evil, they decided to go their own way.

When we do things motivated by our selfishness, we sin. We reject God's way.

But God sent His Son as our Savior. Jesus didn't sin, although He was tempted. He paid for our sins—all the times we have gone against God's way—on the cross. He made us right in God's eyes. And for eternity God's way will be our way.

_____Let's talk: What happens when we do things our own way?
How does God make His way our way?

_____Let's pray: Help us remember Your way in everything we do, Lord. Guide us by Your Spirit so the way we choose may be pleasing to You. Amen.

T. R.

Old Things and New Things

Read from God's Word

"Forget the former things; do not dwell on the past. See, I am doing a new thing! Now it springs up; do you not perceive it? I am making a way in the desert and streams in the wasteland. ... I, even I, am He who blots out your transgressions, for My own sake, and remembers your sins no more." Isaiah 43:18–19, 25 ༄

Imagine how the people of Israel felt when they were blocked by the Red Sea, with hundreds of mighty chariots bearing down on them.

Then something new and different happened. God parted the sea, and the Israelites safely walked to the other side.

God did many new and unheard-of things for the people of the Bible. He told them, as He tells us today, "Forget the former things; do not dwell on the past."

The people of Israel had rejected God. They worshiped idols rather than the all-powerful living God.

But God told them not to remember or despair over the old events. He would not hold these things against the people. He would do something new for them—send His Son to earth to become a human being.

And then this God-man Jesus died on a cross and rose again for our sins. Because of our Savior's death and resurrection, God doesn't remember our sins and they have no power over us.

The God who did all those new things for the people of Israel is still doing them for us today in our Baptism, when we hear His Word preached, and when He serves us from His altar. Each day He forgives our sins and renews His promise of eternal life. What a great God we have!

———Let's talk: What things have we done that are better off forgotten? How does God do His new thing in us?

———Let's pray: Jesus, Your death on the cross saved us. Help us always treasure the salvation that You offer us through it. Amen.

T. R.

Read from God's Word

When the people saw that Moses was so long in coming down from the mountain, they gathered around Aaron and said, "Come, make us gods who will go before us. As for this fellow Moses who brought us up out of Egypt, we don't know what has happened to him." Aaron answered them, "Take off the gold earrings that your wives, your sons and your daughters are wearing, and bring them to me." So all the people took off their earrings and brought them to Aaron. He took what they handed him and made it into an idol cast in the shape of a calf, fashioning it with a tool. Then they said, "These are your gods, O Israel, who brought you up out of Egypt." Exodus 32:1–4 ✍

Idol Makers

Mrs. Alcott read her class the story of the golden calf. While Moses was on Mount Sinai for 40 days, the people of Israel grew impatient. To replace God they built an idol like those they had seen in Egypt, thinking that an idol could help them.

Mrs. Alcott asked the students what they thought of the story.

"The children of Israel were stupid," Mandy said. "How could anyone worship a statue?"

A statue can't move or think. It's made of metal, wood, or stone.

The idols of today are things we begin to trust in more than God. Perhaps our idols are money, fame, sports, or good looks.

It's easy to let these things become more important than God. But they can never help us with our greatest needs—forgiveness of sins, strength for daily living, and the sure hope of heaven.

Only God can help us. God is as close as His Word and Sacraments. He speaks to us, comforts us, and tells us of His great plan for us. He turns our hearts toward Jesus, our dearest treasure, who shed His blood to win us back to the true God.

He can and will see us through the most difficult times.

_____Let's talk: What things serve as idols for us today? How can we keep from worshiping these idols?

_____Let's pray: Your Word, O Lord, is a light to our path. Give us the strength and wisdom to follow Your way. Amen.

T. R.

No More Revenge

The boys were playing touch football. Anthony had the ball and another boy tackled him to the ground.

Three other boys on Anthony's team were urging him to get revenge against the boy who had tackled him. It was his right, they said.

There was a person in the Old Testament who seemed to have every right for revenge. Joseph's brothers were jealous of the affection he received from their father, Jacob. They planned to kill Joseph, but instead they sold him into slavery, thinking they would never see him again.

Years later Joseph became the second most powerful person in all of Egypt. When his brothers traveled to Egypt to buy food, he could easily have gotten his revenge and made them pay for the horrible way they had treated him.

But Joseph forgave his brothers. He showed them love and forgiveness.

Read from God's Word

Then Joseph said to his brothers, "Come close to me." When they had done so, he said, "I am your brother Joseph, the one you sold into Egypt! And now, do not be distressed and do not be angry with yourselves for selling me here, because it was to save lives that God sent me ahead of you." ... And he kissed all his brothers and wept over them. Afterward his brothers talked with him. Genesis 45:4–5, 15

God doesn't try to get back at us for our sins either. God hates sin and He has every right to punish us. But Jesus came into the world to be our Savior.

By His death and resurrection, Jesus took all our sins away. How great that God did not seek revenge against us for our sins, but rather came after us to give His life for us.

——Let's talk: Why is it wrong to try to take revenge against someone? How should we act instead? Why?

——Let's pray: Thank You, Lord, for not getting revenge against us for our sins. Help us treasure the love and forgiveness You showed in sending Jesus to die for our sins. Amen.

T. R.

Read from God's Word

That my heart may sing to you and not be silent. O LORD my God, I will give You thanks forever. Psalm 30:12 ༆

Thanksgiving in September

People in the United States celebrate Thanksgiving on the fourth Thursday in November. Canada celebrates on the second Monday in October. When do you start getting ready?

Carolyn and Michael's family started to prepare for their Thanksgiving dinner during the summer. They visited a turkey farm and chose a young turkey from the farmer's large flock. The farmer printed their name on a band and put it on the turkey's leg. He would raise the turkey for the family. "By November he should be just the right size for your Thanksgiving dinner," said the farmer.

Carolyn and Michael's family visited their turkey several times that summer. Just after school started in September, the farmer phoned them. "Your turkey's already 24 pounds. Would you like to have Thanksgiving early this year?"

So the last Sunday in September they invited their relatives over for a turkey dinner! Grandma and Grandpa even brought pumpkin pie.

We don't have to celebrate Thanksgiving on a certain day. We don't even have to serve turkey! Every day we have reason to be thankful. We can celebrate and be thankful today. We can thank God for blessings anytime and anywhere. Since the greatest blessing of all is Jesus, our Savior from sin, every day can be Thanksgiving!

_____Let's talk: If you would celebrate Thanksgiving today, for what specific blessings would you thank God?

_____Let's pray: Dear Father, we thank You for all Your blessings, especially for the gift of Your Son, our Savior. Amen.

A. S.

Leader of the Flock

Susan learned a lot when she wrote a report on wild turkeys. Susan knew that only the males gobble, which surprised her classmates. She also told them that within a flock there is an order, where one turkey is the leader. Most of the time older birds dominate smaller birds and males usually dominate females.

We need order and leaders in our lives too. Often our leaders are older than we are—pastors, parents, teachers, brothers, sisters, or grandparents. Peer pressure also influences us. This means that peers (friends your age) can try to influence how you do things, making choices hard for you.

Leadership can be good or bad. Bad leadership can happen when kids convince their friends to skip classes, take drugs, or steal, or when adults use curse words (especially in front of their children). Sadly, the world is filled with sinful people who lead other sinful people into sinful acts. That's why God sent Jesus.

He was tempted in all ways like us, but He did not sin. However, Jesus didn't come to give us an example of how to live. He came to bring us forgiveness for our sins and now lives in us through Baptism, as our Savior.

Read from God's Word

"My command is this: Love each other as I have loved you. Greater love has no one than this, that he lay down his life for his friends." John 15:12–13 ✍

———Let's talk: Who are your leaders? How can you be a Christlike leader to others?

———Let's pray: Dear Jesus, help me to follow only You and to be a loving leader and friend to others. Amen.

A. S.

Pumpkin Teeth

Read from God's Word

A happy heart makes the face cheerful, but heartache crushes the spirit. Proverbs 15:13

"You have orange braces on your teeth!" said Grandpa.

Eric smiled. "I know, Grandpa. I had the orthodontist put orange bands on my braces right before Halloween. The kids at school called me pumpkin teeth. I like to make kids laugh!"

Grandma and Grandpa laughed too.

"Orange is a good color for Thanksgiving too," said Eric's little brother, Brian. "It reminds me of pumpkin pie. Yum!"

"I suppose you'll have red and green bands when we see you at Christmas," suggested Grandpa.

"That's a good idea!" said Eric.

God appreciates humor too. He says, "A happy heart makes the face cheerful." Think of all the funny-looking animals He created and the funny noises they make.

Who got the last laugh when Satan thought Jesus had lost the battle against sin on the cross? God's defeat was actually God's victory. Jesus conquered sin, death, and the devil—the ultimate last laugh about serious stuff.

Maybe you have a relative or friend who enjoys making people laugh. Maybe you are the class clown at school. Bringing joy and laughter are good gifts from God that we should enjoy—even more so when they provide new opportunities for us to talk about the Good News of Jesus.

_____Let's do: Just for fun, think about other times in the Bible when God the Father, or His Son, Jesus, must have had a good laugh. Share about these times with a friend. Have a good laugh!

_____Let's pray: Dear Creator, thank You for the gift of humor. Thank You also for refreshing our spirit with the joyful news of Jesus, our Savior. Amen.

A. S.

Christt the King

Paul noticed his brother's trombone by the door while the two were eating breakfast. "Dave, why are you taking your trombone to church?"

"I'm playing special music for Christ the King Sunday," answered Dave.

"What's that?" asked Paul.

"It's the day we celebrate that Jesus will come again at the end of the world. Some people call it Judgment Day," said Dave.

"So why is the brass ensemble playing today?" asked Paul.

Dave chewed his cereal thoughtfully. "Probably because the Bible says Jesus will come with trumpets on the Last Day."

"Bet that brass band will be better than yours!"

Dave smiled at his little brother. "Probably!"

Later in church, Paul and his family listened to the brass ensemble play the opening music. Paul thought, *Not bad! But if Dave wants to play in Christ the King's brass ensemble on Judgment Day, he'd better practice!*

Perhaps a brass ensemble plays at your church on special days like Easter, Pentecost, or Christ the King Sunday. Special music adds joy to the celebration of Christ's victory over sin and eternal death. We celebrate because Christ's victory makes it possible for us to join our King in our heavenly home.

Read from God's Word

Listen, I tell you a mystery: We will not all sleep, but we will all be changed—in a flash, in the twinkling of an eye, at the last trumpet. For the trumpet will sound, the dead will be raised imperishable, and we will be changed. For the perishable must clothe itself with the imperishable, and the mortal with immortality. When the perishable has been clothed with the imperishable, and the mortal with immortality, then the saying that is written will come true: "Death has been swallowed up in victory." "Where, O death, is your victory? Where, O death, is your sting?" The sting of death is sin, and the power of sin is the law. But thanks be to God! He gives us the victory through our Lord Jesus Christ. 1 Corinthians 15:51–57 ✎

———Let's do: Go to the Internet and listen to some of Handel's *Messiah*. It includes music based on 1 Corinthians 15:51–57. When you listen to the trumpet solo (and any other time you hear trumpets or trombones play), remember Christ the King and the celebration we'll have together in heaven.

———Let's pray: Dear Christ, my King, thank You for Your promise to prepare a place for me in heaven. Amen.

A. S.

Pilgrims in the New World

Read from God's Word

Then Jesus came to them and said, "All authority in heaven and on earth has been given to Me. Therefore go and make disciples of all nations, baptizing them in the name of the Father and of the Son and of the Holy Spirit, and teaching them to obey everything I have commanded you. And surely I am with you always, to the very end of the age." Matthew 28:18–20 ✍

If April showers bring May flowers, what do May flowers bring? (Pilgrims, of course!)

A ship called the *Mayflower* brought the Pilgrims to America in 1620. Today a replica of the *Mayflower* can be seen in Plymouth, Massachusetts.

Dressed like a Pilgrim, one actor on the ship tells this story: "We sailed from Plymouth, England, with 102 men, women, and children. Because the ship was only 90 feet long, beds were short, food grew scarce, and people became sick. After 65 days at sea, we finally landed. Praise the Lord!"

The Lord was with those Pilgrims as they sailed across the ocean and made their homes in the new world. God blessed them with food, protection from storms and enemies, and freedom to worship Him as they wished.

God brought them new life—not only through the Pilgrim babies but, more important, through the death and resurrection of Jesus. The Pilgrims had many reasons to celebrate the first Thanksgiving Day. They were Christians who rejoiced in God's grace in a new land.

God brings us this same Jesus by His Gospel. Like the Pilgrims we have freedom to attend church. In the Divine Service we hear the pastor proclaim the forgiveness of sins and give Christ's body and blood for our eternal life and salvation. All are reasons to celebrate.

———Let's talk: The Pilgrims saw only water for two months. How would you have felt? In what ways did God help the Pilgrims survive their journey? How is He helping you?

———Let's pray: Dear Lord, thank You for Your blessings, especially for Your great love in Jesus. Amen.

A. S.

Plymouth Rock

P lymouth Rock is a big boulder with "1620" carved in it. According to legend, the *Mayflower* Pilgrims stepped onto this rock when they landed in America on December 21, 1620. It had been months since the little ship set sail from Plymouth Harbor in England.

The stepping-stone was significant at the time, but that sure, solid footing did not last. Hidden at the end of a fencerow, the rock was considered nothing special for years. Then, over time sections of the boulder were moved for celebrations, cracking or breaking in the process.

Our Lord is both solid and sure. He is called the rock of our salvation. He is a rock that never splits or chips. Like the psalmist says in Psalm 62:2, "He is my fortress, I will never be shaken." Our lives can be shaken and treacherous, just like the Pilgrims' journey. Our lives are sinful and sin-filled with sickness, injury, guilt, or sadness.

Read from God's Word

My soul finds rest in God alone; my salvation comes from Him. He alone is my rock and my salvation; He is my fortress, I will never be shaken. Psalm 62:1–2 ∽

God sent His Son, Jesus, to secure a place for us in heaven by His perfect victory over sin, death, and the devil. Jesus is the rock who invites and empowers each of us to stand firm on Him. His Spirit gives us a lasting faith and shows us mercy throughout our long journey to heaven.

_____Let's talk: Imagine how the weary Pilgrims felt when they finally stepped onto Plymouth Rock. Can you think of a time when you've felt that weary? How was Jesus a comfort then?

_____Let's pray: Dear God, thank You for being my rock and my salvation. Keep my faith strong until I reach my heavenly home. In Jesus' name. Amen.

A. S.

Read from God's Word

"In My Father's house are many rooms; if it were not so, I would have told you. I am going there to prepare a place for you. And if I go and prepare a place for you, I will come back and take you to be with Me that you also may be where I am." John 14:2–3

Home for the Holiday

Hurry, Janna! We'll miss the plane!" shouted Lindsey. Just then Janna dropped the fruit basket she was carrying. Other passengers stopped to help the girls pick up the fruit.

"Thanks!" shouted the sisters. "Happy Thanksgiving!"

"We made it just in time!" said Janna as the two girls collapsed in their seats.

"What people will go through to get home for Thanksgiving! Remember the year we drove to Grandma and Grandpa's?" asked Lindsey. "The car stalled, and we had to be towed 90 miles."

The day before Thanksgiving is one of the busiest travel days in the United States. That's because many people travel many miles to spend Thanksgiving Day at home with their families.

Someday we'll be with family and friends in another home, the Father's mansion. Not only do we have Jesus with us now in His Word along with the water, bread, and wine, but also we will have an eternal holiday with Jesus.

Traveling to heaven isn't always easy. Hardships often make the journey difficult and temptations can put us off course. But our heavenly Father sent His Son to pay for our ticket and to help us overcome the obstacles.

Jesus promises to come again and take us home with Him, where we will have Thanksgiving eternally.

─────Let's do: Write out the letters to the word *Thanksgiving*. Think of one of God's gifts that starts with each letter. (Don't forget heaven.)

─────Let's pray: Dear heavenly Father, thank You for providing a way to heaven for us in Jesus. Guard and keep us as we travel home. Amen.

A. S.

No Way

Neither Jeff nor Tom had a car, and they needed one for a special project. They were planning to deliver groceries for Thanksgiving Day to needy families.

The friends began their search for a neighbor who would lend them a car or a ride. Several people wished them good luck but none agreed to help. Jeff and Tom were about to give up when they spotted a van with a flat tire slowing to a stop. A man in a business suit got out and examined the van's flat tire.

"May we change it for you?" Tom offered. "You're not dressed for changing that tire."

How do you think this story ended?

Thanksgiving Day is a time when we remember many blessings and thank God for them. Some blessings are taken for granted—like food, a place to live, and a family. Other bless-ings are special, like a new car or help from two friendly young men. Still others are blessings we will enjoy eternally, like God's love and forgiveness in Jesus.

Giving thanks is not just an annual event. It is a timeless response that comes from God. In worship, God reveals His blessings. He helps us enjoy them, give thanks for them, and share them with others.

———Let's talk: Who is the "least of these brothers of Mine" in your life? How will you thank God this Thanksgiving?

———Let's pray: Dear Jesus, thank You for all Your blessings. Help us use them to benefit others. Amen.

A. S.

Read from God's Word

"The King will reply, 'I tell you the truth, whatever you did for one of the least of these brothers of Mine, you did for Me.'"
Matthew 25:40

Thanksgiving to Christmas

Gail opened the front door for Aunt Ellen.

"Good morning, Gail. Are you ready?"

Aunt Ellen usually did all her Christmas shopping the day after Thanksgiving. She once said, "With my shopping out of the way I can concentrate on the real Christmas in December."

Gail was finally old enough to go on the long day's venture. She'd saved her allowance and made her list.

As Gail and her aunt studied ads in the newspaper, Gail's mom walked into the room. "How can you two rush into Christmas so soon?"

Sometimes we get so caught up in November and December activities that the real reason we celebrate Thanksgiving and Christmas can get lost.

Many years ago God used a star to lead some Wise Men to Jesus. They didn't know where the star would lead them, and they were distracted and delayed a short while in Jerusalem. Still, they never lost sight of the reason for their journey. God's star led them to Bethlehem, where they worshiped the Savior.

When you flip your calendar to next month, draw a star on December 25. This star can help you think about how the heavenly Father lovingly gave up His Son, Jesus. This baby is born to die. Celebrate the Father's love.

———Let's talk: Does your church have Advent services? How do these services prepare you for the coming Christ?

———Let's pray: Dear Jesus, as the Wise Men were led to You by the Christmas star, help us to keep our eyes on You. Amen.

A. S.

Decorated for Christmas

Read from God's Word

The ransomed of the LORD will return. They will enter Zion with singing; everlasting joy will crown their heads. Gladness and joy will overtake them, and sorrow and sighing will flee away. Isaiah 51:11

Sid and Kay look forward to the Saturday after Thanksgiving. Their family travels to cut down their Christmas tree on that day.

Sid and Kay live in Wisconsin, where the November weather is unpredictable. Sometimes it's cold and snowy. Other times it's warm and sunny. Whatever the weather, their family hikes through the tree farm until they find just the right Christmas tree. The trunk may be crooked on one side or rather bare. But after Sid and Kay decorate their tree with ornaments and bright lights, it is beautiful. They always declare it "the perfect tree."

Without Jesus, we're all like an ordinary evergreen tree. We're not perfect. We sin every day. God sent Jesus for all people. He forgives our crooked sinfulness and fills in our bare lives with love and forgiveness. God makes us beautiful, decorating us with the righteousness and love of our Savior. Once decorated, we reflect His love.

Our lives are just as unpredictable as Wisconsin weather. They may be filled with sorrow and sighing or gladness and joy. Through it all, God is always with us. In happy times and in sad times, He decorates our lives with the light and righteousness of His Son and declares us "perfect."

———Let's talk: What special Christmas ornaments or decorations does your family have that remind you of God's love in Jesus? What might be a good design for a new ornament? How do the decorations you put on your tree remind you of Jesus and God's love?

———Let's pray: Loving Father, thank You for making me Your own child and decorating me with Jesus' love and forgiveness. Amen.

A. S.

december

Contributors for this month:

Kim Bejot

Loreene Bell

Lawrence Eatherton

Steven Graebner

Ruth Maschke

Countdown!

Engineers use a countdown to check off items in preparation for a rocket launch. When they have checked each detail and gotten to zero, all systems are "go," ready for launch. Children might count off the days until a birthday party or a Christmas holiday. When there is a countdown, excitement builds. Important jobs get done.

Before Jesus was born, God began a countdown with Adam and Eve, and it continued with the prophets. It was close to zero when John was born. He was part of God's detailed preparations for the coming of the Savior. John would "go on before the Lord." He would "make ready a people."

Advent is a church season of waiting and preparing. We wait, lighting candles on the Advent wreath. We wait, listening to Old Testament prophecies that point to Christ's coming. We prepare, remembering our sinful condition and our sinful acts—showing our need for a Savior.

God works each Advent and year-round through His Word and Sacraments to bring people to Christ. He prepares hearts to receive His Son as the Savior of the world. He works through choirs of children as they practice singing the Christmas news and join in worshiping the Christ Child. And His countdown will continue until He returns on the Last Day.

> **Read from God's Word**
>
> *Then an angel of the Lord appeared to him, standing at the right side of the altar of incense. When Zechariah saw him, he was startled and was gripped with fear. But the angel said to him: "Do not be afraid, Zechariah; your prayer has been heard. Your wife Elizabeth will bear you a son, and you are to give him the name John. He will be a joy and delight to you, and many will rejoice because of his birth, for he will be great in the sight of the Lord. He is never to take wine or other fermented drink, and he will be filled with the Holy Spirit even from birth. Many of the people of Israel will he bring back to the Lord their God. And he will go on before the Lord, in the spirit and power of Elijah, to turn the hearts of the fathers to their children and the disobedient to the wisdom of the righteous—to make ready a people prepared for the Lord." Luke 1:11–17*

_____Let's do: List ways to help point others to the Christ Child.

_____Let's pray: Dear Jesus, thank You for the opportunities You
provide to tell the Good News of Your birth. Amen.

K. B.

Read from God's Word

For the wages of sin is death, but the gift of God is eternal life in Christ Jesus our Lord. Romans 6:23

The Unexpected

The snow started falling in the middle of the night. Will there be a snow day? The whole area was holding its breath. Finally the announcement came. No school!

Parents were thankful to have an extra day at home to catch up on laundry and bake Christmas cookies. Children started reading books, playing video games, bundling up for a trek in the snow, and eating cookies with hot cocoa. Teachers had an unexpected day at home. Many people looked at the unexpected snowstorm as a gift.

Jesus was both expected and unexpected. God's people had been waiting for the promised Savior from the wages (the price that had to be paid) of their sins. God sent Jesus at just the right time. During that "right time," He lived without sin and then died for our sins and the sins of all people, rising victorious on Easter morn. Now, through faith, we receive forgiveness of sins and life eternal.

Daily life is full of unexpected events—divorces, broken legs, lost pets—that alter future plans. But God's people never have to worry about their future because God has given them the long-expected gift, Jesus. He is with them now and forever, even when we might not expect Him to be there.

_____Let's talk: What are some of the unexpected blessings God gives you?

_____Let's pray: Dear heavenly Father, thank You for a world of unexpected gifts. Thank You for Jesus, Your greatest gift of all! Amen.

K. B.

Noteworthy Help

R ight away Miss B. could tell something was wrong with Kate.

"I can't get a note out of my flute." Kate was slumped in despair. "I've tried all week by myself. Maybe I should just quit."

Miss B. replied, "Let me hold the mouthpiece. You blow while I position it against your lips. Keep the air coming evenly," directed her teacher. Kate blew, and Miss B. adjusted the mouthpiece until the first sound occurred.

Kate learned how to hold the mouthpiece correctly and how to play other notes.

God sends many kinds of helpers for us. The Fourth Commandment reminds us of how our parents, teachers, police officers, pastors, coaches, and others are helpers sent by God. These people help us learn new things in life. They take care of many of our needs. Many of them teach us God's Word and show us how to live as God's children.

Read from God's Word

He is the atoning sacrifice for our sins, and not only for ours but also for the sins of the whole world. 1 John 2:2 ✑

No one can help us with righteousness (living perfectly). And we certainly can't help ourselves, because we are sinful. The only helper who can make us righteous before the Father is Jesus, the promised Savior. He is the only One who could atone (pay) for our sin. He's the Righteous One. He came to be our perfect helper.

_____Let's do: Make a list of the people God has given you as helpers. Don't forget Jesus. Thank each one.

_____Let's pray: Dear Father, thank You for helpers, especially those who tell me about You. Thank You for sending Jesus. In His name I pray. Amen.

K. B.

Read from God's Word

"For God did not send His Son into the world to condemn the world, but to save the world through Him. Whoever believes in Him is not condemned, but whoever does not believe stands condemned already because he has not believed in the name of God's one and only Son." John 3:17–18 ⌒

A Different Point of View

The percussion group's performance had been one of the most interesting assemblies the students had ever attended. The performers didn't use regular instruments—drums, cymbals, or maracas. They used everyday farm tools.

They played their first song on old plastic buckets. The group continued to amaze the audience using shovels, hammers, water coolers, car parts, and trash cans.

The "Cow-Barn Cha-Cha" was great. Milking stools, cowbells, milk jugs, an old cream, and even a cow skull can became musical instruments. Band members even aimed a large squirt gun at a bucket to create a sound like someone milking a cow.

When the show was over, the audience learned how the group had come up with so many different instruments. The director said, "We just look at things from a different point of view."

God sees us from a different point of view too. Jesus changes the way the heavenly Father looks at us. Through Jesus' work on the cross, the Father doesn't see His children as sinners without hope. He sees us as His redeemed children. Jesus saved us through His perfect life, death, and resurrection. Through faith in Jesus, made certain in Holy Baptism, we become God's beloved children. We are no longer condemned by our sins. We become instruments fit for service in His kingdom.

_____Let's do: Think of new ways that God sees you through Jesus. Then think of new ways God can use the new you to serve others.

_____Let's pray: Dear Jesus, thank You for dying and rising so the Father sees me through You. Thank You for the promise of heaven. Amen.

K. B.

Who Loves Me?

The day had gone badly from the beginning. First Janice couldn't find her left shoe. When she finally got to school, she remembered she was supposed to return her best friend's nail polish—the one on her dresser at home. Not only that, the cooks made salmon casserole with peas for lunch.

Janice felt like the entire school was ignoring her. When everyone piled into the car after school, Janice was in a horrible mood.

"How was school?" asked their mother.

"Awful!" cried Janice. "No one even cared that I was there."

"Oh, come on, sis," Jake said. "We saw you pouting at lunch. Maybe your friends were scared they would catch your attitude."

The fact is, often we may make it hard for others to love us. Our sin even separated us from God. He is the only One who cares about us *no matter what*. He loves us in good moods or bad. But this kind of love doesn't give us permission to be in a bad mood with Him or others.

God's love comes to us because of Jesus. He suffered and died on the cross for our sins while we were sinners. He changes our eternity and makes all things new in the light of His love and forgiveness and hope.

Read from God's Word

The LORD appeared to us in the past, saying: "I have loved you with an everlasting love; I have drawn you with loving-kindness. I will build you up again and you will be rebuilt, O Virgin Israel. Again you will take up your tambourines and go out to dance with the joyful." Jeremiah 31:3–4 ✍

———Let's do: Have you had a day like Janice? Write about ways God reminds you that He loves you.

———Let's pray: Dear Father, thank You for loving me even when I'm at my worst. Help me to rejoice in all things. In Jesus' name. Amen.

K. B.

A Heavenly Celebration

Kevin sat on the edge of his bed, staring at the floor, thinking. *Maybe, if I'm still, they won't take me along.*

"Kevin, it's time to go," Dad called.

Kevin didn't move. Soon he heard Dad coming up the stairs. "Why didn't you come when I called you?" Dad asked.

"I don't want to go. Every time I go, I cry," Kevin sighed.

"So do I, Big Guy," said Dad as he sat down.

"It's not that I don't want to think about Kendall. He was the best brother a kid could ever have," Kevin began.

"Then what is it, son?" his dad asked.

"Look around, Dad. I have Kendall's baseball glove, the model airplane he built when he was my age, and his stuffed bear. When I think about him here, it's always with happy thoughts. But when we go to the cemetery, I only think about him dying."

"Kevin, I feel mixed up too," Dad began. "The ache of missing Kendall is still strong, but we can celebrate his new life. Kendall died and rose with Jesus, in Baptism. We know Kendall is in heaven with Him right now. One day we will all be together in heaven."

"That will be the best celebration," Kevin said. "Let's call this the 'Anniversary of Kendall's Entry into Heaven.'"

_____Let's do: Think about someone you know who has been hurt by a loss. Write and tell them the ways Jesus is with them.

_____Let's pray: Dear Jesus, thank You for Your promise of eternal life. Amen.

K. B.

A Worldview

Read from God's Word

That if you confess with your mouth, "Jesus is Lord," and believe in your heart that God raised Him from the dead, you will be saved. For it is with your heart that you believe and are justified, and it is with your mouth that you confess and are saved. Romans 10:9–10

B rent collected key chains. He bought one every time he and his family took a trip. If his parents went somewhere, they brought one home as a souvenir.

He had key chains from all over the world. He had one with his name on it from Disney World, a model of the Sears Tower in Chicago, a surfboard from Florida, a revolving coin from Mount Rushmore, and many more. They were strung together in one long chain across his bedroom wall. At the very beginning of the chain was his favorite—the cutout of a cross.

One day he showed them all to his grandmother. She asked why the cross was first. He told her that seeing the cross reminded him that Jesus had died on the cross so he could be forgiven. He said that if you looked through the cutout of the cross, you could see the world differently.

God looks at us differently because of the cross. Jesus paid the price for our sins there. Now God gives us a new life and a new look, through faith in Jesus, calling us His and forgiving our sins. It doesn't matter where we are—Berlin or Mount Rushmore. We are different because of God's love in Jesus, the key of our salvation.

_____Let's do: Write a letter of thanks to Jesus for being with you wherever you go. Name at least five places you've been.

_____Let's pray: Dear Jesus, thank You for being with me wherever I go. Help me to remember Your promise of forgiveness and salvation. Amen.

K. B.

Read from God's Word

"And I will put enmity between you and the woman, and between your offspring and hers; He will crush your head, and you will strike His heel." Genesis 3:15 ⌇

A Clue for Christmas

Ben and Sam came into the house with smiles on their faces. They had a secret. Mom knew Dad had taken them shopping.

"So," she said, "did you get me something for Christmas?"

"Yes," Sam answered, "but we can't tell you what it is."

"But if you want a clue," Ben said, "they're blue and furry, and you put them on your feet."

Mom and Dad both burst out laughing. Ben didn't really tell Mom the secret, but he gave a pretty good clue, didn't he?

Mom said, "Just what I need and just what I want."

God promised Adam and Eve a Christmas gift too. He didn't tell them exactly what it was. But He gave them a pretty good clue in Genesis 3:15.

The Christmas gift was going to be a Savior. The Savior was going to suffer. But He was also going to crush the power of sin and Satan. That meant that Adam and Eve would not have to die forever. Adam and Eve probably never guessed that the Savior would be born in a manger. But they knew that God would give them life forever. That's just what they needed. That's just what they wanted. Jesus is God's Christmas gift to Adam and Eve and everyone. And He is wonderful!

_____Let's do: Look around you. Listen. What clues do you see and hear that tell you Christmas is coming soon?

_____Let's pray: Dear God, thank You for Your wonderful gift of Jesus. Forgive our sins and help us to tell the secret of Your love to others. In Jesus' name. Amen.

L. E.

No Mistake Here

Read from God's Word

"I am the Lord's servant," *Mary answered. "May it be to me as you have said." Then the angel left her.* Luke 1:38 ⮌

$\mathcal{S}$upper was over. Dad read the Advent devotion. It was about how God chose Mary to be the mother of God. She said, "I am the handmaid of the Lord" (Luke 1:38 RSV).

Then it was time to open the door on the Advent calendar. Today it was Beth's turn. Each day there was a Bible passage about Jesus' coming. There was one day, however, that had a mistake printed inside. Beth read the Bible passage. "I am the handmaid of tee Lord."

The two boys congratulated their sister. "Beth, you got the special door!"

Advent calendars can have a printing mistake, but God didn't make a mistake when He chose Mary to be the mother of Jesus. Mary was a sinful person just like you and me. She needed Jesus to be her Savior. But God also chose her to be Jesus' mother.

Mary was surprised, but she was ready to do whatever God asked her to do. She was honored to be the handmaid of the Lord. She was glad that her Savior was going to be born.

There are many things that make us happy at Christmastime. We make special things. We get ready in special ways. The most special thing is this. Jesus was born to be our Savior. And that makes all of us happy.

——Let's talk: God also chose you as His child. Tell about something you would like to do to help others.

——Let's pray: Dear God, thank You for choosing Mary to be the mother of Jesus. Forgive our sins and make us happy in serving You. For Jesus' sake. Amen.

L. E.

Read from God's Word

"For God so loved the world that He gave His one and only Son, that whoever believes in Him shall not perish but have eternal life." John 3:16

A Christmas Surprise

I know what you're getting for Christmas," Al whispered after school one day. "You're going to get a trumpet."

Leon just smiled and said, "Oh." You see, Al and Leon were cousins. He knew that Al was the one who was going to get a trumpet for Christmas. *Wow*, Leon thought, *he's sure going to be surprised on Christmas morning.*

Christmas morning came, and guess who was surprised?

They both got a trumpet! That was a Christmas Leon will always remember.

On the first Christmas many years ago, God surprised the world with a gift. The gift was the baby Jesus. But Jesus was not an ordinary baby; He was also true God, the Savior of the world.

Some people still don't believe that Jesus is the gift for them. They give gifts. They receive gifts. They may think that Jesus is a gift for someone else, but not for them.

Then it happens. A father attends a Christmas program. He listens to his son speak his part about a baby born in Bethlehem. He's heard the story before, but today by God's mercy he understands that gift is for him. The Holy Spirit uses the Word to tell this father that Jesus is his Savior too! God's mercy helps it be the best Christmas gift he ever received.

_____Let's do: Were you ever surprised to get a certain gift? Write about it.

_____Let's pray: Dear God, thank You for the Christmas surprise that happens when someone believes in You for the first time. Help us to share the story of Jesus with someone this Christmas. Amen.

L. E.

Watching for Christmas

I t was Wednesday evening. Little Jasmine was in church for an Advent worship service.

She knew that Christmas was coming soon. This worship service was a special way to get ready for Jesus' birthday. Jasmine listened and she watched. But soon she was tired. She leaned against Dad and he put his arm around her. Soon she was asleep.

Suddenly the people were singing. Jasmine woke up and looked around. "Is it Christmas?" she asked. "No," her father answered. "Not yet, but soon."

Long before Jesus was born, God told the people that Christmas was coming. He was going to send a Savior to take away all their sins. The people were excited. But soon, many of them were tired of watching and waiting. Was the Savior *ever* going to come?

Sometimes it's hard to wait for Christmas. We are like all those people who watched and waited for Jesus for so many years.

Finally Jesus came as a baby. That same Jesus comes to us now in His Word, and He gives Himself in Holy Communion.

We don't have to wait very long for Christmas. Keep your eyes open. Watch and wait. Be ready to sing for joy and celebrate Jesus' birth!

Read from God's Word

In the past God spoke to our forefathers through the prophets at many times and in various ways, but in these last days He has spoken to us by His Son, whom He appointed heir of all things, and through whom He made the universe. Hebrews 1:1–2

——Let's talk: What do you like most about Christmas? How can you help others remember that it is Jesus' birthday?

——Let's pray: Thank You, God, for all the people who waited and watched so many years for the birth of Jesus. Forgive our sins. Help us to be patient and trust in You. Amen.

L. E.

Read from God's Word

While they were there, the time came for the baby to be born, and she gave birth to her first-born, a son. She wrapped Him in cloths and placed Him in a manger, because there was no room for them in the inn. Luke 2:6–7 ✍

Inside the Wrapping

Brittany was wrapping Christmas gifts for her younger brothers and sisters the best that she could. When finished, she looked at the four little presents she had wrapped. The paper stuck out on the corners. There were wrinkles where it should have been smooth. But at least her brothers and sisters wouldn't be able to tell what was inside.

When God gave us the gift of Jesus, He let Mary wrap the gift. All she had was strips of cloth to wrap Him in. He was not the best-wrapped gift in the world. If you looked at that baby, all wrapped up in strips of cloth, what would you think? You might not be able to tell what was really inside. From the simple wrapping, that baby did not look special at all. But inside those swaddling clothes was the Savior of the world. He was God's special gift to everybody.

When Brittany's brothers and sisters opened up their gifts on Christmas morning, they were as happy as could be. Each gift was a special sign of love.

It is almost impossible for us to understand that God was wrapped in swaddling clothes. Jesus looked so weak and small. Yet inside the wrapping was God's gift of love. Born to die for sinners. Born to save you.

_____Let's do: Imagine three gifts all wrapped up. Imagine one more that could remind you of Jesus. What could it be?

_____Let's pray: Dear God, with each gift we wrap or unwrap this Christmas, help us to remember Your gift to us, wrapped in swaddling clothes. Thank You for Your gift of love and forgiveness. Amen.

L. E.

Come, Lord Jesus!

This year Tom had a special role in the Christmas program at church. He was the innkeeper. When Mary and Joseph came up to him, he was to say, "Stop! There's no room in the inn!"

Tom put both his hands up just like a police officer. He looked at Mary and Joseph with a frown on his face. Mrs. Brown said he was doing a very good job.

But Tom's sister Abby didn't agree. On the way home from practice, she said, "Tom, why were you so mean to Mary and Joseph? You were supposed to say, 'Come, Lord Jesus, be our guest!'"

Abby was too young to understand. The innkeeper just didn't know who Jesus really was! But Abby knew that things should have been different. Because Jesus loves everyone and gave so much for them, everyone should have room for Jesus.

Do you know someone who doesn't have room for Jesus? Maybe they just don't know about Jesus yet. How are you going to tell someone about Jesus this year? Whom will you invite to church? Whom will you send a Christmas card? These are ways to tell people about Jesus our Savior. When people realize that Jesus is their Savior, they don't say, "Stop! No room!" They say, "Come, Lord Jesus, be our guest."

_____Let's talk: Are you going to sing or speak in a Christmas program? What will you do to tell people about Jesus this Christmas?

_____Let's pray: Come, Lord Jesus, be our guest, and let Your gifts to us be blessed. Amen.

L. E.

Read from God's Word
And she gave birth to her first-born, a son. She wrapped Him in cloths and placed Him in a manger, because there was no room for them in the inn. Luke 2:7 ✍

Where Is Jesus?

The day finally arrived when the Christmas tree could go up. First the lights went on. Then the ornaments, each one with a special memory. Finally the star was placed on the top.

But there was still one thing more. It was the nativity scene. Dad set it in place under the tree.

Ben and Sam and Beth began arranging the figures. There were Wise Men, shepherds, a cow, a donkey, a sheep, and, of course, Mary and Joseph kneeling by the manger. But where was Jesus? "Look in the box! Did He get lost behind something? We can't have Christmas without Jesus!"

"Here He is!" Dad said. He opened his hand, and there was Jesus. "I was saving Him for just the right time," Dad said with a smile.

That's what our heavenly Father did. At just the right time, Jesus was born. God had been holding Him back until everything was ready. Then God opened His hand, and there was Jesus.

On Christmas morning, Beth got to put the figure of baby Jesus in the manger. Then they were ready to celebrate Christmas.

It's true. You can't have Christmas without Jesus. Jesus was born to be our Savior from sin. Christmas is all about Jesus, who still comes to us in the Divine Service.

_____Let's do: Write about your Christmas tree. What makes it special?

_____Let's pray: Thank You, God, for giving us Jesus at just the right time. Thank You for sending Him to die for our sins and save us. Thank You for opening Your hand of love and giving us Jesus. Amen.

L. E.

We Two Kings

Read from God's Word

The Lord will rescue me from every evil attack and will bring me safely to His heavenly kindom. To Him be glory for ever and ever. Amen. 2 Timothy 4:18 ✍

E verything was okay until the 'We Three Kings' song," reported Shawana, who had been Mary in the Christmas play. "When I heard the second king whisper, 'We *two* kings—number 3 is missing,' I laughed."

"It sounds like one of those two kings got you into trouble," suggested Mom.

"The real Mary was concerned about two kings—Jesus and King Herod," said Grandpa. "King Herod was jealous of Jesus, the newborn King. Herod tried to trick the Magi into finding Jesus for him. 'I want to worship the baby too!' he lied. God protected our Savior by whisking Him away to Egypt. Herod killed all the boy babies in Bethlehem, thinking he'd destroyed the new King."

"I sure wouldn't want to be like Herod," said Shawana.

"Me neither," answered Grandpa. "But there are times when we are jealous, deceitful, or mean to others. Like King Herod, we want things *our* way. Sin is in our earthly kingdom and our very being. We have no hope to rescue ourselves."

"That's why Christmas is so wonderful. The newborn King came to be our Savior—to die on the cross for our sins," Shawana said. "He forgives our jealousy, deceitfulness, and anger. And He will bring us safely through this life to His heavenly kingdom, where we will be with Him in glory."

_____Let's talk: Which word/words in each pair describe Jesus? Rich/poor; died/died and rose; murdered many/died for all; kept promises/lied; proud/humble; hateful/loving; forgiving/jealous; all-powerful/power-hungry.

_____Let's pray: Dear Lord, help us follow and worship Jesus, our light and our salvation. Amen.

R. M.

Read from God's Word

For to us a child is born, to us a son is given, and the government will be on His shoulders. And He will be called Wonderful Counselor, Mighty God, Everlasting Father, Prince of Peace. Of the increase of His government and peace there will be no end. He will reign on David's throne and over His kingdom, establishing and upholding it with justice and righteousness from that time on and forever. The zeal of the LORD Almighty will accomplish this. Isaiah 9:6–7

Great News!

Some people claim they know what's going to happen in the future. They use some very silly objects to help them do that—tea leaves, glass balls, even the lines in the palm of someone's hand.

Only God knows the future. Long ago He chose prophets to warn His chosen people about their sinfulness and to promise them God's mercy and pardon.

A prophet named Isaiah carried a special message from God to His people. We read that message in Isaiah 9, where God said He was going to send someone to set up a kingdom that would last forever.

Do you know who Isaiah was talking about? It was to be a newborn baby boy, a human descendant of King David. He would be God too.

The prophet was talking about the baby Jesus. What God had said hundreds of years before, through Isaiah, finally came true. God sent His Son to save us from eternal punishment for our sins.

God told us through His prophets that He loves us. He showed us this through the gift of His only Son. We don't know why God loves us so much. We only know He does. He said so and proved it by sending Jesus to die for our sin. What great news to share!

_____Let's talk: Why is God's good news the best message we can ever receive? What do you think Jesus' four names in Isaiah 9:6 mean?

_____Let's pray: Dear God, thank You for Your Word, which tells of Your love. And thanks for sending Jesus to be my Savior. Amen.

L. B.

What's Missing

Y ou may call the nativity scene a manger scene (American); *crèche* (French); *krippe* (German); *praesepio* (Italian); *nacimiento* or *pesebre* (Spanish); *svokka* (Polish); *steaua* (Romanian); *putz* (Moravian). No matter what you call it, are you sure you have all the pieces to tell the whole story?

Read verse 17 again. What figure of the Christmas story is shown one way but not another in the typical nativity scene? Most manger scenes don't tell the end of the story.

The shepherds are usually shown kneeling or worshiping the Christ Child. But it's not the whole story. The shepherds were so happy that they left the stable and told everyone the good news! There should be a nativity piece showing shepherds telling someone the good news.

A Chinese carol by Fan T'en-hsiang says,

Wondrous news through streets resounds, Poor man's Savior; peasant's Friend.

An Austrian carol also tells what verse 17 says:

Then shepherds be joyful, salute your great King. Let hills and dales ring to the song that you sing, Blest be the hour, welcome the morn, For Christ, our dear Savior, on earth now is born.

The shepherds spread the good news that the Savior was born. We can too! Christmas believers become Christmas missionaries, telling others about the Savior, who has paid for our sins and given us new life.

Read from God's Word

So they hurried off and found Mary and Joseph, and the baby, who was lying in the manger. When they had seen Him, they spread the word concerning what had been told them about this child, and all who heard it were amazed at what the shepherds said to them. But Mary treasured up all these things and pondered them in her heart. The shepherds returned, glorifying and praising God for all the things they had heard and seen, which were just as they had been told. Luke 2:16–20 ✐

_____Let's do: What joyful news about Jesus coming to save sinners could you spread on a Christmas card? Design one.

_____Let's pray: Heavenly Father, help me glorify and praise You, so others may know Jesus. Amen.

R. M.

Read from God's Word

"Today in the town of David a Savior has been born to you; He is Christ the Lord. This will be a sign to you: You will find a baby wrapped in cloths and lying in a manger." Suddenly a great company of the heavenly host appeared with the angel, praising God and saying, "Glory to God in the highest, and on earth peace to men on whom His favor rests." Luke 2:11–14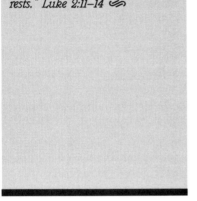

What's a Polyglot?

No, a polyglot isn't a friend of a pollywog. It isn't a many-sided inkblot. Nor does it mean "many angels." It isn't about Christmas—though it could be. The following example may help you figure out its meaning.

> Latin—*pax*
> Greek—*irene*
> Hebrew—*shalom*
> English—*peace*
> French—*paix*
> Italian—*pace*
> Spanish—*paz*
> German—*Friede*

Polyglot means "many tongues." A polyglot is a book or part of a book, especially a Bible, in which the text is written in two or more languages. Two to ten languages, or tongues, are printed in columns on each page. The most famous polyglot, printed in Spain in the 1500s, was in Hebrew, Latin, Greek, and Aramaic. In 1645, Syriac and Arabic were added. If you opened this polyglot to Luke 2:11, you could read the angel's announcement in six languages!

Whatever language the angels spoke, we know they announced the birth of the Prince of Peace. They gave glory to God for sending His Son to be our Savior from sin and death. Because of God's gift, we have peace—peace that comes from knowing Jesus, our Savior.

Like the angels, we can share God's peace in any language! So whether you speak ten languages or one, you can spread God's message of love and peace to all the world.

_____Let's do: Make two parallel columns. Label one "God's Peace" and the other "Earthly Peace." Then list words that describe God's and people's ideas of peace. Do they share the same concepts? What is your idea of peace?

_____Let's pray: Holy Spirit, we pray that this Christmas "many tongues" will announce that Jesus Christ is Lord and more people may come to know His peace. Amen.

R. M.

Christmas Questions

What decorations should we put up? What carols shall we sing? These Christmas questions are important, but the most important question is, What Child is this?

William Dix asked that question while writing the hymn "What Child Is This." Dix wonders why God was born into such a humble setting.

Another song, a spiritual, asks the question "What you goin' to name that pretty little baby?" The answer was given to Joseph by an angel of the Lord, "You are to give Him the name Jesus, because He will save His people from their sins" (Matthew 1:21). The person, character, and work of Jesus were described by the prophet Isaiah some 700 years before Jesus was born: "Wonderful Counselor, Mighty God, Everlasting Father, Prince of Peace." Jesus was no ordinary baby. He is the Word of God made flesh.

What Child is this? The answer can also be found at Easter. Dix's hymn continues: "Nails, spear shall pierce Him through, The cross be borne for me, for you!" The spiritual asks, "O Mary, where is your baby?" The answer: "They took Him from a manger and carried Him to a throne."

He is Jesus, the King of kings. He is God's Son, a gift from our loving Father, our Savior from sin and death.

Read from God's Word

This is how the birth of Jesus Christ came about: His mother Mary was pledged to be married to Joseph, but before they came together, she was found to be with child through the Holy Spirit. Because Joseph her husband was a righteous man and did not want to expose her to public disgrace, he had in mind to divorce her quietly. But after he had considered this, an angel of the Lord appeared to him in a dream and said, "Joseph son of David, do not be afraid to take Mary home as your wife, because what is conceived in her is from the Holy Spirit. She will give birth to a son, and you are to give Him the name Jesus, because He will save His people from their sins." Matthew 1:18–21 ✐

———Let's do: Tell the whole story with one simple picture!
Draw a manger and a cross.

———Let's pray: O dearest Jesus, holy child, Prepare a bed,
soft, undefiled, A holy shrine, within my heart,
That You and I need never part. (*LW* 38:5) Amen.

R. M.

Christmas A-Mail

When you were born, your parents announced the happy news of your birth. They may have used mail, telephone, telegram, fax, or e-mail. A-mail, although older, is the fastest. A-mail, by angel messenger, is instantaneous!

In Luke we are told of angel announcements——a-mail——to Zechariah, Mary, and the shepherds. Luke describes how:

1. Angels are God's messengers, serving His purposes. For example, they were sent to announce the birth of John and of Jesus.
2. Angels appear suddenly. Zechariah, Mary, and the shepherds were "startled," "gripped with fear," "greatly troubled," even "terrified." The angel always said, "Do not be afraid."
3. Angel messages proclaim peace and bring joyful news. Each message points to Jesus, our Savior.

If a-mail is from the angels, s-mail is from God the Holy Spirit. Whenever you receive God's absolution, hear the Gospel preached, and study the Bible, you are touched by the God of the angels. He announces that because Jesus was born and died for your sins, you are forgiven. The Holy Spirit gave you faith and continues to send messages through His Word.

Praise and worship Jesus, your Savior, joyfully this Christmas!

_____Let's talk: Read Luke 1:11–31 and 2:1–14. What can God's Christmas angels tell you about worship, fear, faith, praise, and serving God? How will you announce the good news?

_____Let's pray: Thank You, Father, for sending Your holy angels to announce the special birth of Your Son. Help me announce to others, "Christ, our Savior, is born!" Amen.

R. M.

Be Prepared!

M ama has been shopping a long time, Papa," Ricardo said.

Just as he finished his sentence, a car drove up. A stranger got out of the car with Mama. He introduced himself and told Papa what happened. "I'm Mr. Scott," the stranger said. "Your wife had an accident on an icy road. I'm glad she wasn't hurt because neither of us was prepared." Then Mr. Scott left.

At devotions, the family read Matthew 11:10: "I will send My messenger ahead of You, who will prepare Your way before You."

"God was prepared even if I wasn't," said Mama. "I prayed when the car began sliding, and God kept me safe. Then He sent Mr. Scott to help me."

"Think how God prepared His people for Jesus' coming," Papa said. "He sent prophets, like Isaiah and Malachi. To be ready for the Savior, the people needed a change of heart that included being sorry for their sins and turning to God. And that's what John preached to prepare the way."

Ricardo wondered, "So when God helps us to be sorry for our sins, we are prepared for Christmas?"

"Yes," said Papa. "Jesus came to save us, and He has made us well-prepared for heaven!"

Read from God's Word

*This is the one about whom it is written: "I will send My messenger ahead of you, who will prepare your way before you.'"
Matthew 11:10* ᴄᴐ

———Let's do: Unscramble these words to find ways to prepare for Christ's coming: ovle, hiorspw, veig gfsti, tiisv eth ciks, dare het eBlib, eb rosyr ofr ym snis, ayrp, elph het oopr.

———Let's pray: Dear Jesus, prepare my heart this Christmas to make way for You. I trust in Your love and mercy. Amen.

R. M.

Read from God's Word

An angel of the Lord appeared to him in a dream and said, "Joseph son of David, do not be afraid to take Mary home as your wife, because what is conceived in her is from the Holy Spirit. She will give birth to a son, and you are to give Him the name Jesus, because He will save His people from their sins." Matthew 1:20–21

The Work Tree

Aressa's family decorates their Christmas tree with ornaments that reminded them of jobs their family members had in the past.

"Mom," Aressa asked as they were hanging the ornaments on the tree, "what does this bouquet of flowers mean?"

"That's for the job your granddad once had," Mom explained. "He worked as a gardener for the cemetery."

"And what about this one?" Aressa continued, touching an ornament that looked like an ice-cream soda. "Is that for the job you had at the ice-cream shop when you met Dad?"

"That's right," said her mom.

"But what about the cross we put on top of the tree?" asked Aressa.

"It is there to remind us of Jesus' job."

"Jesus' *job*?" wondered Aressa. "But He was just a baby at Christmas. What job did He have?"

"The most important job in the world," said Mom. "He was born to be our Savior. To do that, He had to die on a cross. Baby Jesus grew up and did His job. He died and rose again. That is why He was born."

Aressa thought for a minute. "That's the hardest job on our tree, Mom. I'm glad it belongs to Jesus. No one else could ever do it!"

_____Let's talk: Why could no one else do the job that Jesus did? What stories do your Christmas ornaments tell?

_____Let's pray: Dear Father, thank You for sending Jesus to do the job only He could do. In Jesus' name I pray. Amen.

S. G.

Follow Your Nose

A s soon as he woke up in the morning, Lamont could tell what the evening meal would be.

Mom was preparing one of their favorite meals in the slow-cooker. The smells in the air that morning told Lamont that a great meal was going to be ready in the evening.

Just as the smells excited Lamont because he knew what to expect for supper, Christmas smells excite us. We know a great celebration is coming soon. The aroma of cookies and cakes sweetens the air. Christmas trees fill our homes with a woodsy, pine scent. In some parts of the country a fresh, clean snowfall will leave its own special smell.

The unique Christmas scents, like the smell of straw in a manger, help us to recall God's gifts. He sent Jesus to pay for the world's sins. He gives us the clean, fresh water of Baptism, which washes away our sins. He gives us His own body and blood through the wine and the bread of Communion. He gives us love for others and helps us share it.

A great celebration is coming! There may be special meals and gift exchanges with family and friends. But the main course of Christmas, the real reason to look forward to celebrating, is God's greatest gift—Jesus!

Read from God's Word

The beginning of the gospel about Jesus Christ, the Son of God. It is written in Isaiah the prophet: "I will send My messenger ahead of you, who will prepare your way"—"a voice of one calling in the desert, 'Prepare the way for the Lord, make straight paths for Him.'" And so John came, baptizing in the desert region and preaching a baptism of repentance for the forgiveness of sins. The whole Judean countryside and all the people of Jerusalem went out to him. Confessing their sins, they were baptized by him in the Jordan River. John wore clothing made of camel's hair, with a leather belt around his waist, and he ate locusts and wild honey. And this was his message: "After me will come one more powerful than I, the thongs of whose sandals I am not worthy to stoop down and untie. I baptize you with water, but He will baptize you with the Holy Spirit." Mark 1:1–8 ✏

_____Let's talk: What do you think Mary and Joseph smelled a few hours before Jesus was born? What are your favorite Christmas smells?

_____Let's pray: Heavenly Father, help us enjoy the Christmas gifts You have given us, especially the gift of Jesus, our Savior. In His name we pray. Amen.

S. G.

A Christmas Drama

Read from God's Word

In those days Caesar Augustus issued a decree that a census should be taken of the entire Roman world. (This was the first census that took place while Quirinius was governor of Syria.) And everyone went to his own town to register. So Joseph also went up from the town of Nazareth in Galilee to Judea, to Bethlehem the town of David, because he belonged to the house and line of David. He went there to register with Mary, who was pledged to be married to him and was expecting a child. While they were there, the time came for the baby to be born, and she gave birth to her firstborn, a son. Luke 2:1–7 ✑

Voice: I know you have plans, but you've got to come!
Group: Where? We've got presents to open, songs to sing, and a feast to eat.
Voice: Come, all of you.
Group: It had better be someplace good.
Voice: Come along. Out this way ...
Group: Out this way? This is nowhere!
Voice: Come to this small town, just a few buildings at a crossroads out in the country, just a few hundred people.
Group: Why did we leave our wonderful Christmas to come out here?
Voice: Come quickly to this field, to this little cave.
Group: But it's muddy and dirty—they keep animals here!
Voice: Come around; come in. There's something to see.
Group: What could be worth seeing here? Can't we go back to our festive Christmas celebration?
Voice: Just come in and see. There, in the dust and straw and dirt. There is the baby.
Group: Who is that? Why is He here? Where are the presents? Why is no one singing carols? Where are the lights?
Voice: Shhh—you'll wake Him. We've come to Bethlehem. We've come to see Jesus in a manger. Here is where everyone learns the true meaning of Christmas.
Group: Here is where Christmas begins!
Voice: Come to see Him!

_____Let's talk: Where in the Divine Service can you see Jesus?

_____Let's pray: God, help me begin my Christmas celebration at Bethlehem's manger. Amen.

S. G.

A New Life

Read from God's Word

"The Spirit of the Lord is on me, because He has anointed me to preach good news to the poor. He has sent me to proclaim freedom for the prisoners and recovery of sight for the blind, to release the oppressed, to proclaim the year of the Lord's favor." Luke 4:18–19

Richard's dad had been in prison for a long time. During holidays—especially at Christmas—he and his mom were lonely.

Richard tried to get excited about Christmas, and his mom tried hard to make things nice. Sometimes the thought of opening presents did make him smile. A few days ago, he saw a large box under a blanket in the attic.

And so, early on Christmas morning, Richard woke up and ran downstairs to see if the large box was under the tree. It was!

Then someone whispered his name. He turned around and there was his father! His dad had been released from prison! This was the best Christmas ever! His dad's freedom was more important than any other gift he could have received. Richard and his parents could begin a new life together.

We have been released from a prison too. Sin put us in a prison, keeping us far away from God. Then God sent His Son to set us free. Because of the Christ Child, we have the most important gift God can give us—freedom from sin and death. Now we can be together with God and have a new life.

Jesus' birth means a new life for us—a life full of love and joy with God!

_____Let's talk: Think about all the gifts you have received. What is your greatest gift? What does Jesus' birth mean to you?

_____Let's pray: Dear Jesus, happy birthday! You have given me a new life full of joy and love. Help me share Your love with others. Amen.

S. G.

Read from God's Word

Yet to all who received Him, to those who believed in His name, He gave the right to become children of God—children born not of natural descent, nor of human decision or a husband's will, but born of God. The Word became flesh and made His dwelling among us. We have seen His glory, the glory of the One and Only, who came from the Father, full of grace and truth. John 1:12–14 ✍

Life-Changing Gifts

Erin was so excited when her baby brother was born—at first. But later on she was disappointed. Everyone was paying attention to Garrett. Daddy didn't even have time to read her usual bedtime story. Erin's whole life had changed!

"Mom," Erin said one day, "can you send Garrett back? I don't think I like having him around."

"I know things are different, Erin," replied her mom. "Someday you'll be glad to have a brother. You'll be surprised at all the ways he'll be able to help you."

Mary and Joseph found that life had changed after Jesus was born too. There were no more shepherds worshiping, no more reports of angels. There was just this baby who needed a lot of care.

Your Christmas excitement may fade soon too. You have chores to do and brothers and sisters to put up with. But God helps you keep celebrating! Jesus is part of your life!

Jesus gives you and all other believers the gifts of forgiveness and eternal life in heaven. Because Jesus gave His life on the cross and the Holy Spirit brought you to faith in Jesus, you are a child of God. You are baptized. Right now, and every day in the future, you can celebrate His life-changing gifts.

_____Let's talk: How does faith in God's promises help you handle disappointments?

_____Let's pray: Dear Father in heaven, help me celebrate the birth of my Savior, Jesus, every day! Amen.

S. G.

Spelling It Out

Match each numbered phrase in the first list with an answer from the second list. Put the answer's letter in order in your journal. When all phrases are matched with their answers, read the letters to discover what the Bible said the Savior's birth would mean.

___1. Told Mary she would have a baby. (Luke 1:26–27)

___2. What the first half of the Bible and Elizabeth have in common. (Luke 1:36)

___3. Jesus' royal ancestor. (Luke 1:32)

___4. You don't read about these worshipers in Luke's Gospel. (Matthew 2:1–2)

___5. Joseph and Mary were not welcome here. (Luke 2:7)

___6. Where Mary and Joseph took Jesus on their first family outing. (Luke 2:27)

___7. Zechariah's earthly ruler. (Luke 1:5)

___8. Mary and Joseph went _____ from Galilee to Bethlehem. (Luke 2:4)

___9. Who, according to the angel, was Mary's baby? (Luke 1:32)

Read from God's Word

Comfort, comfort My people, says your God. Speak tenderly to Jerusalem, and proclaim to her that her hard service has been completed, that her sin has been paid for, that she has received from the LORD's hand double for all her sins. A voice of one calling: "In the desert prepare the way for the LORD; make straight in the wilderness a highway for our God. Every valley shall be raised up, every mountain and hill made low; the rough ground shall become level, the rugged places a plain. And the glory of the LORD will be revealed, and all mankind together will see it. For the mouth of the LORD has spoken." Isaiah 40:1–5 ✍

D. David

E. East

G. Gabriel the angel

H. Herod

I. The inn

J. Joseph

O. They are both old

R. Rome

S. The Son of the Most High

T. The temple

U. up

W. Wise Men (Magi)

_____ Let's talk: The name "Immanuel" has special meaning. The answer to the puzzle above will tell you. What does it mean to you as a baptized child of God?

_____ Let's pray: Dear Father in heaven, thank You for spelling out the meaning of the birth of Jesus for me. Amen.

S. G.

Read from God's Word

Yet the LORD longs to be gracious to you; He rises to show you compassion. For the LORD is a God of justice. Blessed are all who wait for Him! Isaiah 30:18

The Right Time

Paul was short and not very fast. He was missing three fingers on his right hand. But Paul loved football. The coach told Paul, "Maybe you could kick field goals for us next fall."

So Paul practiced every day. He worked with his coach. Finally, in the fall, he was ready to start the new season with the team. But they didn't need him the first game. Or the second. Game after game went by. Paul waited to be needed. Finally his moment came. The field goal he kicked helped his team win. How cool!

Jesus had to wait for the right time too. After He was born, Jesus waited years before the right time for His ministry to begin. But when the time was right, Jesus was ready for the job. Jesus fulfilled the needs of all the world by suffering and dying to take away our sins.

We all wait. God makes us part of His team in Holy Baptism. He enlightens us with His gifts, sanctifies and keeps us in the true faith. Sometimes it's very hard to be on God's team. We worry that He's forgotten about us. But by Baptism, we can know God will not forget us. He will help us fulfill our important role—our vocation—that He gives us.

_____Let's talk: What are some special things you are waiting for? How can Jesus help you while you wait?

_____Let's pray: Dear God, give us patience when we must wait for things in this life. Give us great joy in knowing we already have Your greatest gift—faith in Your Son, Jesus Christ, our Lord, through whom we have salvation. Amen.

S. G.

Water, Water Everywhere

S plash it. Watch it. Spray it. Throw it. Slurp it. Pour it. Drink it. Spill it. Freeze it. Boil it. Bubble it. Mop it. Carry it. Mix it. Wash with it. Plant with it. Cook with it. Clean with it. Play with it. Fish in it. Swim in it. Cool off in it. Warm up in it.

What is it? It's water, of course! It's part of our life every single day. Water touches you daily. When it does, let it refresh you. Let it remind you of Baptism, where it isn't just simple water but water joined to God's Word, which brings a gift from God to you.

Baptism provides a great gift— new life in God's family. It washes your sins away so you become God's child. Your life is changed forever. Your new life as God's child cannot be achieved by your efforts. God freely gives you this gift. Your new life is full of forgiveness, love, and joy in knowing that He is with you always and someday you will be living with your Father in heaven.

Read from God's Word

But when the kindness and love of God our Savior appeared, He saved us, not because of righteous things we had done, but because of His mercy. He saved us through the washing of rebirth and renewal by the Holy Spirit, whom He poured out on us generously through Jesus Christ our Savior. Titus 3:4–6

Just as you can do many things with water, you can do many things through your Baptism. As you remember it, you can celebrate how you died and rose with Christ in that baptismal water.

_____Let's talk: Why do you think God chose to use something as ordinary and plain as water to bring His gifts to us? If you have been baptized, what is the date of that re-birthday? How can you celebrate your Baptism today and every day?

_____Let's pray: Almighty Father, in Baptism—a washing with water joined to Your Word—You brought new life to me. Help me remember Your great gift as I use water today. For all Your gifts, thank You! Amen.

S. G.

Read from God's Word

Now there was a man in Jerusalem called Simeon, who was righteous and devout. He was waiting for the consolation of Israel, and the Holy Spirit was upon him. It had been revealed to him by the Holy Spirit that he would not die before he had seen the Lord's Christ. Moved by the Spirit, he went into the temple courts. When the parents brought in the child Jesus to do for Him what the custom of the Law required, Simeon took Him in his arms and praised God, saying: "Sovereign Lord, as You have promised, You now dismiss Your servant in peace. For my eyes have seen Your salvation, which You have prepared in the sight of all people, a light for revelation to the Gentiles and for glory to Your people Israel." Luke 2:25–32 ᑌ

Too Sick

Josiah's nose was running, his head hurt, he was coughing, and he felt sick to his stomach.

It wouldn't have been so bad, except that it was the weekend after Christmas. This was the weekend that Josiah always spent with his dad and his grandparents. There would be presents, his favorite foods, cousins to play with, and fun times. But Josiah felt so sick he didn't even want to move.

Josiah's dad gave him some medicine and a cup of juice. Then he let Josiah sleep a little more. After his nap Josiah felt better—good enough, anyway, to go to his grandparents' house for the weekend.

The illness Josiah had would soon go away, but he had another sickness that would not go away. We also have this sickness. It's called sin. God has some "medicine" for our sin-sick souls. It's the Gospel.

God's Gospel medicine does more than cover up the symptoms of sin; it cures us of our sin. And, best of all, the Gospel is free! The Gospel not only tells us that Jesus died and then came alive again, but it also brings Jesus to us. Because of what Jesus did, our sins are forgiven and we will live forever in heaven!

_____Let's talk: In today's Bible reading, what effect did the Gospel "medicine" have on Simeon? What effect does the Gospel have?

_____Let's pray: Heavenly Father, thank You for all the ways You bring the Gospel medicine to us. In Jesus' name. Amen.

S. G.

When Time Runs Out

Read from God's Word

When I saw Him, I fell at His feet as though dead. Then He placed His right hand on me and said: "Do not be afraid. I am the First and the Last. I am the Living One; I was dead, and behold I am alive for ever and ever! And I hold the keys of death and Hades." Revelation 1:17–18

Here it was, the very last day of the year, and Maureen still had many thank-you notes to write. Time was running out!

Adam's basketball team was playing a team that they were supposed to beat easily. But Adam's team was losing by 18 points, with only 30 seconds to go! Time was running out!

Sometimes the hours and days seem to pass slowly, while at other times they seem to go so quickly. And sooner or later, our time on earth will run out.

It's a good thing we have a God who is in charge of time. He is at the beginning, at the end, and at every moment in-between. God the Father sent His Son at just the right time. He hung on the cross and, when the time came for Him to pay for our sins, He died.

After Jesus died, He overcame the power of death and rose from the grave. He is Lord of all things—time, space, even death.

God makes all our time—every year, every month, and every single day—new for us by His forgiveness. Even when we die, our time with God will have a new beginning in heaven. The year may come to an end, but our lives with God will never end.

———Let's talk: Have you made plans for the times to come during the New Year? How can you include Jesus in your time?

———Let's pray: Lord Jesus, help me celebrate the times You have given. Thank You for my past and present times. Be with me every day in the coming New Year. Amen.

S. G.